El Salvador in the Eighties

COUNTERINSURGENCY AND REVOLUTION

El Salvador in the Eighties

COUNTERINSURGENCY AND REVOLUTION

Mario Lungo Uclés

Edited with an Introduction
by **Arthur Schmidt**

Translated by **Amelia F. Shogan**

Temple University Press
Philadelphia

Originally published as *El Salvador en los 80:
contrainsurgencia y revolución,* by Mario Lungo Uclés,
© 1990 by EDUCA-FLACSO

Temple University Press, Philadelphia 19122

Published 1996

Printed in the United States of America

⊛ The paper used in this publication meets the requirements of the American
National Standard for Information Sciences—Permanence of Paper for Printed Library Materials, ANSI Z39.48–1984

Text design by Anne O'Donnell

Library of Congress Cataloging-in-Publication Data

Lungo, Mario.
    [Salvador en los 80. English]
    El Salvador in the eighties : counterinsurgency and revolution /
Mario Lungo Uclés ; edited with an introduction by Arthur Schmidt ;
translated by Amelia F. Shogan.
        p.   cm.
    Includes bibliographical references and index.
    ISBN 1-56639-431-7 (alk. paper). — ISBN 1-56639-432-5
(pbk. : alk. paper)
    1. El Salvador—History—1979–1992.   2. Social change—El Salvador.
I. Schmidt, Arthur, 1943–   .   II. Title.
F1488.3.L8713   1996
972.8405'3—dc20   96-33806

Contents

El Salvador in the Eighties

COUNTERINSURGENCY AND REVOLUTION

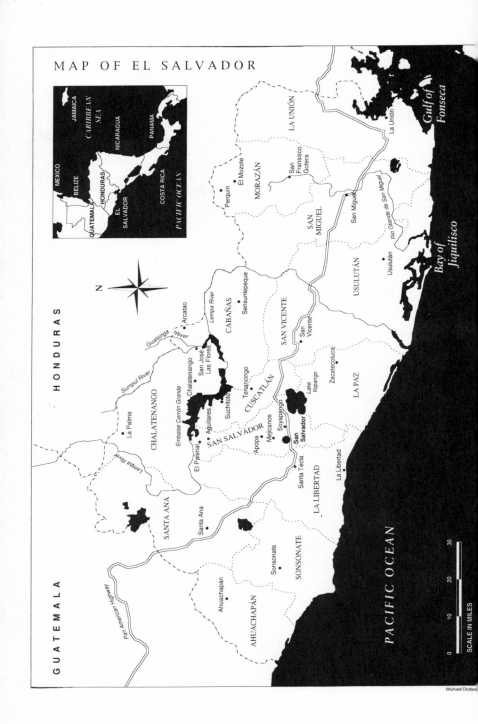

MAP OF EL SALVADOR

Introduction
The Continuing Significance
of El Salvador

Arthur Schmidt

The Relevance of *El Salvador in the Eighties*

Readers in the United States in the late 1990s might ask why they should bother paying any attention to this book. After all, they might note, the revolutionary wars in Central America that so preoccupied U.S. foreign policy during the 1980s have become a thing of the past.[1] They might read that the Salvadoran government, "thanks to American support, has now brought peace, without totalitarianism, to El Salvador."[2] With the Cold War over, they might regard relations between the United States and Latin America as similar to "the relations that prevail between the United States and Canada. Security matters have been displaced from the top of the agenda by the search for positive outcomes and mutual gains in the economic sphere."[3] Moreover, they might ask, are not changes in social customs and in technology more important for the twenty-first century than wars, politics, and ideologies?[4]

It may be hard for some to give credence to the idea that understanding a small and poor nation like El Salvador can provide anything vital for comprehending the rapidly changing contemporary world. Yet a careful reading of *El Salvador in the Eighties* indicates that the work of Mario Lungo Uclés carries substantial weight. To begin with, Lungo is no ideological leftover from yesterday's Central American politics. He is a serious social scientist who has long been fascinated with the social complexities of El Salvador. A former director of the School of Architecture at the University of El Salvador, Lungo has established himself internationally as an expert on the issues of contemporary Latin American urbanization.[5] At the same time, he has be-

1

come known as one of the most acute analysts of his country's conflictive social and political processes. *El Salvador in the Eighties,* winner of the 1990 Casa de las Américas prize, is his third book-length study of El Salvador's revolutionary civil war.[6] Here Lungo combines his analysis of economic and technological forces of a modern, global character with a deep appreciation of the specific political and historical circumstances of Salvadoran society.

It is precisely this mixture that makes his work valuable. The economic and technological imperatives of the late twentieth century neither transform the world by themselves nor operate in a vacuum. *El Salvador in the Eighties* remains relevant at the end of the century because it bridges the world-historical contexts of the Cold War, national liberation movements, and welfare-state capitalism, on the one hand, and the new age of nation-state diminution, neoliberal politics, and economic globalization, on the other. There is no fundamental reason to suppose that insurgencies have ended forever just because the Cold War is over. Readers in the United States should appreciate the importance of reading Lungo in order to understand something about the underlying sources of social conflict in Central America and in parts of Mexico. Although the recent Central American revolutionary wars may be fading into the past, many of their long-term causes—particularly those stemming from landlessness, political marginalization, and social inequalities—are not. Economic modernization, considered by many experts (somewhat uncritically) to be the solution to poverty and political unrest, may prove in some cases to make unequal social conditions even more acute. Over the next decade, unfettered integration into the global economy is expected to uproot millions of people from rural areas in Central America and Mexico. For them, there are no clear alternative economic opportunities.[7]

Conditions like these can provide new ground for guerrilla revolts, as in the case of the insurgency of the Zapatista National Liberation Army in the southern Mexican state of Chiapas. Timed to begin on January 1, 1994, the date of the formal commencement of the North American Free Trade Agreement (NAFTA), the uprising of the EZLN promptly became part of a wider and, as yet, unresolved set of political and economic difficulties for Mexico.[8] The rebellion derived both from such long-standing causes as peasant demands for land and the severe oppression of indigenous groups in Chiapas and from the more recent consequences of economic integration into the global economy: agricultural debts, dropping coffee prices, and the 1992 reform of Article 27 of the Mexican constitution (which had served as the legal basis for peasant claims for access to land). The Chiapas revolt soon became, in the words of the Mexican novelist Carlos Fuentes, "Latin America's first post-Communist rebellion." The uprising reflected Mexico's position as "a country trying to establish democracy while coping with two contradictory pulls—cultural self-determination demanded by the likes of the Chiapas Indians on the one hand, and integration into the world market, exemplified by NAFTA, on the other."[9] Although relatively small in numbers and very poorly armed, the Zapatistas succeeded in holding the Mexican government at bay by rallying domestic and international sympathy to their cause. The newly internationalized character of Mexican politics, the result of economic globalization, provided the insurgents with new points of leverage through their ability to use modern means of communication and to make use of international human rights standards and public sympathies about the plight of indigenous peoples. The statements of Subcomandante Marcos, faxed to the press from insurgent points of refuge in the Lancandon jungle, developed into a literary and political sensation throughout the rest of Mexico.[10]

While the fortunes of the insurgents have been far from entirely happy ones, the Chiapas rebellion illustrates the continued relevance of Lungo's analysis in *El Salvador in the Eighties,* in particular his emphasis upon the opportunities open to insurgent groups through the use of innovative tactics, their connections to the popular organizations of civil society, and the centrality of the negotiation process. The Zapatistas appear to have created a strategy to use action on the battlefield as a means to mobilize support from civil society. They seem to have concluded that globalization offered them the opportunity to checkmate the government through their ability to frighten away the foreign investment that Mexico's economic restructuring has been predicated upon. They may have hoped that the new post–Cold War global context would make it possible for negotiations to open up the country's political system and to put into place a structure of social reform in a relatively short period of time, something that had taken the Salvadoran insurgents many more years of organizing and open warfare.

El Salvador in the Eighties remains relevant reading for people in the United States since the U.S. political system remains far more disposed to become involved in the affairs of Central America and Mexico than it does to understand them. Some have asked, for example, whether the Clinton administration's hasty extension of financial support to

Mexico after the December 1994 devaluation of the peso might become a "financial Vietnam" for the U.S. dollar.[11] Understanding the critical conditions of Central America and Mexico has become even more necessary for the United States now that the domestic and international realities of the late-twentieth-century world have become so inseparably intertwined.[12] Yet journalism and politics in the United States show relatively little comprehension of the critical social conditions prevailing in Central America and Mexico after the Cold War. Audiences in the United States seldom encounter the opportunity to hear direct voices from regions upon which their country exercises an overwhelmingly strong impact. Although Central Americans and Mexicans have produced a vast literature on their own problems, very little of it has been translated. The mass communications media in the United States provide only "a propaganda model" of interpretation of other societies, an "invented reality" that "manufactures domestic consent" for worldviews reinforcing the policies and business interests of the U.S. political establishment and economic elites.[13] The faith of present-day U.S. leaders in the capacity of expanding trade to resolve all significant Latin American issues reflects their long-established habit of viewing the influence of the United States as an uplifting, civilizing element in the Western Hemisphere.[14]

Lungo's analysis should warn U.S. readers against the fashionable assumption that economic globalization and democracy necessarily walk hand in hand. As Ronald Steel has noted, "there is no necessary correlation between market success and democracy. The idea that there is one is at best wishful thinking, and at base a provincial conceit, a delusion rather than a policy."[15] The Central American past should also warn against presuming any correlation between U.S. intervention and democracy.[16] The United States has historically dominated Central America through a structure of political-military interference and economic dependency that Walter LaFeber has labeled "the system."[17] A policy of opposition to Central American revolutions under the administrations of Jimmy Carter, Ronald Reagan, and George Bush was simply the most recent and most costly example in a long history of destructive U.S. interventions in the region. The United States disbursed about ten billion dollars in military and economic aid as part of its efforts to prevent revolution in Central America between 1980 and 1992.[18] To its shame, the United States trained officers and troops who were guilty of massacres and other human rights abuses. Officials of various administrations covered up evidence of those abuses, deliberately broke international and U.S. law, supported covert trafficking in arms and drugs, and exercised unconstitutional powers, finally provoking a crisis of survival for the Reagan presidency in the Iran-contra affair in 1986.[19]

Readers in the United States must understand the importance of overcoming this destructive legacy if their country is to cope with the regional foreign policy issues of the new era of economic globalization. Lungo counters many of the facile journalistic assumptions about U.S. accomplishments in the Central American wars, showing how Pentagon counterinsurgency tactics had an enormous impact upon El Salvador yet failed to achieve their goals. *El Salvador in the Eighties* offers more than just an examination of political and military strategies. As a study of social change under wartime conditions and shifting global realities, it opens up for the reader the connections between the Salvadoran revolutionary struggles, which the United States has seen only in the framework of the Cold War, and the economic and demographic trends of the post–Cold War world. Lungo highlights the importance of his country's new economic dependence upon the monetary support given family members by Salvadorans who had fled abroad from war and persecution. He argues that this income from the remittances of Salvadoran exiles in the United States enabled El Salvador to avoid a terminal economic crisis, thereby obligating the guerrillas to rethink the limits of their military and political strategy. He sees Salvadoran migration to the United States as a dynamic phenomenon that at once transforms social, economic, and cultural conditions in both societies. These views underscore the argument that international refugee and undocumented-labor flows constitute inevitable parts of present-day worldwide economic and political reorganization, not separate trends that can be coped with by repressive legislation like Proposition 187 in California.[20]

Lungo's analysis is valuable for readers who wish to think about the politics of economic globalization. *El Salvador in the Eighties* warns that social conflicts linked to the reorganization of the world economic order will lie at the heart of world politics as the next century opens. Lungo asks what type of constructive democratic politics will be possible in that context. He devotes extensive sections of *El Salvador in the Eighties* to a discussion of new forms of organization within El Salvador, particularly the emergence of an autonomous popular movement whose demands for democratization, basic rights, and peace pitted the government against large segments of civil society.

Lungo's treatment shows how the combined actions of the guerrillas and the popular movement altered national politics in ways that forced the government into negotiations to end the war.

Lungo's analysis reflects the complex interrelationships that now exist between worldwide economic and technological forces, on the one hand, and specific social groups and geographical places, on the other. Economic globalization has displaced the former centrality of nation-states as units of production, consumption, and economic policy making.[21] The undeniable importance of electronic technology has fostered a widespread view of economic globalization as "a more advanced and complex form of internationalization which implies a degree of functional integration between internationally dispersed economic activities."[22] Although accurate, this remains too limited a view. In the words of Saskia Sassen:

> *This narrow focus has the effect of excluding from the account the place-boundedness of significant components of the global information economy; it thereby also excludes a whole array of activities and types of workers from the story of globalization that are as vital to it as international finance and global telecommunications are. By failing to include these activities and workers, it ignores the variety of cultural contexts within which they exist, a diversity as present in the processes of globalization as the new international corporate culture.[23]*

Lungo would agree. His social perspective refuses to concede omnipotent causal power to technology. In his view, the causes of economic globalization remain rooted in the social and political dynamics that link the population of a country like El Salvador with the institutions and interests of the more powerful centers of capital and technological innovation. Moreover, he contends that contemporary global analysis cannot exclude popular elements as protagonists of change if it is to remain accurate. His insistence upon the need for economic and social democratization calls into question the incompleteness and the elite bias of any definition of globalization as simply a technologically driven process of economic rationalization.

El Salvador in the Eighties poses the question of how new forms of popular participation in politics might contribute to the eradication of critical socioeconomic inequalities. The book relentlessly questions old revolutionary tactics, stressing the success of innovation over orthodoxy in the waging of the revolutionary war, in the forging of the peace process, and in planning for the future rebuilding of the nation. Lungo maintains that globalization has made an anachronism out of the past left-wing emphasis on the capture of state power for the purposes of effecting a radical reorganization of society. At the same time, however, he would agree with the observation of Manuel Castells and Roberto Laserna that "our world is characterized by the simultaneous integration of economies and disintegration of societies. In between, national states must cope with the crisis of legitimacy of the political system as well as with the economic crisis of the developmental process."[24] For Lungo, the individualistic and limited character of popular participation under Western constitutionalism remains woefully insufficient to undertake this task. His opinions reflect the incomplete character of the Latin American "transition to democracy" that has been under way since 1982. Electoral civilian regimes have replaced military rule throughout much of Latin America, but they have often remained weak in the face of institutional deficiencies, severe social inequalities, and public alienation.[25] Instead of reliance upon electoralism, Lungo stresses the significance of popular movements as potential avenues toward more comprehensive forms of social justice and democratization. During the present age of diminished state authority over society, popular movements, by his account, become a new basis for political action.[26]

In *El Salvador in the Eighties* and in his subsequent work, Lungo specifically warns about the dangers of the income polarization and social decomposition that have accompanied globalization.

> *By now it is becoming increasingly clear to most Salvadorans that after fifteen years of bitter conflict, it is necessary to construct a national project which involves both the wealthy and the poor in a process of consensus-building. The war has proven that the organized poor are capable of resisting the project of the dominant classes; yet, the war has also proven that the popular project cannot be successfully imposed by force. By building a national project, neither the "project of capital" nor the popular project would dominate. In a sense, for El Salvador to survive as an intact society, both sides need each other. Without capital, technological and managerial experience, El Salvador would be destined to generations of extreme misery. However, without democratization of production, of the political system and of culture, El Salvador would be headed for a renewed and perhaps more prolonged civil war.[27]*

Lungo's views parallel the worries of other analysts that the world of the late twentieth and early twenty-first centuries is becoming increasingly characterized by endemic violence as economic change shreds the ties of social stability, particularly in regions where geographical, class, racial, or ethnic divisions have historically predominated.[28] Many fear that contemporary economic patterns are creating a world ahead in which

> *a huge and increasing proportion of human beings are not needed and will never be needed to make goods or to provide services because too many people in the world are too poor to buy them. The fundamental political conflict in the opening decades of the new century . . . will not be between nations or even between trading blocs but between the forces of globalization and the territorially based forces of local survival seeking to preserve and to redefine community.*[29]

While the most fearful consequences of such a context will most likely affect the poorer regions of the world, the internal social fabric of economically powerful countries like the United States will not remain exempt from their influence. Ever more unequal distribution of income, wealth, opportunity, and tax benefits have characterized the political economy of the United States over the last quarter century, accompanied by increasing degrees of urban decay, crime, incarceration, social intolerance, and political alienation.[30] In the midst of this situation, U.S. readers should find Lungo's insistence upon the importance of popular organization and the negotiation of social consensus illuminating.

Lungo tells a tale in *El Salvador in the Eighties* that is both heroic and sobering. It is the story of how a determined and inventive insurgent force emerged out of the social struggle of a downtrodden people in a country usually deemed too small for successful guerrilla warfare. It relates how the insurgents battled for several years against both domestic and U.S. determination to eradicate them, adjusting to new circumstances, and eventually using their military power to extract significant reforms from the Salvadoran power structure through peace talks mediated by the United Nations. Sometimes referred to as a "negotiated revolution," the 1992 peace accords ended the revolutionary war, and promised an end to El Salvador's historic exclusion of the mass of society from the political system, to its structures of tyranny, and to the landlessness that had made the lives of its rural population ones of endemic poverty.[31] Lungo's tale is also a story about the human costs of war (more than 75,000 people died in the Salvadoran conflict), about the limitations of what popular organization can achieve even after the most arduous struggle, and about the difficulties of creating meaningful social and economic democracy in the context of economic globalization.

The Unfolding of Revolution in El Salvador

The recent experiences of countries undergoing economic liberalization and political democratization have demonstrated the power of historically rooted political and social contexts in shaping patterns of change.[32] Lungo opens *El Salvador in the Eighties* with the example of two long-standing political and social patterns of enormous influence, what he calls the "hegemonic crisis inside the dominant bloc" and "the fifty-year-old general hegemonic crisis of Salvadoran society." Understanding this dual phenomenon will require going back historically to another period of global economic restructuring, the last quarter of the nineteenth century, when El Salvador became a coffee-exporting society. It is a case whereby economic modernization simultaneously produced material progress and an increased social injustice whose ultimate legacy was the revolutionary war of *El Salvador in the Eighties*.

The five countries of Central America—Costa Rica, El Salvador, Guatemala, Honduras, and Nicaragua—emerged somewhat insecurely into the international arena after the demise of the authority of Spain in 1821, the failure of Mexico's attempt to incorporate them into a wider empire in 1823, and the collapse of the Central American Federation after 1838. While conservative practices could provide some stability for a limited time, national consolidation generally awaited the adoption of liberal reforms and the creation of more lucrative export economies.[33] In El Salvador, as in many other parts of Latin America between 1830 and 1930, "coffee production was associated with a profound transformation of landscape and society." Unlike most other countries in the region, however, El Salvador's coffee growing occurred in agricultural areas that had been densely settled since the colonial period.[34] By the mid-1870s, the value of coffee exports began to surpass those of indigo, the principal colonial cash crop, provoking a demand among landowners and liberal political circles that the new crop be allowed to displace its competitors for land and labor.

Unlike the slow and uncertain growth of planation indigo, the rewards of coffee farming were great, immediate and available to those who could produce the greatest amount of fruit in the shortest time. After initial attempts to convert the existing structure of landholding for commercial purposes, the decision was taken, by a coffee planters' government, to abolish any aspect of man's ownership, use or settlement of the land that hindered the rapid establishment of coffee plantations.[35]

Legislation between 1879 and 1882 resulted in the abolition of collective village landholding. As world coffee prices doubled in the 1880s, large estates dedicated to this crop became the basis of the wealth of the famous "fourteen families," a new oligarchy whose grip over Salvadoran life later contributed so substantially to the development of revolutionary conditions.[36]

Despite some armed resistance by the peasantry, the new social order soon consolidated itself, largely monopolizing the land and labor of the coffee-growing areas of central and western El Salvador. As James Dunkerley has observed, "[T]he form of both settlement and labor made the Salvadoran coffee *finca* [farm] much more directly the locus of social control than elsewhere."[37] The nation's oligarchy possessed such considerable social and economic power in the late nineteenth and early twentieth centuries that it did not at first have to rely heavily on the agency of the state to discipline the country's lower classes, whose wages and working conditions were among the poorest in Central America. Deals among elite families securely controlled the country's electoral politics, permitting governments in the prosperous 1920s the luxury of occasionally flirting with political reforms to appeal to emerging urban middle-class and labor elements.[38] This sense of security changed, however, when coffee prices fell drastically as a result of the Great Depression and social disturbances began to rise. Prices in 1935 were just a third of those of 1925, while the per capita GDP of El Salvador in 1939 remained below its pre-depression level, even after some years of nominal economic recovery.[39] After a military coup in December 1931 and an abortive Communist uprising the following month, the oligarchy ceded political control to the army, opening the way to "the fifty-year-old general hegemonic crisis of Salvadoran society" that plays such a prominent role in Lungo's account.

While the immediate causes of the revolt of January 1932 remain complex, its long-term roots lie in the social conflicts of the Salvadoran coffee-exporting order. One recent account has stressed the interplay between class and ethnic tensions:

> *Agrarian unrest in the coffee-growing zones and social agitation, with plenty of opportunities for the actions of the Communists, were both factors in El Salvador in 1932. The peasant rebellion, nonetheless, took place almost exclusively in heavily Indian zones. The bloody repression that ensued was felt most in the same region, leading to the virtual extinction of those visibly Indian, on the pretext of the existence of a Communist threat. The patterns of social confrontation are intertwined and, therefore, difficult to interpret. At the base, there is a serious conflict between landowners, peons, and peasants, made even worse by the economic crisis and the rapid changes in the distribution of land that took place in the decades prior to and because of the expansion of coffee cultivation. This conflict, however, . . . was not enough to cause the insurrection. This took place in areas heavily populated with Indians and was an expression of another basic conflict: the clash between Indians and mestizos.[40]*

The savagery of the suppression of the revolt killed some ten thousand to forty thousand Salvadorans, virtually extinguishing indigenous ethnic identity, and leaving thereafter a lasting memory of terror among the lower classes and a rigid hostility to reform among major segments of the oligarchy.[41]

The leader of the 1932 repression, General Maximiliano Hernández Martínez, continued to govern El Salvador until his overthrow in 1944. Under his personal dictatorship, the authority of the Salvadoran state expanded and a new "reactionary despotism" emerged; it would survive through various modifications to govern El Salvador until the revolutionary crisis emerged in the 1970s.[42] Under this system, the landowning oligarchy retained dominant economic power and a controlling influence over economic policy making. Although the country's economy grew and diversified, particularly in the decades after World War II, coffee remained El Salvador's dominant product, still accounting for some 43 to 57 percent of its commodity exports for the years between 1960 and 1979.[43] The coffee-growing oligarchy extended its power into other realms of the economy, such as finance and industry, creating a highly concentrated pattern of ownership that prevented the emergence of a "modernizing elite" or a bourgeoisie free from dependent ties to the oligarchy. El Salvador could thus industrialize significantly within the Central American Common Market during the 1960s without the oligarchy "having to accept the social and political consequences of that transformation."[44]

Lungo's use of the term "dominant bloc" reflects the absence in El Salvador of a distinct ruling class with its own political apparatus. After the overthrow of Hernández Martínez, the officer corps as an institution took the reins of government, operating the Salvadoran political system in accord with the interests of the dominant bloc, a "reactionary coalition" whose nucleus

> *was composed of the 240 or so largest agricultural planters, the twenty-six major groups engaged in export agriculture and specializing in coffee exports, cattle ranchers with interests in the banking sector, large merchants dedicated to the supply of agricultural machinery and other agricultural inputs, financiers and bankers associated with export agriculturalists, the major speculators in real estate, and some entrepreneurs of the food-processing and textile industries. Linked very closely to these were former military officers who had retired at the top of the ranks and who had played key roles in pacifying the country during one or more of the periodic political crises; former high government officials who because of their legal or technocratic skills could fill managerial functions in the private sector; and, on a lesser scale, local commanders of the National Guard who offered protection to the largest farms, and individuals connected to the repression of opposition elements.[45]*

As the military coups of 1944, 1948, 1960, 1961, and 1972 indicated, tensions and divergent political interests could exist within this coalition. In fact, El Salvador became known for political cycles in which dissident progressive elements in the officer corps would effectuate a coup, promulgate reforms, and then lose power to conservative elements again.[46] While elements in the military and its satellite political party, the Partido de Conciliación Nacional (PCN—Party of National Conciliation), liked to pose as political modernizers, the postwar system of military rule severely restricted civilian political power and prohibited any significant deviation from the interests of the oligarchy. The lack of clear hegemony by any group within the dominant bloc persisted. Nevertheless, the repressive qualities of "reactionary despotism" were sufficiently effective to prevent "the general hegemonic crisis of Salvadoran society" from presenting a serious political challenge until the 1970s.

New political pressures emerged out of the country's pattern of economic successes in the three decades after World War II, during which El Salvador's gross domestic product multiplied sixfold.[47] The revival of the agro-export economy retained the preeminence of coffee, but the degree of Salvadoran monoculture was reduced through the power of such new exports as cotton, sugar, and beef. The operation of the Central American Common Market after 1961 created new regional opportunities. Between 1960 and 1979, Salvadoran industry expanded at an average rate of better than 6 percent per year, almost twice the pace of growth of the agricultural sector.[48] Few of these benefits reached the Salvadoran lower classes, however, particularly those in the countryside. Large landowners gained the benefits of export expansion, increasing their dominant role over the rural economy. About 12 percent of rural families were landless in El Salvador in 1961, a figure that is said to have risen to 29 percent in 1971, to have topped 40 percent in 1975, and to have continued rising thereafter.[49] A young, rapidly growing, increasingly urban Salvadoran population now emerged into a world of dismal opportunities and repressive regimentation. Income distribution was highly unequal: 63 percent of Salvadoran families earned slightly more than 28 percent of total income, averaging less than 100 dollars per month per family; the wealthiest 6.2 percent of families, on the other hand, gained the same share of total income, averaging about 650 dollars each. The poorest 20 percent of Salvadorans earned one-fiftieth of the country's income, while the most comfortable 20 percent earned two-thirds.[50]

Despite these highly oppressive socioeconomic conditions, the Left, as Lungo notes in Chapter two, had generally not considered tiny El Salvador to be suitable terrain for guerrilla warfare prior to the 1970s. The Partido Comunista de El Salvador (PCS—Salvadoran Communist Party) did not see a splinter faction take up arms following the success of the Cuban Revolution in 1959, as occurred in so many other Latin American countries. El Salvador's population density and its geographical limits seemed to make it a poor location for the development of a guerrilla *foco* that would force the country into a revolutionary crisis. So did the power of the Organización Democrática Nacionalista (ORDEN—Democratic Nationalist Organization), a right-wing vigilante group in the countryside that enjoyed official patronage in the late 1960s, especially through the influence of the head of the National Guard, General José Alberto "Chele" Medrano.[51] The Left would not take up guerrilla warfare in El Salvador until the 1970s, by which time all other forms of political activity seemed to have proven notoriously unsuccessful.

Before then, the PCS kept to reformist political tactics and sought electoral allies among other forces that had gained a measure of tolerance within the system. The mildly reformist Partido Demócrata Cristiano (PDC—Christian Democratic Party), founded in 1960, had gained seats in the national legislature in 1964, and its candidate, José Napoleón Duarte, won the mayoralty of San Salvador in 1966. The Movimiento Nacional Revolucionario (MNR—National Revolutionary Movement), headed by Guillermo Manuel Ungo, openly promoted a social democratic program that gained support from banned political organizations on the Left. The possibilities of major political gains by the opposition seemed greater after the 1969 conflict with Honduras had forcefully repatriated 130,000 Salvadorans, adding to the country's tense social conditions and publicly raising the previously forbidden issue of agrarian reform.[52] But in 1972 and in 1977, the government bloodily imposed Colonel Arturo Molina and General Carlos Romero, the respective PCN presidential candidates, thus preventing the possible victory of the National Opposition Union coalition of the Communists, the Christian Democrats, and the MNR. Government manipulation of the voting in municipal and legislative elections in 1974 and 1976 further discredited the idea of meaningful reform under the existing political process and thus "set the stage for revolutionary guerrilla movements whose leaders had learned many lessons from the military failures of their brethren in other Latin American nations in the 1960s."[53]

Ultimately, the increasingly polarized Salvadoran context of the 1970s resulted in the creation of a broad, well-organized network of support for revolutionary struggle, what Lungo calls an "extended rear guard." The popular foundations for revolution were constructed out of two separate but interrelated sources: socially minded reformers within the Christian churches, particularly the Roman Catholic Church, and the membership of mass organizations. In the spirit of renovation of the Second Vatican Council, the Latin American bishops met at Medellín, Colombia, in 1968 in a historic conference that reoriented the church toward the task of uprooting the structures of sin embedded within society, in particular the injustices stemming from widespread poverty and oppression.[54] Influenced by the theology of liberation, new initiatives like the development of Christian base communities (CEBs) provided the organizational structures within which grassroots leadership could emerge. Traditional religious teachings were now reread as calls to action against injustice.[55] The CEBs found fertile ground amid the oppressive social and political conditions of El Salvador. Religious activism soon brought down increased repression upon the church and such related institutions as the Universidad Centroamericana (UCA), including the beating, torture, and assassination of clergy. The new archbishop of San Salvador, Oscar Romero, emerged in 1977 as a prophetic voice of conscience, denouncing government abuses, defining norms of justice, and calling the rapidly polarizing society to take the path of dialogue and peace.[56]

The social ferment within church-related organizations interacted powerfully with a simultaneous outburst of radical organizing in El Salvador. In 1970, the secretary-general of the PCS, Salvador Cayetano Carpio, broke with the party over the issue of armed struggle and helped to form the Fuerzas Populares de Liberación (FPL—Popular Liberation Forces), the first of five political-military bodies that emerged to support guerrilla warfare. All five would ultimately unite as the Frente Farabundo Martí para la Liberación Nacional (FMLN—Farabundo Martí National Liberation Front) in 1980. At the same time that these groups established the bases for an armed struggle, a host of grassroots organizations sprang up throughout El Salvador to try to meet the day-to-day needs of ordinary people and to resist repression. These, in turn, coalesced into mass popular organizations that affiliated with one of the five political-military groups.[57] This welter of organizing activity amid the tumult of the 1970s proved, in the words of Lungo, "absolutely crucial" for the emergence and maintenance of a popular revolutionary guerrilla struggle in El Salvador.

The Salvadoran Revolutionary Struggle, 1979–92

When he first published *El Salvador in the Eighties* in 1989, Lungo argued that the year 1979 opened a new political period in Salvadoran history that became clearly defined by the FMLN offensive of January 1981. "Because this new period sprang from the accumulated successes and failures of the revolutionary movement of the 1970s," he contended, "it must end in either the triumph or the defeat of the revolutionary forces." By the time he wrote Chapters six and seven in 1991–92, Lungo had been obliged to admit the error of his earlier conclusion: "The peace accords signed in the first days of 1992 by the FMLN and the ARENA government closed this political period without either the victory or the strategic defeat of the revolutionary forces." His original conclusion may have proven wrong, but his analysis in fact had retained its validity. It was precisely the three factors that he had given so much weight to in his diagnosis—changes in the political organization of the dominant classes, the innovative shifts in the thinking of the FMLN, and the radically changing global context—that had required negotiations rather than bringing outright victory for either the guerrillas or the government.

The tenacity and originality of the insurgents underscored the importance of the organizing that had taken place in the 1970s and the depth of support that the FMLN could count on among significant segments of the population.[58] Without that support, as Lungo contends, an insurgent force in such a small country would soon have been effectively wiped out. Acute political organization and tactical originality had to make up for more than severe geographical adversity. These factors also had to counter the ample support that the Salvadoran government received from the United States, the negative ramifications of the Latin American debt crisis after 1982, and, by the late 1980s, the implications of the Central American peace process, the disintegration of the Soviet bloc, and the dominance of economic globalization. For convenience, the complex, highly eventful years of the revolutionary war can be divided into four periods: 1979–81, polarization into the revolutionary-counterrevolutionary dynamic; 1981–84, large-scale armed conflict in the countryside amid the establishment and consolidation of electoral politics in El Salvador; 1984–89, dispersed but intense insurgent and counterinsurgent military activity, demands for peace, and shifting national and international political contexts; and 1989–92, the establishment and fulfillment of a negotiated process to end the war.

1979–81

While revolutionary conditions developed simultaneously in El Salvador, Guatemala, and Nicaragua during the 1970s, the victory of the insurgent Sandinistas over the Somoza dictatorship in Nicaragua in July immediately added a sense of urgency to the tensions prevalent throughout Central America. This was especially true in El Salvador, which "was buffeted by a rising spiral of mass demonstrations and protests, government repression, left-wing kidnappings, occupations of public buildings, labor strikes, and death-squad murders" between July 1977 and October 1979.[59] In a context of serious divisions within the dominant bloc and widespread fear of the spread of revolution in Central America, a group of reform-minded civilians and younger military officers plotted a coup. They sought to remove the regime of General Romero and to introduce fundamental reforms intended to circumvent the increasing possibility of revolutionary war. They easily succeeded in ousting Romero on October 15, 1979, but soon the reform-minded elements lost control of the army to reactionary officers who subverted their efforts to bring about serious change.

The climate of repression worsened rapidly. Government and death-squad killings soon approximated a thousand per month, an atrocious degree of violence that continued throughout much of the following year, spreading terror and poisoning all possibilities of political compromise.[60] Right-wing violence spared no perceived "subversives," no matter what their status: victims included Mario Zamora, the government's *procurador general de los pobres,* killed on February 23, 1980; Archbishop Romero, assassinated on March 24, 1980; Enrique Alvarez Córdova, former minister of agriculture and president of the Frente Democrático Revolucionario (FDR—Democratic Revolutionary Front), murdered along with five other FDR members on November 27, 1980; and Maryknoll sisters Maura Clark and Ita Ford, Ursuline sister Dorothy Kazel, and lay missioner Jean Donovan, all from the United States, raped and killed by the National Guard on December 2, 1980.[61]

Under these conditions, 1980 became a year of division into revolutionary and counterrevolutionary poles. The consolidation of the revolutionary camp unfolded through the development of new organizations that united different leftist factions as right-wing violence closed off all other alternatives. In January 1980 the popular organizations brought themselves together as the Coordinadora Revolucionaria de Masas (CRM—Revolutionary Coordinator of the Masses). On January 11, the coalition made public a comprehensive revolutionary program that promised agrarian reform and nationalization of key elements of the economic infrastructure, including foreign trade and the banks. A few days later it mobilized a demonstration of two hundred thousand people, who were then attacked by the National Guard, the National Police, and others, leaving many dead and hundreds injured.

By now, the reform-minded civilians who had originally supported the October coup had left the government. Following the assassination of Archbishop Romero, some, like Guillermo Ungo, joined with the CRM, political parties, labor unions, professionals, and others to form the Democratic Revolutionary Front. After a strategy of demonstrations, general strikes, and recruitment of international solidarity failed to alter government conduct, the FDR moved closer to support for a strategy of insurrection. Over the same months, guerrilla groups established greater unity among themselves, forming a partially unified directorate in May before establishing the FMLN in October 1980.

The counterrevolutionary pole consisted of an uneasy amalgam of the armed forces (the army and other security forces like the National Guard, Treasury Police, and National Police), the principal components of the former governing bloc, the remaining factions of the splintered Christian Democratic Party, and the United States. Leaders of the Christian Democrats, the most prominent of whom was José Napoleón Duarte, joined the junta as other civilian reformers left it. Through military aid and financial support, the United States now played a significant role in holding the counterrevolutionary pole together. After the July 1979 Sandinista victory in Nicaragua, the administration of Jimmy Carter had tried to contain revolution in Central America through military assistance and the promotion of reforms intended to undercut the appeal of radicalism. In past years, the United States had supported the Salvadoran military as part of its Cold War policies in Latin America. It thus bore responsibility for helping to create the military-linked intelligence networks that fostered the death squads.[62] Nevertheless, assistance from the United States had not previously amounted to substantial sums of money.

All that changed quickly in 1980, despite the plea to Carter of Archbishop Romero, a month before his death, that the United States not send military assistance. (Prophetically, Romero asserted that U.S. funds would only widen the circle of violence in El Salvador.)[63] Carter gave El Salvador fifteen million dollars of war-related aid in 1980, an amount that was more than quintupled the following year. Over the next decade, 1981–90, U.S. aid to El Salvador totaled close to four billion dollars, more than 70 percent of which was made up of war-related funds.[64] Taking the Christian Democrats under its wing, the United States supported the government's initiatives that nationalized the finance and coffee-exporting sectors, created a three-tier process of agrarian reform, and promised electoral democracy.[65] With the strong support of the United States, Duarte took the title of president in December 1980.

1981–84

On the eve of the Reagan administration's taking office, the FMLN launched its January 1980 "general offensive." Lungo offers a lengthy discussion in Chapter two of this controversial decision. As he shows, the offensive was neither a victory nor a defeat for the FMLN. While it proved that the insurgents could not topple the government through an all-out insurrection at that moment, the offensive helped to equip the guerrillas to wage a long-term conflict under adverse conditions against a much larger armed forces establishment.[66] Since the mass organizations had been decimated by the repression during 1980, the contribution of the offensive to creating new logistical mechanisms of popular support was highly important.

The FMLN soon proved its capacity to survive as the war expanded within El Salvador and as the dynamics of revolutionary and counter-revolutionary conflict took on an increasingly regional character in Central America. Wide areas in the eastern, northern, and central parts of El Salvador remained subject to strong FMLN influence despite a rapid expansion in the size of the government armed forces, their use of air power, and the introduction of comprehensive new counterinsurgency techniques known under the rubric of "low-intensity warfare."[67] As Lungo points out, the FMLN's development of control zones and new forms of political organization enabled it to expand and prolong the conflict. By 1984, the FMLN had a formed a revolutionary army between nine thousand and twelve thousand strong; it had repeatedly demonstrated its capacity to mount large-scale offensives during 1982 and 1983. In the words of Lungo, "the FMLN military campaign forced the government to interrupt plans and reorganize forces, thus causing it to lose the military initiative taken toward the end of August 1981." The FMLN was able to obtain arms on the international market and from the Salvadoran armed forces via bribery or capture; it no longer relied upon the arms from Cuba and Nicaragua that previously had been important in the preparation of the January 1981 general offensive.[68]

The United States continued to insist, however, that arms shipments from Cuba and Nicaragua not only sustained the FMLN but were the cause of the revolution itself. Initially, the Reagan administration had looked forward to a quick victory in El Salvador, which it saw as a test case of U.S. resolve in the conflict between East and West.[69] But as the situation in El Salvador proved surprisingly intractable and opposition arose from Congress and the U.S. public over intervention, the new administration began to adopt a more comprehensive strategy. Washington's counterinsurgency experts soon discovered the need to do more than just train new Salvadoran battalions in the United States. The adoption of U.S. tactics in the war required a significant remaking of the entire Salvadoran officer corps, an ambitious project that would require time and support from Congress.[70] Moreover, tactics adopted in El Salvador had to be compatible with other aspects of counterinsurgency policy in the entire Central American region. In the end, Reagan followed Carter's lead in El Salvador, proclaiming a U.S. position of "promoting democracy" in Central America and throughout the world. What U.S. neoconservatives had previously labeled a liberal Democratic "hallucination" became the centerpiece of Reagan policy, eventually coming to be known as the "Reagan doctrine."[71] An alliance with elected civilian regimes in Central America allowed the Reagan administration to label the Sandinistas as "totalitarians"; it also provided the political cover under which U.S. policy withstood the impact of continued flagrant human rights abuses by government forces in El Salvador and Guatemala and by the Nicaraguan contras without the loss of congressional funding for counterinsurgency efforts in Central America.[72]

As Lungo's analysis explains, the Reagan strategy may have served domestic political purposes in gaining continued funding for U.S. policy in Central America, but it contributed to a dynamic of change in which the administration saw its objectives of military victory in El Salvador frustrated, eventually obliging the United States to accept negotiations as the means to end the war. Four factors contributed to this result. First, despite all the money and training spent upon them, the army and security forces of El Salvador never fully abandoned their abusive character, nor did they completely adopt U.S. counterinsurgency tactics. Second, the FMLN learned how to retain the military and political initiative after 1981, never fully ceding it to the government despite changing national and international circumstances. Third, the Christian Democratic land and financial reforms did not break the economic power of the oligarchy, particularly since stage two of the land reform, the part that would have affected the most important coffee farms, was never implemented. Fourth, U.S. support for civilian elections failed to create the "political center" identified with the Christian Democrats that Carter and Reagan administration policy had been predicated upon. Initially, the United States found itself having to claim that the Salvadoran government represented a beleaguered "democratic center" against the extremes of the Right and the Left, a fiction that proved hard to sustain when government security forces were so strongly linked to widespread human rights abuses and when government troops were involved in massive search-and-destroy missions.[73] Large-scale voter participation in the 1982 constitutional assembly elections might seem to have offered the U.S. position a veneer of credibility (despite the documented fraudulent official inflation of the size of the turnout) were it not for the significant power gained by the Right in those elections. With the notorious Roberto D'Aubuisson as head of the assembly, the Right was able to use its newfound respectability to subvert the Christian Democratic reform process said to be the essence of the democratic alternative to FMLN revolution.[74]

As Lungo emphasizes in *El Salvador in the Eighties,* the founding of the Alianza Republicana Nacionalista (ARENA—Nationalist Republican Alliance) by D'Aubuisson and others in 1981 possessed major historical significance. "Toward the end of 1981," Lungo notes, "there were more than a few who underestimated the significance of D'Aubuisson and ARENA, dismissing them as a fascist group with little potential inside El Salvador." Yet, for the first time in half a century, ARENA offered the Salvadoran bourgeoisie the possibility of "a party that could collect the ideas, intentions, and expectations of the broadest range of the Right." Although Duarte and the Christian Democrats won the presidential elections of 1984 and the legislative and municipal elections of 1985, thereafter the electoral field would belong to ARENA, converting the Right to the use of elections and fundamentally altering the character of Salvadoran politics.

1984–89

During these years, the war entered into a state of "dynamic equilibrium" in which the two adversaries constantly tried out new initiatives but in which neither could triumph. Ultimately, this condition of unending warfare opened the way for negotiations to end the conflict, a process that took several years. As Salvador's first elected civilian president since 1931, Duarte received significant amounts of fresh military and economic assistance from the United States. Appreciating the indispensability of a legitimate electoral regime as a prerequisite for U.S. assistance, the Salvadoran armed forces supported Duarte's government and initiated a series of political and military campaigns intended to strengthen the government's position in areas of FMLN influence. Fattened by U.S. assistance, the Salvadoran armed forces found the condition of "dynamic equilibrium" a prosperous if corrupt existence.[75] For Duarte's government and the Salvadoran economy, however, these circumstances proved a dead end. The armed forces blocked the president's effort at a peace dialogue with the FMLN, while the war and the 1986 earthquake meant continued harsh living conditions for the Salvadoran public.[76]

For its part, the FMLN developed tactics that allowed it to mount significant operations but then disperse rapidly to avoid government air power. In the process, it reduced its number of combatants to about six thousand while reemphasizing, as Lungo notes, the importance of political work. With its 1984 proposal for a broad coalition government, the FDR/FMLN began placing more emphasis upon political alliances, offers of negotiation, and international diplomacy as serious complements to guerrilla activity. Having surmounted the 1983 murder of Mélida Anaya Montes and the suicide of Salvador Cayetano Carpio, the leadership of the FMLN became more flexible, cooperating in the return of some FDR leaders like Rubén Zamora and Guillermo Ungo to political participation in El Salvador and reevaluating its previous opposition to elections. In January 1989, the FMLN offered to participate in the presidential elections of that year and to honor their results if the voting were postponed six months. In negotiations in February with the government and representatives of Salvadoran political parties, the FMLN offered to abandon armed struggle, join the political process, and recognize a single national army in exchange for a series of significant military reforms.[77]

While these talks failed, the FMLN proposal formed the germ of the subsequent move toward peace between 1990 and 1992. Although the antagonists were not yet ready for permanent dialogue, the international setting increasingly favored a negotiated solution. The Iran-contra scandal in 1986 and the 1988 elections had left the U.S. government with a weaker commitment to the conflict. The end of the Cold War and the breakup of the Soviet bloc altered the international setting fundamentally. The new Bush administration began to perceive advantages to a negotiated settlement in El Salvador early in 1989, a view that was strengthened by the Sandinista defeat in the

February 1990 elections in Nicaragua. International relations were in the process of adaptation to economic globalization, in which governments would pay more attention to markets and investment than to Cold War versions of security against perceived "Communist threats." The Contadora/Caraballeda peace process between 1984 and 1987 emphasized the importance of internal negotiations and the end of external military assistance to parties in conflict. After 1987, the Central American Equipulas peace process reemphasized internal negotiation and participation in open domestic electoral processes, a formula that by 1989 held open the prospect of ending the war in Nicaragua.[78]

Moreover, as Lungo emphasizes so strongly in *El Salvador in the Eighties*, the war had transformed the country so extensively as to prevent victory for either side. The disintegration of Duarte's administration and the rise of ARENA's electoral power meant that the U.S. project of a "democratic center" regime as an alternative to revolution had failed. In the meantime, ARENA had seized the opportunities afforded by modern electoral politics to become the civilian political expression of a bourgeois governing bloc. After 1985, party leaders from business backgrounds like Alfredo Cristiani began to dominate ARENA and benefited from its voting successes. ARENA gained control of the legislature (in coalition with the minority representation of the PCN) in the 1988 elections, and Cristiani won the presidency for the party in 1989 with 54 percent of the vote. At the same time, popular organizations and labor groups, most of which were not affiliated with the Christian Democrats, were rebuilding their positions (which had been almost destroyed by the repression of 1980). By 1986, the popular movement had achieved notable strength and, despite severe risks, played an important and vocal role in politics. Increasingly, popular groups connected their assertion of the basic needs of their members with the question of peace. In 1987, with the support of popular organizations and ecumenical religious groups, the Permanent Commission on the National Debate emerged to plant the question of peace at the center of Salvadoran public life.

The war had also powerfully changed the country's economy. Although the Christian Democratic reforms had not broken the economic power of the oligarchy, they had created a reformed segment of the rural economy sympathetic to the FMLN negotiating position and had galvanized the new bourgeois economic thinking, as Lungo points out. Economic globalization, plus El Salvador's dependency upon the remissions from the approximately one million Salvadorans in the United States, obligated the forces to rethink their political strategies for the war. For the FMLN, the implication was clear: remissions from exiles would prevent any final economic crisis that would give the FMLN military victory, while globalization meant that no party could govern successfully without the cooperation of domestic and foreign sources of capital.

1989–92

Shortly after having been voted into office, President-elect Cristiani called for talks with the FMLN, following up on the preelection negotiations that had ensued from the guerrillas' offer to quit the war and enter the political process (subject to certain major institutional reforms). As Lungo sets forth in Chapter six, a tentative but definite process of negotiation began that would result in the signing of the peace accords on January 16, 1992. The process became more institutionalized when representatives of the government and the FMLN met in September 1989 and invited the participation of the office of the secretary-general of the United Nations. Talks in the following month began the role of the United Nations as the broker of peace negotiations in El Salvador.

In other words, by 1989 the objective conditions for a comprehensive negotiated settlement to the war had largely emerged. Both camps, however, had yet to realize with sufficient depth that negotiations constituted their only way out. Cristiani's initiatives did not fully represent the position of his government and political base. Important segments of ARENA remained to be convinced of the impossibility of a total political-military victory over the FMLN. Some continued to harbor the illusion that ARENA could go on prosecuting the war while implementing the government's program for economic recuperation—a position that elements of the Bush administration shared as well. Thus, officials of both governments claimed at times that the FMLN was an exhausted and increasingly irrelevant political and military force. Despite the negotiations of September and October, the ARENA government directed more repression against popular organizations and unions. Bombings against well-known opposition elements culminated in the powerful October 31 explosion at the headquarters of the Federación Nacional Sindical de Trabajadores Salvadoreños (FENASTRAS—National Trade Union Federation of Salvadoran Workers). It killed ten people (including the secretary-general of the union) and wounded thirty. To the FMLN, and to many others, it hardly seemed that the historic attitude of the government had changed.[79]

The response of the FMLN was to launch a daring offensive in the city of San Salvador itself, which had hitherto been spared the destructive presence of the war. Two years in the planning, the offensive of November 1989 failed to overthrow the government as some insurgents had hoped, yet it dealt a fatal blow to the illusion that the FMLN could simply be dismissed as a spent force. The attack proved the strategic vulnerability of the government, discredited counterinsurgent intelligence gathering, and revealed the savage underpinnings of the regime. Government armed forces bombed and strafed lower-class neighborhoods in the capital in retaliation. The U.S.-trained Atlacatl battalion entered the grounds of the Central American University on the fourth night of the offensive and killed the rector and vice-rector, four other Jesuits, their housekeeper, and her daughter.[80]

As Lungo emphasizes in his analysis, the FMLN offensive profoundly modified the structure of the Salvadoran political situation in 1989, "not so much between the two principal contending blocs in themselves but rather among various tendencies within them, favoring those on each side who argued for a negotiated political solution to the conflict." As a result, the previously tentative negotiation process now became the political focus for the Salvadoran government, the United States, and the FMLN. (Chapter six of *El Salvador in the Eighties* contains a calendar of the talks during 1990 and 1991, information that need not be repeated here.) The negotiations survived some very difficult threats during late 1990 and early 1991, an important turning point that was reinforced by outcome of the March 1991 assembly and mayoral elections. In July 1991 the United Nations Observer Mission in El Salvador (ONUSAL) began monitoring human rights in the country. Tense and complex rounds of negotiations between September 1991 and January 1992 resulted in the agreement upon a ceasefire and the final terms of the peace accords that officially ended the war. In February 1992 major public celebrations welcomed the return of FMLN figures from abroad and from clandestine life.[81]

El Salvador since 1992

The peace accords were intended to be the foundation for a new future for El Salvador after its bloody revolutionary war. The accords were the product of negotiations between two warring parties, each of which had become convinced of its inability to prevail militarily and had come to see the war as an obstacle to other important objectives it held. The FMLN realized that the post–Cold War world of economic globalization posed new challenges that could not be met through guerrilla struggle. Political survival for the Left required adapting to electoral participation, a process already initiated by Guillermo Ungo, Rubén Zamora, and others from the FDR by standing for election in 1989.[82] Therefore, the leadership of the FMLN decided to negotiate the renunciation of the group's armed power in exchange for a demilitarization of Salvadoran public life and the creation of a more open political system in which it could compete as a party. For its part, the ARENA government of Alfredo Cristiani saw the war as an obstacle to successful Salvadoran participation in the contemporary world economy. As Lungo notes in *El Salvador in the Eighties,* the spread of the new bourgeois philosophy of a competitive, modernizing economic elite meant that the old pattern of reliance upon the armed forces to control the political system was now viewed as an anachronism. ARENA's electoral success had convinced important elements in the governing bloc that demilitarization and a more open political system were both safe and desirable concessions in exchange for the disbanding of the FMLN's guerrilla army.

Fulfilling the promise of the peace accords proved to be an arduous task, and the optimism of early 1992 soon dimmed. During the negotiations, neither the government nor the FMLN had consulted or educated their bases of support in any depth. Both found it difficult to deal with recalcitrant or confused elements within their own ranks, a reality that led to the schedule for the fulfillment of the accords being readjusted with some frequency. Moreover, full compliance was complicated by the significantly different vantage points of the revolutionary and government blocs. The government held the advantage of incumbency; its adherents often tended to define the demobilization of the FMLN as the only legitimate stipulation of the accords. Furthermore, supporters of the military dug in their heels, dragging out the timetable for demilitarization. Bureaucratic inertia, subtle forms of sabotage, and simple bad faith on the part of the government bloc characterized its resistance to full implementation. Once its demobilization was well under way, the FMLN found that its leverage over the enforcement of the accords had diminished, leaving full implementation precariously dependent upon the limited power of international agencies. Serious divisions within the ranks of the

FMLN, particularly the tendency of the ERP to deal with the government independently, undermined the ability of the guerrillas to enforce their interpretation of the provisions they had gained through negotiation. The FMLN's adjustment to peacetime politics proved confused and uncertain.

The international pressure that been vital to progress in negotiations weakened after January 1992. As John Coatsworth notes, the Bush administration sought "to translate U.S. power into a restoration of the country's traditional dominance in Central America while simultaneously moving to reduce the time and resources devoted to the region."[83] This objective had largely been achieved by the time the accords were signed, and the United States lessened its pressure on the Salvadoran government. The U.S. embassy in El Salvador possessed neither an ambassador nor a deputy chief of mission for six months during 1992.[84] Even though the principal international force involved in the implementation of the accords was the United Nations, much of its leverage with the Salvadoran government depended upon being backed up forcefully by the United States and by other governments helping to fund postwar reconstruction.

The peace accords established a complex set of mechanisms to achieve the two fundamental objectives of demilitarizing Salvadoran life and opening up the country's political system.[85] Demilitarization began with a ceasefire that ended action on the battlefield. It continued with a fixed timetable for the demobilization of the FMLN in stages in congruence with reforms in El Salvador's military and political structures. The accords called for the Salvadoran armed forces to be reduced from 60,000 to 30,000 men; the rapid-reaction battalions, the Treasury Police, the National Guard, and the intelligence bureaus, all of which were associated with political repression and extensive human rights abuses, were to be eliminated. In addition, an Ad-hoc Commission would review the records of the senior 10 percent of the officer corps and present a list of those to be dismissed because of abuse of authority and of human rights. Finally, a Truth Commission would investigate some of the most notorious past cases of human rights abuses, fix responsibility for them, and offer recommendations about the cases and about how to prevent such acts.

The most notable areas of compliance with the accords since 1992 have been those that concerned demilitarization. The ceasefire held, a considerable achievement in itself. The guerrilla forces of the FMLN underwent complete demobilization in stages. The ranks of the army were halved, and the rapid-reaction battalions, the Treasury Police, the National Guard, and the intelligence bureaus were dissolved. Despite considerable furor, the officers cited on the list of the Ad-hoc Commission were purged. However, the work of the Truth Commission was less successful. While it compiled devastating information about the responsibility of military figures in some of El Salvador's most notorious massacres and killings, its recommendations were largely ignored. Less than a week after the commission's report was made public, ARENA pushed a broad amnesty bill through the Legislative Assembly over the opposition of the PDC, CD, and UDN. Perhaps more clearly than any other act, the amnesty bill revealed the depth of division in the country's political forces and the serious lack of consensus about what had occurred in its recent history. Despite the peace accords, past abuses of power still enjoyed impunity. Ordinary people and their families who had been victims of human rights abuses did not have the opportunity to go on record as part of a system of national accountability; they received neither an apology nor any admission of official wrongdoing.

Other provisions of the accords aimed to open up El Salvador's political system and to provide opportunities for former soldiers and guerrillas. Protecting human rights and reintegrating onetime combatants into civilian life were major concerns in the peace agreements. ONUSAL was given a major role in monitoring human rights conditions in El Salvador and helped to train personnel of a new legal office, the Procuraduría de Derechos Humanos, that would be established as an independent agency of the national government. The U.N. agency was also designated to assist in the formation and training of a new Policia Nacional Civil (PNC—National Civilian Police); it would be composed of former FMLN combatants (20 percent), former National Police (20 percent), and civilians (60 percent). Once in full operation, the PNC would replace the National Police and would be the sole agency responsible for maintaining law and order in El Salvador. The accords also called for major judicial reform to upgrade the country's woeful legal and criminal-justice systems. Political liberalization was to operate under the supervision of the Comisión para la Consolidación de la Paz (COPAZ—Commission for the Consolidation of Peace), composed of representatives of the government, the FMLN, and every political party in the national legislature. Opening up the political system would require new legislation, including amendments to the constitution, modification of Salvador's electoral system, and legalization of the FMLN as a political party. The accords also provided for stipends, training, and land redistribution for demobilized soldiers and guerrillas. People who had cultivated abandoned farmland for a certain number of years would also be eligible to benefit under the redistribution. Agencies of the United Nations and international funding were to assist the government and nongovernmental agencies in El Salvador's physical reconstruction from the war. A Social and Economic Forum would bring together representatives of government, business, and labor to discuss the country's economic needs and to foster agreement on basic issues.

These measures to open El Salvador's political system and to broaden its social base achieved mixed success. Internal divisions rendered both COPAZ and the Social and Economic Forum cumbersome and ineffective. Although ONUSAL helped human rights conditions to improve notably, the new institution of the Procuraduría de Derechos Humanos lacked funds and power. Judicial reforms progressed only slightly and encountered serious political obstacles. Land transfers to eligible former combatants and peasants lagged way behind schedule. In addition, the numbers of former soldiers and guerrillas demobilized far outran opportunities for training and employment. A rise in criminal activity became one of the principal issues of the postwar environment, causing the government to breach the April 1992 constitutional provision that restricted the armed forces from enforcing internal law and order. With the support of ONUSAL, the fledgling PNC gradually went into operation, replacing the National Police, but it suffered from inexperience, from insufficient funding and equipment, and from the actions of some former National Police within its ranks.

Even at the time of their signing, the peace accords looked ahead to the simultaneous presidential, legislative, and municipal elections of 1994 as a significant instrument of the country's postwar political normalization. The FMLN gained recognition as a legal political party and cooperated with the CD in supporting Rubén Zamora as a joint presidential candidate, although its approach to civilian politics was at times uncertain and confused. The election resulted in a major victory for ARENA, with 49.3 percent of the presidential vote in the first round (68 percent in the second round, a two-person runoff), 39 legislative seats, and control of 206 municipalities. ARENA had far more money and organizational capacity than any other party in El Salvador. The FMLN, having won 21 seats in the legislature, was considered by many to be the country's second-largest political force until further, seemingly irrevocable splits took place within its ranks, dividing the ERP and the Resistencia Nacional (RN) from the FPL, PCS, and PRTC. The experience of El Salvador underscores the importance, as Lungo argues, of understanding democracy as more than just elections. Given the country's history and the intensity of the revolutionary war, the successful participation of the FMLN in the 1994 elections was remarkable. Nevertheless, as was the case in the aftermath of the Truth Commission's report, the elections revealed the depth of divisions in Salvadoran society. Fear of governmental authority and a general lack of trust in the mechanisms of the electoral process overshadowed the voting. Abstentions ran high (43 and 50 percent in the two electoral rounds of March 20 and April 24, respectively), indicating the remoteness of the electoral process from the lives of many people and spoiling ARENA's expectation that a high voter turnout would provide the government with overwhelming international legitimacy. Serious charges arose that FMLN sympathizers had been excluded from the registration process and that voting on election day had been sullied by manipulatory tricks in favor of ARENA. At the very least, the voting process suffered from ineptitude on the part of the Supreme Electoral Council, cumbersome procedures, and enormous confusion.

Events in El Salvador since the signing of the peace accords demonstrate that a condition of peace requires more than the simple absence of war. There must be a significant level of trust about a society's institutions. There must also be a basic consensus about the nature of a country's past and the purpose of its future. This trust and consensus do not yet exist in El Salvador. The peace accords achieved some remarkable changes, opening a new historical period for the country, as Lungo notes. Individual rights and opportunities for political participation are far greater than they were before the revolutionary war. Yet the promise of the accords remains incomplete and the permanency of some of their achievements open to question, particularly in the political realm. Public institutions in El Salvador, especially those of the judicial system, remain weak. Salvadorans can still seriously wonder whether there will be justice for ordinary citizens and whether the powerful will be held accountable for their actions. The lopsided power of ARENA, the internal disarray within the FMLN, the weakness of other political parties, and the disaffection of major segments of the population from the political system all reduce the competitive balances necessary to prevent abuses. With the departure of ONUSAL and a reduction in the international funding for postwar reconstruction, institutional improvement will stem more heavily than before from the quality of the country's internal processes. As Lungo argues in *El Salvador in the Eighties,* much of the future will depend upon the ability of popular movements to organize groups to press forward with their needs and to strengthen the internal fabric of civil society. This is particularly crucial since the country's historical legacy of social inequality remains as alive as ever. As Carlos Vilas has stated, "[T]he challenge of democratization in Central America is to combine the institutionalization of ongoing conflict resolution with the effective transformation of socioeconomic structures and of cultural rigidities."[86] The accords concentrated upon demilitarization and creating a political opening, not upon renegotiating economic power. The socioeconomic elements of the accords—the Social and Economic Forum, the land redistribution, and the training and employment provisions for demobilized combatants—have been the least effective parts of the agreement. Widespread unemployment has contributed to a rising crime rate, resulting in a climate of public insecurity and fear. As Lungo and others have long argued, meaningful democracy in El Salvador requires far greater social equity and more highly developed popular structures of opportunity than the concentrated economic power of the country's elite has been willing to concede, either before the revolutionary war or since its negotiated ending in 1992.[87] It would be a tragic irony if the political accomplishments of the peace accords simply created a modernized, civilian electoral politics in which the Salvadoran wealthy used their disproportionate economic power to control the system and retain their historical privileges. Looking at the experience of El Salvador since 1992, Lungo now argues that "defending the political, social, and economic interests of the poor within the context of civil society is infinitely more complex than defending the poor in the context of guerrilla struggle."[88] This contention simultaneously modifies and builds upon his earlier views presented in *El Salvador in the Eighties.* Even as it downgrades some of his hopes for the viability of alternative politics, it reemphasizes both the long-term nature of popular struggles in El Salvador and the inseparable connection between political power and social power:

> *In recent years the issues of the rights of citizens and the rights of individuals have predominated in the political and human rights debate in El Salvador. These discussions are undeniably*

legitimate; however, the fundamental question of social justice has often been overlooked. . . . A truly democratic political culture must apply the rigors of democracy not only to politics but also to . . . private enterprise. Restricting the application of democracy only to the sphere of electoral politics and not dealing with the issue of the lack of democracy within the market system only contributes to social fragmentation.[89]

The post–Cold War world has been celebrated, prematurely, as one of triumphant democracy and unleashed economic prosperity. In actuality, the social and political foundations of rapid economic globalization remain unstable. "Social fragmentation" is a frightening prospect in many parts of the world. While "the vogue of revolution" may be over, the realities that provoke insurgency are not.[90] The experience of El Salvador warns the twenty-first century of the costs of ignoring social needs. It shows that a society of peace constitutes more than just the absence of war and that democracy is more than simply holding elections. El Salvador emphasizes the capacity of oppressed peoples to carry on long-term social struggles under highly adverse conditions. It suggests that the most vital global task in the years ahead should be to defend political democracy by promoting social democracy.

NOTES

1. Saul Landau, *The Guerrilla Wars of Central America: Nicaragua, El Salvador, and Guatemala* (New York: St. Martin's Press, 1993), 205–11.
2. Charles Krauthammer, "The Neoconservatives Hope Clinton Will Deal Them at Least One Key Foreign Post," *Philadelphia Inquirer*, January 19, 1993, A-10. Of similar import is David Broder's hasty post–Cold War gloss to the foreign policy of the administrations of Ronald Reagan and George Bush: "From Afghanistan to El Salvador, the United States under the leadership of these Republicans effectively supported the people whose values and aspirations came closest to our own—and helped them prevail." See David S. Broder, "As the Long Tenure of Republicans Comes to an End, History May Well Be Kind," *Philadelphia Inquirer*, January 17, 1993, C-6.
3. Isaac Cohen, "A New Latin American and Caribbean Nationalism," in *Free Trade in the Western Hemisphere*, ed. Sidney Weintraub (Newbury Park, Calif.: Sage Periodicals Press, 1993), 45.
4. See Peter F. Drucker, "The Age of Social Transformation," *Atlantic*, November 1994, 53–80.
5. See, for example, Mario Lungo Uclés, coord., *La planificación de la ciudad: Experiencias latinoamericanas* (San Salvador: FLACSO, 1993).
6. *El Salvador en los 80: Contrainsurgencia y revolución* (San José: EDUCA-FLACSO, 1990) followed *El Salvador, 1981–84: La dimensión política de la*

guerra (San Salvador: UCA Editores, 1985) and *La lucha de las masas en El Salvador* (San Salvador: UCA Editores, 1987).

7. See Juan Hernández Pico, S.J., "Central America's Challenge: Produce and Participate," *Envío* 14 (February–March 1995): 41–50; Raúl H. Mora Lomelí, S.J., "The Cycles of Crisis Are Narrowing," *Envío* 14 (May 1995): 31–36; and Edelberto Torres Escobar, "Will Central America's Farmers Survive the Export Boom?" *NACLA Report on the Americas* 28, no. 3 (November–December 1994): 28–33.

8. On the situation in Chiapas, see Tom Barry, *Zapata's Revenge: Free Trade and the Farm Crisis in Mexico* (Boston: South End Press, 1995); George Collier with Elizabeth Lowery Quaratiello, *Basta! Land and the Zapatista Rebellion in Chiapas* (Oakland: Institute for Food and Development Policy, 1994); and Physicians for Human Rights and Human Rights Watch/Americas, *Mexico, Waiting for Justice in Chiapas* (Boston and San Francisco: Physicians for Human Rights, 1994).

9. Carlos Fuentes, "Chiapas: Latin America's First Post-Communist Rebellion," *New Perspectives Quarterly* 11, no. 2 (Spring 1994): 56, 58.

10. Alma Guillermoprieto, "Letter from Mexico," *New Yorker* March 13, 1995, 40–46.

11. See two articles by Tim Carrington, "Mexico's Woes Show Risks of Partial Reform," *Wall Street Journal* February 13, 1995, A-1, and "Ties to Mexico Are Becoming Burden for U.S.," *Wall Street Journal*, March 9, 1995, A-2.

12. See Ronald Steel, "The Domestic Core of Foreign Policy," *Atlantic Monthly*, June 1995, 84–92.

13. See Michael Parenti, *Inventing Reality: The Politics of the Mass Media* (New York: St. Martin's Press, 1986), and Edward S. Herman and Noam Chomsky, *Manufacturing Consent: The Political Economy of the Mass Media* (New York: Pantheon Books, 1988).

14. See Fredrick B. Pike, *The United States and Latin America: Myths and Stereotypes of Civilization and Nature* (Austin: University of Texas Press, 1992).

15. Steel, "Domestic Core of Foreign Policy," 87.

16. Tony Smith provides a foolishly optimistic view of the ability of U.S. power to construct happy conditions in other societies through intervention. See his "In Defense of Intervention," *Foreign Affairs*, November–December 1994, 34–46. For a very different view, see T. D. Allman, *Unmanifest Destiny: Mayhem and Illusion in American Foreign Policy—From the Monroe Doctrine to Reagan's War in El Salvador* (Garden City, N.Y.: Dial Press, 1984).

17. Walter LaFeber, *Inevitable Revolutions: The United States in Central America*, 2d ed., rev. and exp. (New York: Norton, 1993), 5–18. See also John H. Coatsworth, *Central America and the United States: The Clients and the Colossus* (New York: Twayne, 1994), in which he argues that U.S. dominance over Central America in the twentieth century has been the primary cause of political instability and violence in the region.

18. Calculated from the tables given in James Dunkerley, *The Pacification of Central America: Political Change in the Isthmus, 1987–1993* (London and New York: Verso, 1994), 145.

19. See, for example, Cynthia Brown, ed., *With Friends Like These: The Americas Watch Report on Human Rights and U.S. Policy in Latin America* (New York:

Pantheon, 1985), 112–204; Mark Danner, *The Massacre at El Mozote: A Parable of the Cold War* (New York: Vintage Books, 1994); Theodore Draper, *A Very Thin Line: The Iran-Contra Affairs* (New York: Hill and Wang, 1991); and Peter Dale Scott and Jonathan Marshall, *Cocaine Politics: Drugs, Armies, and the CIA in Central America* (Berkeley and Los Angeles: University of California Press, 1991).

20. For analyses of contemporary international migrations, see Louise Lamphere, Alex Stepick, and Guillermo Grenier, eds., *Newcomers in the Workplace: Immigrants and the Restructuring of the U.S. Economy* (Philadelphia: Temple University Press, 1994); Paul Ong, Edna Bonacich, and Lucie Cheng, eds., *The New Asian Immigration in Los Angeles and Global Restructuring* (Philadelphia: Temple University Press, 1994); Alejandro Portes and Rubén G. Rumbaut, *Immigrant America: A Portrait* (Berkeley and Los Angeles: University of California Press, 1990); and two works by Saskia Sassen, *The Mobility of Labor and Capital: A Study in International Investment and Labor Flow* (London: Cambridge University Press, 1988), and *Global Cities* (Princeton: Princeton University Press, 1992).

21. Martin Carnoy, Manuel Castells, Stephen S. Cohen, and Fernando Henrique Cardoso, *The New Global Economy in the Information Age: Reflections on Our Changing World* (University Park: Pennsylvania State University Press, 1993), 1–3.

22. Peter Dicken, *Global Shift: The Internationalization of Economic Activity*, 2d ed. (New York: Guilford Press, 1992), 1.

23. Saskia Sassen, *Cities in a World Economy* (Thousand Oaks, Calif.: Pine Forge Press, 1994), 7. The analyses of Dicken, as well as those of Carnoy, Castells, Cohen, and Cardoso, would support Sassen's statement.

24. Manuel Castells and Roberto Laserna, "The New Dependency: Technological Change and Socioeconomic Restructuring in Latin America," *Sociological Forum* 4, no. 4 (1989): 556.

25. For some of the issues facing democratization in Latin America, see Jorge Castañeda, *Utopia Unarmed: The Latin American Left after the Cold War* (New York: Knopf, 1993), and Jorge I. Domínguez and Abraham F. Lowenthal, "The Challenges of Democratic Governance in Latin America and the Caribbean: Sounding an Alarm," *Inter-American Dialogue Policy Brief,* September 1994.

26. The literature on popular movements in Latin America is extensive. See Susan Eckstein, ed., *Power and Popular Protest: Latin American Social Movements* (Berkeley and Los Angeles: University of California Press, 1989); Arturo Escobar and Sonia E. Alvarez, eds., *The Making of Social Movements in Latin America: Identity, Strategy, and Democracy* (Boulder, Colo.: Westview Press, 1992); and Minor Sinclair, ed., *The New Politics of Survival: Grassroots Movements in Central America* (New York: Monthly Review Press, 1995).

27. Mario Lungo Uclés, "Building an Alternative: The Formation of a Popular Project," in *The New Politics of Survival: Grassroots Movements in Central America,* ed. Minor Sinclair (New York: Monthly Review Press, 1995), 178. See also his "Redefining Democracy in El Salvador: New Spaces and New Practices for the 1990s," in *Latin America Faces the Twenty-First Century: Reconstructing a Social Justice Agenda,* ed. Susanne Jonas and Edward J. McCaughan (Boulder, Colo.: Westview Press, 1994), 142–57.

28. See Benjamin R. Barber, "Jihad vs. McWorld," *Atlantic*, March 1992, 53–65.

29. Richard J. Barnet and John Cavanagh, *Global Dreams: Imperial Corporations and the New World Order* (New York: Simon and Schuster, 1994), 17, 22.

30. See Michael Lind, "To Have and Have Not: Notes on the Progress of the American Class War," *Harper's*, June 1995, 35–47.

31. Terry Lynn Karl, "El Salvador's Negotiated Revolution," *Foreign Affairs*, Spring 1992, 147–64. According to Tommie Sue Montgomery, *Revolution in El Salvador: From Civil Strife to Civil Peace*, 2d ed. (Boulder, Colo.: Westview Press, 1995), 261, Secretary-General Boutros Boutros-Ghali of the United Nations used the phrase "negotiated revolution" at the signing of the peace accords in Mexico City.

32. See Barbara Geddes, "The Politics of Economic Liberalization," *Latin American Research Review* 30, no. 2 (1995): 195–214; and Ben Ross Schneider, "Democratic Consolidations: Some Broad Comparisons and Sweeping Arguments," *Latin American Research Review* 30, no. 2 (1995): 215–34. For essays stressing the importance of respecting specific Latin American circumstances in the context of comparative and statistical-research approaches, see Peter H. Smith, ed., *Latin America in Comparative Perspective: New Approaches to Methods and Analysis* (Boulder, Colo.: Westview Press, 1995).

33. See Héctor Pérez Brignoli, *A Brief History of Central America*, trans. Ricardo B. Sawrey A. and Susana Stettri de Sawrey (Berkeley and Los Angeles: University of California Press, 1989), 92–105, and Ralph Lee Woodward, Jr., *Central America, a Nation Divided*, 2d ed. (New York: Oxford University Press, 1985), 149–76.

34. William Roseberry, introduction to *Coffee, Society, and Power in Latin America,* ed. William Roseberry, Lowell Gudmundson, and Mario Samper Kutzbach (Baltimore: Johns Hopkins University Press, 1995), 3, 5.

35. David Browning, *El Salvador, Landscape and Society* (Oxford: Clarendon Press, 1971), 165, 174.

36. The power of the oligarchy remained concentrated, even as its membership increased over time. Research in the 1980s calculated the size of the oligarchy at 114 family groups containing 1,309 individuals. See Montgomery, *Revolution in El Salvador*, 69.

37. James Dunkerley, *Power in the Isthmus: A Political History of Central America* (London and New York: Verso, 1988), 32.

38. Leon Zamosc, "Class Conflict in an Export Economy: The Social Roots of the Salvadoran Insurrection of 1932," in *Central America*, ed. Jan L. Flora and Edelberto Torres-Rivas (New York: Monthly Review Press, 1989), 65–70.

39. James Dunkerley, "El Salvador since 1930," in *Central America since Independence*, ed. Leslie Bethell (Cambridge: Cambridge University Press, 1991), 162–63.

40. Héctor Pérez Brignoli, "Indians, Communists, and Peasants: The 1932 Rebellion in El Salvador," in *Coffee, Society, and Power in Latin America*, ed. William Roseberry, Lowell Gudmundson, and Mario Samper Kutzbach (Baltimore: Johns Hopkins University Press, 1995), 256.

41. Although estimates of the number killed vary widely, most investigators agree that more than 90 percent of the casualties can be attributed to the government side, reprisals outweighing killings by the rebels on the order of 100 to

1 or more. See Thomas P. Anderson, *Matanza: El Salvador's Communist Revolt of 1932* (Lincoln: University of Nebraska Press, 1971), 136.

42. See Enrique A. Baloyra, "Reactionary Despotism in El Salvador: An Impediment to Democratic Tradition," in *Trouble in Our Backyard: Central America and the United States in the Eighties,* ed. Martin Diskin (New York: Pantheon, 1983), 101–23.

43. John Weeks, *The Economies of Central America* (New York: Holmes and Meier, 1985), 76.

44. Enrique A. Baloyra, *El Salvador in Transition* (Chapel Hill: University of North Carolina Press, 1982), 28; Dunkerley, "El Salvador since 1930," 170. The example of El Salvador flagrantly contradicted the faith of U.S. political-development theorists in the emergence of "modernizing elites" that would guide political, economic, and social change in the Third World. See Irene L. Gendzier, *Managing Political Change: Social Scientists and the Third World* (Boulder, Colo.: Westview Press, 1985).

45. Baloyra, "Reactionary Despotism in El Salvador," 109.

46. Montgomery, *Revolution in El Salvador,* 37–38. See also Roberto Turcios, *Autoritarismo y modernización: El Salvador, 1950–1960* (San Salvador: Ediciones Tendencias, 1993).

47. Over the same period, 1946–79, per capita economic output rose 2.5 times. See Victor Bulmer-Thomas, *The Political Economy of Central America since 1920* (New York: Cambridge University Press, 1987), 308–9, 312–13.

48. Weeks, *The Economics of Central America,* 64.

49. Charles D. Brockett, *Land, Power, and Poverty: Agrarian Transformation and Political Conflict in Central America* (Boston: Unwin Hyman, 1988), 75.

50. Montgomery, *Revolution in El Salvador,* 73; Edelberto Torres Rivas, *History and Society in Central America,* trans. Douglass Sullivan-González (Austin: University of Texas Press, 1993), 121.

51. Alastair White, *El Salvador* (New York: Praeger, 1973), 257. Allan Nairn detailed the role of the United States in creating ORDEN in "Behind the Death Squads," *Progressive,* May 1984, 20–29.

52. See William H. Durham, *Scarcity and Survival in Central America: The Ecological Origins of the Soccer War* (Stanford: Stanford University Press, 1979), and Thomas P. Anderson, *The War of the Dispossessed: Honduras and El Salvador, 1969* (Lincoln: University of Nebraska Press, 1981).

53. Che Guevara, *Guerrilla Warfare,* introduction and case studies by Brian Loveman and Thomas M. Davies, Jr. (Lincoln: University of Nebraska Press, 1985), 403.

54. A good, concise account of the impact of the bishops' sessions in Medellín upon the church in Central America is Tommie Sue Montgomery, "Liberation and Revolution: Christianity as a Subversive Activity in Central America," in *Trouble in Our Backyard: Central America and the United States in the Eighties,* ed. Martin Diskin (New York: Pantheon, 1983), 75–99; see also the comprehensive examination in Phillip Berryman, *The Religious Roots of Rebellion: Christians in Central American Revolutions* (Maryknoll, N.Y.: Orbis Books, 1984).

55. On the theology of liberation, see Phillip Berryman, *Liberation Theology: Essential Facts about the Revolutionary Religious Movement in Latin America and Beyond* (Philadelphia: Temple University Press; New York: Pantheon, 1987).

56. For an account of the actions of CEBs and resulting government repression, see Montgomery, *Revolution in El Salvador,* 86–97. On Monseñor Romero, see James R. Brockman, *The Word Remains: A Life of Oscar Romero* (Maryknoll, N.Y.: Orbis Books, 1982), and Jon Sobrino, *Archbishop Romero: Memories and Reflections,* trans. Robert R. Barr (Maryknoll, N.Y.: Orbis Books, 1990).

57. The five political-military organizations, with their component popular organizations (here listed first) and armed forces (listed second), were: the Popular Forces of Liberation (FPL, founded 1970), affiliated with the Popular Revolutionary Bloc (BPR, 1975) and the Popular Forces of Liberation (FPL, 1970); the National Resistance (RN, 1975), affiliated with the United Popular Action Front (FAPU, 1974) and the Armed Forces of National Resistance (FARN, 1975); the Party of the Salvadoran Revolution (PRS, 1977), affiliated with the 28th of February Popular Leagues (LP–28, 1978) and the Revolutionary Army of the People (ERP, 1972); the Communist Party of El Salvador (PCS, 1930), affiliated with the Nationalist Democratic Union (UDN, 1967) and the Armed Forces of Liberation (FAL, 1979); and the Revolutionary Party of Central American Workers (PRTC, 1976), affiliated with the Popular Liberation Movement (MLP, 1979) and the Revolutionary Party of Central American Workers (PRTC, 1976). Taken from Montgomery, *Revolution in El Salvador,* 102. The popular organizations had ceased to exist by late 1980.

58. Montgomery, *Revolution in El Salvador,* 115.

59. Ibid., 72.

60. Americas Watch Committee and the American Civil Liberties Union, *Report on Human Rights in El Salvador* (New York: Vintage Books, 1982), 278–81.

61. These killings are all covered in Raymond Bonner, *Weakness and Deceit: U.S. Policy and El Salvador* (New York: Times Books, 1984), 72–76, 103–4, 178–79, and 213–14. On the death of Romero, see also Brockman, *The Word Remains,* 217–23; on the deaths of the four U.S. churchwomen, see Allman, *Unmanifest Destiny,* 1–18, and Ana Carrigan, *Salvador Witness: The Life and Calling of Jean Donovan* (New York: Simon and Schuster, 1984), 221–317.

62. See Nairn, "Behind the Death Squads," and also Michael McClintock, *The American Connection,* vol. 1, *State Terror and Popular Resistance in El Salvador* (London: Zed Books, 1985).

63. Brockman, *The Word Remains,* 205–6.

64. Calculated from "Trends in U.S. Aid to the Region," *Envío,* December 1990, 18. The figure of more than 70 percent combines military aid (27 percent) with economic support funds (45 percent). Development assistance made up 16 percent of total U.S. funds. Economic support funds are often defined as a form of war assistance; see Rep. Jim Leach, Rep. George Miller, and Sen. Mark O. Hatfield, "U.S. Aid to El Salvador. An Evaluation of the Past, a Proposal for the Future," *A Report to the Arms Control and Foreign Policy Caucus* (February 1985); Tom Barry and Deb Preusch, *The Soft War: The Uses and Abuses of U.S. Economic Aid in Central America* (New York: Grove Press, 1988), 21–32. On the linkages between U.S. food policy and political-military objectives in Central America, see Rachael Garst and Tom Barry, *Feeding the Crisis: U.S. Food Aid and Farm Policy in Central America* (Lincoln: University of Nebraska Press, 1990).

65. On the reforms, see Montgomery, *Revolution in El Salvador,* 136–42.

66. The Salvadoran army expanded from 10,000 men in 1979 to 24,000 in 1982 to a peak of 56,000 in 1987. The FMLN increased from a few hundred combatants in January 1981 to an estimated total of 9,000 to 12,000 in 1984; thereafter, it deliberately reduced its force under arms to about 6,000 by 1987. See Montgomery, *Revolution in El Salvador,* 118, 149, 169, 198.

67. On low-intensity-warfare doctrines in El Salvador, see Daniel Siegel and Joy Hackel, "El Salvador: Counterinsurgency Revisited," in *Low-Intensity Warfare: Counterinsurgency, Proinsurgency, and Antiterrorism in the 1980s,* ed. Michael T. Klare and Peter Kornbluh (New York: Pantheon, 1988), 112–35.

68. Montgomery, *Revolution in El Salvador,* 117.

69. See "'Communist Interference in El Salvador': The U.S. State Department White Paper," in *El Salvador: Central America in the New Cold War,* ed. Marvin E. Gettleman et al., rev. ed. (New York: Grove Press, 1986), 314–24. Opponents of the war in the United States also failed to appreciate the particular qualities of the struggle in El Salvador—an early anti-war bumper sticker claimed that El Salvador Is Spanish for Vietnam.

70. Murat Williams, a retired veteran diplomat and a former U.S. ambassador to El Salvador, argued that remaking the Salvadoran officer corps was a pipe dream. See "Limits in Aiding Salvador," *New York Times,* June 17, 1983, A-27.

71. See Jeane Kirkpatrick's critique of the Carter administration's illusion that it could create democracy in "Dictatorships and Double Standards," in *El Salvador: Central America in the New Cold War,* ed. Marvin E. Gettleman et al., rev. ed. (New York: Grove Press, 1986), 14–35. For how the Reagan administration changed its mind on the "promotion of democracy," see Thomas Carothers, "The Reagan Years: The 1980s," in *Exporting Democracy: The United States and Latin America. Themes and Issues,* ed. Abraham F. Lowenthal (Baltimore: Johns Hopkins University Press, 1991), 90–122.

72. See Cynthia J. Arnson, *Crossroads: Congress, the Reagan Administration, and Central America* (New York: Pantheon Books, 1989).

73. For a comprehensive look at human rights issues in El Salvador during the 1980s, see Americas Watch, *El Salvador's Decade of Terror: Human Rights since the Assassination of Archbishop Romero* (New Haven: Yale University Press, 1991).

74. Dunkerley offers an excellent, succinct treatment of these years in *Power in the Isthmus,* chapter eight.

75. Joel Millman, "A Force Unto Itself: El Salvador's Army," *New York Times Magazine,* December 10, 1989, 46–47, 95, 97.

76. Geske Kijkstra, "Broken Promises: Duarte's Economic Policy," in *A Decade of War: El Salvador Confronts the Future,* ed. Anjali Sundaram and George Gelber (New York: Monthly Review Press, 1991), 85–101.

77. Montgomery, *Revolution in El Salvador,* 213–14.

78. On the Contadora/Caraballeda peace initiative, see Adolfo Aguilar Zinzer, "Negotiation in Conflict: Central America and Contadora," in *Crisis in Central America: Regional Dynamics and U.S. Policy in the 1980s,* ed. Nora Hamilton et al. (Boulder, Colo.: Westview Press, 1988), 97–115; Dario Moreno, *The Struggle for Peace in Central America* (Gainesville: University Press of Florida, 1994), covers the Contadora/Caraballeda and the Esquipulas processes.

79. Dunkerley, *The Pacification of Central America*, 65–68.
80. On the murdered Jesuits, see Teresa Whitfield, *Paying the Price. Ignacio Ellacuría and the Murdered Jesuits of El Salvador* (Philadelphia: Temple University Press, 1995), and John Hassett and Hugh Lacey, eds., *Towards a Society That Serves Its People: The Intellectual Contribution of El Salvador's Murdered Jesuits* (Washington: Georgetown University Press, 1991).
81. Dunkerley, *The Pacification of Central America*, 69–74.
82. Ungo and Zamora ran as candidates for president and vice-president for the Convergencia Democrática (CD—Democratic Convergence) in 1989, obtaining 3.8 percent of the vote. In the election for the Legislative Assembly in 1991, the CD gained 12.2 percent of the vote and eight assembly seats.
83. Coatsworth, *Central America and the United States*, 210.
84. Montgomery, *Revolution in El Salvador*, 228.
85. A summary of the provisions of the peace accords and a discussion of their implementation appears in Montgomery, *Revolution in El Salvador*, 226–48. More extended discussions can be found in the following reports issued by Hemispheric Initiatives of Cambridge, Massachusetts: Margaret Popkin, George Vickers, and Jack Spence, *Justice Impugned: The Salvadoran Peace Accords and the Problem of Impunity* (June 1993); William Stanley, *Risking Failure: The Problems and Promise of the New Civilian Police in El Salvador* (September 1993); Jack Spence and George Vickers, *Toward a Level Playing Field? A Report on the Post-War Salvadoran Electoral Process* (January 1994); Jack Spence and George Vickers, *A Negotiated Revolution? A Two Year Progress Report on the Salvadoran Peace Accords* (March 1994); Kevin Murray, *Rescuing Reconstruction: The Debate on Post-War Economic Recovery in El Salvador* (May 1994); and Jack Spence, David R. Dye, and George Vickers, *El Salvador: Elections of the Century* (July 1994); Margaret Popkin, *Justice Delayed: The Slow Pace of Judicial Reform in El Salvador* (December 1994); Jack Spence, George Vickers, and David Dye, *The Salvadoran Peace Accords and Democratization: A Three Year Progress Report and Recommendations* (March 1995).
86. Carlos M. Vilas, *Between Earthquakes and Volcanoes: Market, State, and the Revolutions in Central America*, trans. Ted Kuster (New York: Monthly Review Press, 1995), 188.
87. For example, see the 1980 essay by Segundo Montes, one of the UCA Jesuits killed in 1989, "Is Democracy Possible in an Underdeveloped Country?" in John Hassett and Hugh Lacey, eds., *Towards a Society That Serves Its People: The Intellectual Contribution of El Salvador's Murdered Jesuits* (Washington: Georgetown University Press, 1991), 141–57.
88. Lungo, "Building an Alternative," 178.
89. Ibid., 177.
90. For a critique of revolutionary ideology, see Forrest D. Colburn, *The Vogue of Revolution in Poor Countries* (Princeton: Princeton University Press, 1994). For other views and issues in the post–Cold War world, see Arif Dirlik, *After the Revolution: Waking to Global Capitalism* (Hanover, N.H.: Wesleyan University Press/University Press of New England, 1994), and Arturo Escobar, *Encountering Development: The Making and Unmaking of the Third World* (Princeton: Princeton University Press, 1995).

1989: A New Era
or Simply a New Phase?

El Salvador began a new period of its political history between the military coup of October 15, 1979, and the general offensive of the FMLN on January 10, 1981. Because this new period evolved from the accumulated successes and failures of the revolutionary movement of the 1970s, it must end in either the triumph or the defeat of the revolutionary forces. Now that this new period is a decade old, we can see how fundamentally it has transformed the Salvadoran political panorama after years of popular revolutionary war, economic changes, and demographic shifts. Two basic processes have stood out: the political recomposition of the dominant classes, a result of the persistent hegemonic crisis of the bloc in power; and the emergence of a lively popular revolutionary alternative.

This book opens with a question: Do the events of 1989, particularly the electoral victory of ARENA, define the start of another historical era, or do they simply mark a new phase in the period initiated in 1979–81? This question derives from my focus upon the structural processes underlying this past decisive decade of Salvadoran history. It colors my analysis of the military aspects of the Salvadoran conflict in Chapter two and my discussion of the major economic and demographic changes of the 1980s in Chapter three. Chapters four and five link the question to the limitations of the political recomposition of the dominant classes and to the political outlook of the popular revolutionary forces.

My question is more than semantic. In an important article, Ignacio Ellacuría argued that 1989 ushered in a new phase in Salvadoran politics, one that had been implicit in the events of the previous "year of gathering transition":

> *This new historical context is no mere conjuncture. The new position of the principal actors in El Salvador and Central America has to be interpreted. Our fundamental hypothesis is that the recent historical process of Central America—especially in Nicaragua and El Salvador—has to be seen as fundamentally determined by the confrontation between the Marxist revolutionary movement and the dominant, capitalist, conservative movement. This well-known confrontation of the last few years has entered into crisis, yielding a fundamentally new and more advanced form whose characteristics can now be appreciated.[1]*

Ellacuría goes on to analyze the crisis of U.S. policy, the evolution of the political framework of the FMLN, the new position of ARENA, the development of social forces, and the significant changes under way in the military. He offers an important overall perspective, one that I share in its analysis of the transformations of recent years. While I do agree that the present context marks a new phase, I would argue that it still lies within the political era that began in 1979–81. That historical period will continue as long as there has been no strategic defeat of the Salvadoran revolutionary movement.

This argument should be evident in the context of the clarity of Ellacuría's exposition of the strong evolution of the FMLN. Important patterns emerge if one visualizes a revolutionary pole and a counterinsurgency pole as the two conflicting elements in the Salvadoran political struggle of the 1980s. While the composition of the revolutionary pole remained the same—the FMLN and the FDR—that of the counterinsurgency pole shifted following the establishment of an ARENA majority in the Legislative Assembly in 1988. This pole originally formed in January 1980 around the PDC, the Salvadoran armed forces, and the U.S. administration of Ronald Reagan; after 1988, its three components became ARENA, the armed forces, and the administration of George Bush.

The precise composition of these two poles is certainly more complex than this brief description allows—among other things, their struggle is influenced by the ever-changing Central American and global political contexts and by the gradual emergence of a new international division of labor arising from changes in the capitalist and socialist economies of the last two decades. Nevertheless, this scheme allows us to focus on the fundamental question of the decade—the unresolved crisis of hegemony in the dominant bloc, an issue that I contend cannot be solved without the strategic defeat of the revolutionary forces.

Changes have also taken place within the components of the two poles. The PDC, for example, is no longer the same political institution it was at the start of the decade, its political character having become quite distant from anything that its founders in the 1960s would have imagined. As an institution, the armed forces have undergone modifications that go well beyond their spectacular growth and their behavior on the battlefield. The same can be said of the Reagan and Bush administrations, whose policies toward El Salvador (particularly those of Reagan) have been so amply studied. Because the newest actor, ARENA, is the least known and least analyzed of all, I have dedicated Chapter four to looking at the recomposition of the dominant classes, the context in which ARENA has emerged as the true party of the Salvadoran bourgeoisie after fifty years during which that class did without one. Likewise, the transcendental changes in the revolutionary forces have barely begun to be analyzed, especially those of the Farabundo Martí National Liberation Front. The organic development of the FMLN, the unfolding of its revolutionary project, and the richness of its political thought can only be explained by analyzing the evolution of its political-military organizations.

It is vital to understand that the process of political and military struggle during the 1980s has at once derived from and expressed itself through the profound transformation taking place in El Salvador's economic, territorial, and demographic foundations. Although these matters have been studied primarily from an economic viewpoint, they need to be related to the political projects of both poles, as Ellacuría has argued:

> *The issue of economic policy is also important. The ARENA government will probably at once be liberal on political questions in order to keep up democratic appearances and very strict on economic questions. . . . It is not a matter of capital having weakened during Duarte's years in office, but rather of capital attempting to grow rapidly. One may suppose that this rapid accumulation of benefits will spill over somehow onto the situation of the popular majorities. If capital achieves its goal without there being any tangible gains for the majority of the population, polarization and confrontation will be inevitable.*

Economic, territorial, and demographic changes also interact closely with the dynamic of military confrontation. Among the most notable developments in this area have been the construction of the rear guard and the revolutionary army on one side and a profound transformation of the government army on the other.

Yet, in the midst of these changes, in 1989 the crisis of hegemony in the dominant bloc still continues. Instead of a solution, a mere replacement of one component of the counterinsurgency pole (the PDC) by another (ARENA) has taken place. This crisis of hegemony has dominated El Salvador since the 1920s and remains, in my opinion, the central characteristic of the country's political system. It stems from the absence (until the 1980s) of a bourgeois party in the strict sense of the term. The political era following 1979 has been characterized by this crisis of hegemony and by the existence of a highly viable revolutionary movement. When added to the experience of the United States in Latin America and elsewhere, these factors have led to a sophisticated and novel counterinsurgency strategy whose main goals are the military defeat of the revolutionary forces and the reconstruction of the Salvadoran political regime. The object is to institutionalize a government that has national and international legitimacy.

The Christian Democratic Party, the armed forces, and the Reagan administration originally agreed on a strategy combining military combat against the FMLN, reform of the country's oligarchic economic structure, and clean elections designed to bring a civilian president into office. The elections of the 1980s did achieve some of the results hoped for by their architects. The Salvadoran government is now endowed with the democratic legitimacy of having been voted into office honestly. Indeed, the legitimation process has been reinforced by the election of civilian presidents, breaking the country's five-decade tradition of military dictatorship. At the same time, however, the counterinsurgency strategy of developing the political center has produced some unforeseen results. It altered the composition of the bloc in power by bringing in the PDC without there being any direct political representation of the dominant classes. This meant that the counterinsurgency pole had to deal with two antagonistic groups between 1980 and 1988, the revolutionaries and the tough bourgeois opposition. By the end of the decade, the bourgeoisie had reconstituted itself as a political class through the emergence of ARENA and its electoral triumphs of 1988 and 1989. This political remaking of the dominant classes constitutes the principal achievement of the elections of the 1980s and of the counterinsurgency strategy pushed by the United States. In the wake of this unexpected result, U.S. policy toward El Salvador has lapsed into a profound inertia from which it has not yet recovered.

The counterinsurgency strategy has resolved neither the hegemonic crisis inside the dominant bloc nor the fifty-year-old general hegemonic crisis of Salvadoran society. It cannot do so without producing a strategic defeat of the FMLN. Yet the FMLN has strengthened itself by developing a more flexible ideology and program. A complex new network of relationships and contradictions now prolongs the crisis of hegemony within the bloc in power even as the potential revolutionary alternative remains. In other words, the political period opened in 1979 still exists. Events since 1988, including ARENA's presidential victory and the FMLN military offensive of 1989, shape a new phase within that period as the rules of the class struggle change within El Salvador.

I shall detail in Chapter four how the fashioning of ARENA as the first legitimate party of the bourgeoisie since the 1920s has been accompanied by a renovation of political thinking among the dominant classes. This renewal is most evident in the economic policy proposals of the Fundación Salvadoreña para el Desarrollo Económico y Social (FUSADES—Salvadoran Foundation for Economic and Social Development) and in the emergence of intellectuals and new publications that truly are the organic representatives of the bourgeoisie. When ARENA took the place of the PDC in the counterinsurgency pole in 1988, the politically reconstituted bourgeoisie assumed a more protagonistic role. Yet, this did not resolve the crisis of hegemony—another key component, the armed forces, had also undergone profound changes that influenced the whole pattern of relationships within the bloc.

The armed forces are no longer the docile servants of the dominant classes as they had been for the last fifty years. The war, with its voluminous military and economic aid from the United States, has enlarged and enriched the Salvadoran military. Engaged in the task of war for which they had been trained and aware that they have suffered the greatest loss of life within the dominant bloc, military men now have the capacity to establish their independence from the bourgeoisie. Only their extreme dependence upon U.S. aid—a source of weakness as well as strength—has prevented coup attempts. Military relations with ARENA are often conflictive, although in ways different from the military's disagreements with the PDC in the last decade.

All of this presents a panorama of extraordinary complexity and dynamism. Moreover, one must situate the political future of El Salvador within the contexts of Central America and the world. In regional politics, dialogue and negotiation prevail, despite the difficulties posed by attempted military solutions. Throughout the world, the recurring crises of the capitalist system and the restructuring of the international division of labor interact with the internal limitations of the socialist countries to create mandatory economic and political changes. All these features of the present moment radically alter spheres of influence and global relationships.

Because it is difficult to predict the future political development of El Salvador with any clarity, I have decided not to posit a group of scenarios. I have chosen instead to offer a perspective on the fundamental structural processes of the country's intense political history during these crucial years.

Key Aspects of
the Military Dimension

Descriptive accounts, communiqués, and propaganda pieces make up the bulk of the extensive body of writings that has emerged about the popular revolutionary war in El Salvador. Far fewer in number are the objective analyses, most of them written by FMLN leaders, some by former U.S. military advisers,[1] and a few by Salvadoran army officers.[2] The reasons should be obvious. It is, for one thing, counterproductive to give away strategic information to the enemy. For another, not enough time has passed to permit drawing conclusions from trends that have only dimly begun to take shape. Even though war has been central to the history of El Salvador over the last ten years, the full dimensions of the conflict still elude analysis.

Nevertheless, there can be no objective basis for political interpretations without an anaylsis of the war. I will address three of its key features that partially explain the central political analysis of this book: first, the armed revolutionary struggle, the territorial constraints on its development, and the formation of the revolutionary army; second, the transformations that have occurred in the armed forces of the Salvadoran government; and third, the problem of insurrection. My analysis will not be exhaustive; I examine in detail only the fundamentals of these three key features as a means of shedding light on the Salvadoran political process during the 1980s.

The Armed Revolutionary Conflict,
Territorial Constraints, and the
Formation of the Revolutionary Army

Any process of armed revolution must deal with the determining characteristics of its own specific context in place and time, with the laws pertaining to all revolutionary wars, and, more generally, with the conditions that apply to all forms of war. For example, the rear guard is critically important. In light of this reality, some Marxist-Leninist groups in El Salvador, especially the PCS undertook a critical examination of the defeats suffered by Latin American revolutionary guerrilla movements in the 1960s and early 1970s. Since their analysis mechanically identified the rear guard with the mountains or the jungle, they doubted the viability of armed struggle in El Salvador. Echoing this, the refrain "The mountains of the Salvadoran revolution are the working masses" became popular many years later, even after the indispensable rear guard had been established. This implicit debate illustrates the importance of examining the process by which the popular forces in El Salvador gradually overcame their country's recognized territorial constraints on armed revolutionary struggle.

Surmounting *Foquismo* and Constructing the Rear Guard

The rear guard was one of the central issues that Salvadoran revolutionaries discussed while planning the establishment of political-military organizations in the early 1970s. They were painfully aware of the defeat of *foquista* guerrilla movements elsewhere in Latin America. [In *Guerrilla Warfare* and other writings, Ernesto "Che" Guevara offered an interpretation of the Cuban Revolution that established the primacy of the guerrilla *foco*, or the guerrilla force itself, in promoting the revolutionary process in Latin America. —Translator] It is a distasteful and paradoxical reality that the relatively late blooming of the Salvadoran revolutionary movement enabled it to avoid the mistakes that had cost the lives of so many nameless, valiant Latin American combatants. The PCS was slower to split than other Latin American Communist parties, and thus the hegemony of its reformist strategy persisted, retarding the development of alternative revolutionary politics. Furthermore, the country's political environment was so closed that it strongly suppressed even liberal ideas and writings. By the time new revolutionary efforts emerged in El Salvador, the era of rural *foquista* guerrilla struggles in other parts of Latin America had already come to an end. Even the cycle of urban guerrilla activities was on the wane, for these groups had failed to generate a revolutionary movement among the working masses of the cities and their compatriots in the countryside.

From the beginning, the need to build a rear guard in El Salvador was as much a political as a key military problem for the fledgling political-military organizations. This reality would soon force out of the struggle those whose militarist leanings prevented them from recognizing the complexity of the issue. The indispensable task of building the rear guard was a terribly difficult and contradictory process. Before the outbreak of open popular revolutionary warfare, revolutionary forces had constructed a political rear guard only in the broadest sense: revolutionary mass organizations. Yet their existence would make the rapid and extended building of a political-military rear guard possible after January 1981, when the military struggle came to predominate.

Following the model provided by General Vo Nguyen Giap,[3] one can distinguish two forms of the rear guard in the Salvadoran case. The "extended rear guard" consists of the broad mass revolutionary movement built after 1974, when the original Frente de Acción Popular Unificada (FAPU—United Popular Action Front) was organized. The "restricted rear guard" is made up of people from the zones under the territorial control of the FMLN. The development of the extended rear guard took place over six years that were absolutely crucial to the Salvadoran revolutionary struggle. Without this initial step, dictated by the historical, social, and political conditions (as well as the territorial characteristics) of El Salvador, the construction of the restricted rear guard after the FMLN general offensive of January 10, 1981, would have been impossible. Peculiar to the Salvadoran revolution, this process constitutes one of the most significant contributions to the liberation struggles of the peoples of Latin America.

After the offensive, which lasted less than a week, the tactical retreat began; this phase ran from the middle of January to June 1981.[4] These months laid the foundation for the final consolidation of the restricted rear guard. Thus, the cycle begun in 1974 reached its completion, having moved through three stages—from (1) the initial construction of a political base among the masses, through (2) the formation of bases of support for specific actions, to (3) the constitution of true zones of political-military control, the specific Salvadoran form of the restricted rear guard. The inability to visualize this complex historical process has produced confusion in understanding the Salvadoran popular revolutionary war. More than a few observers, particularly U.S. military advisers, have underestimated the capacity and development of the Salvadoran revolutionary forces. A brief look at the January 1981 FMLN general offensive and the subsequent tactical military reorganization will show how the revolutionary movement prepared the ground for consolidating its restricted rear guard during this phase.[5]

Above all, I emphasize the overall political and military success achieved by the FMLN. With the general offensive, the revolutionaries brought to an end a historical political era whose final moments obliged them to make a qualitative leap foward, a maximum concentrated effort to alter the correlation of political and military forces in El Salvador. The FMLN offensive created a new political period marked by the start of open revolutionary conflict. Not to have taken this step would have produced a strategic defeat, a point overlooked by analysts who focus exclusively on the military actions of January 1981.

The alteration in the balance of forces appears highly positive today, even in strictly military terms. The offensive was marked by several fundamental accomplishments:

- For the first time since the popular insurrection of 1932, revolutionary forces were able to assume an offensive strategy; this enabled the masses to regain a previously repressed confidence in their capabilities and potential.
- For the first time, the military units of the various revolutionary organizations acted in coordination.
- Although the general offensive covered nearly the entire country, its operations were uneven since inequalities and disequilibriums are an inevitable law of history.
- Tactically, revolutionary forces for the first time executed military actions whose breadth surprised the government armed forces, driving them into fixed positions; many of these were surrounded and nearly fell into revolutionary hands.
- The people learned how to handle arms, enabling them to rapidly form a true revolutionary army, which would be solidly in place by 1983.

And, to reiterate a fundamental point, the January 10 offensive made the building of a restricted rear guard possible:

> *Besides containing the offensive actions of the enemy, after January 10 the revolutionary forces passed from political control to military control of some zones. This shift was vital enough in the development of the war to be considered the principal military accomplishment of the revolutionary forces: the guarantee of an effective rear guard within their own territory.*

> *This constituted an irreversible advance that allowed the revolutionary forces both to adapt to and to prepare themselves for any eventual military situation. Without this military accomplishment, it would be very difficult to think of reaching any decisive phase in the armed struggle.*[6]

This judgment was reaffirmed by analyses made three years later:

> *This action (the offensive of January 10), despite its tardy development with regard to the critical point of the revolutionary situation (January–June of 1980), constituted an active leap forward in the accumulation of forces. It prefaced a continuous, immediate phase of resistance and development, a great strategic success that allowed the FMLN to assure itself of a rear guard. The building and defense of support bases (rear guard territories that were simultaneously battlefronts) were the element necessary in order to win and to consolidate territory after the attrition suffered by the army in each cleanup operation during this phase.*[7]

Following the success of the offensive, the leadership of the revolutionary vanguard analyzed the situation. The fundamental strategic problem of the rear guard (particularly the question of its restricted component) emerged again. It was urgent to establish the bases for its later definitive consolidation. Reflection and discussion brought up a host of questions: How could the formation of this restricted rear guard be prevented from becoming an end in itself, thus locking the revolutionary armed forces into a passive and defensive stance? How could the unavoidable retreat and the time needed for tactical readjustment be combined without incurring a level of disorganization that would provoke counterinsurgency sieges and offensives? What attention should be paid to territorial constraints during these months? How should the armed struggle deal with such constraints? From then on, the leadership decided to operate on the principle that only the defeat of enemy attacks and incursions could guarantee the construction of a relatively stable guerrilla base capable of fulfilling the functions of a rear guard. This official line of approach, whose correctness can be fully appreciated today, was synthesized in an FMLN slogan of the time—Resist, Develop, and Advance.

During the struggle of the following months, the government army launched numerous offensives against the zones of revolutionary control and influence, most notably the nearly two-month siege of Guazapa. This experience proved that topography is never the decisive factor in a revolutionary war. Here, the fundamental deciding element instead proved to be the political work that had been carried out earlier among the working masses in the countryside. As a leader of the FMLN indicated:

> *The entire period before the armed struggle made its "boom" was preceded by an intense struggle of the masses, as much in the city as in the countryside. . . . There is no question that without the organization and activity of the masses, which permitted the Salvadoran revolutionaries to gain political control over extensive peasant zones, the armed struggle would never have gathered force.*[8]

The existence of this work in areas of local, relatively self-sufficent agricultural economies independent of urban centers combined with El Salvador's extraordinary population density to guarantee the fulfillment of the first part of the plan: "resist." The accumulated experience and revolutionary political-military strategy assured the achievement of the other two goals: "develop and advance."

During these months the foundation was established for what would come to be known as "control zones," or, in the propaganda literature, "battlefronts"—a name that does little to convey the rich, complex, and novel social dynamic that developed within them. If, in the week from January 10 to January 17, 1981, "the zones of political activity in the country were suddenly transformed into broad battlefronts" in a series of explosive and simultaneous "peasant insurrections," then from mid-January to mid-June these battlefronts became zones of political-military control, the particular Salvadoran form of the restricted rear guard.

Zones of political-military control cannot be measured solely by whose military forces operate in and around them. The army high command and their U.S. military advisers still continue to disregard this old truism of popular revolutionary wars. At first, it appeared that the government forces had taken this fact into account when designing and executing their plans. How many times, for instance, did they refuse to mention "taking the fish out of the water" or pursuing similar goals? Ultimately, however, all their offensives peaked and lost strength. In fact, a revolutionary political-military strategy does not automatically transform itself from a political strategy into a military one or vice versa. Through struggle, the construction of a revolutionary alternative of power follows a dialectical process between political acts and military acts that does not always mesh with preconceived designs.

Someday, when a historian describes the control zones of the Salvadoran revolution, it will be clear that the specific history of each of them—the history of the exploitation of their workers, of their struggles, of their culture, in sum, the history of all their contradictions and political revolutionary work—not their topographical conditions, constitutes the main reason for their impregnability. Although my purpose here is not to write such a history, I have already touched upon some aspects of it; among others that might be noted are the organizational development of particular zones before the beginning of the war,[9] the role of religion and the popular church in consolidating the rear guard of the FMLN,[10] and the development of an alternative popular culture.[11]

On this last point for example, consider some findings from research into the music of the rear guard in the departments of Chalatenango and Morazán:

> *The content of the songs shows that the politicized peasant sectors have developed a structured group of concepts that have come to be considered a coherent and functional frame of reference for their particular way of life, that is, for the war and their struggle for social transformation. . . .*
>
> *We find the substrata of their concepts as much in the religious sense as in the political sense. . . .*
>
> *The songs convey a sense of collective participation and develop elements of identity and solidarity that reinforce their community and organizational connections (ideological sympathies). Music is an extremely important mechanism within the symbolic strategy of the sectors belonging to the FMLN's political project; it conveys messages and orientations that facilitate the expression of the FMLN's goals, not only within the politicized sectors, but also within the broad sectors of the population in zones of guerrilla influence and zones under dispute.[12]*

From the Restricted to the Extended Rear Guard

By creating zones of control, the restricted rear guard not only achieved consolidation but also a linkage to the extended rear guard that had no rigid territorial limits. The revolutionary forces refused to conceive of the control zones as fixed and definitive, a vision whose positive results became increasingly apparent during the phase known as "starting the seizure of political and military initiative" (July–August 1981), and particularly so during the subsequent phase of "starting the seizure of the strategic military initiative" (June 1982–April 1983). During the first two years of the war, 1981 and 1982, this strategy had to overcome the highly important obstacle of localism. Popularly known as *ombligismo* [literally, "focusing upon one's navel" —Translator], this phenomenon was particularly strong in areas characterized by the social predominance of impoverished *minifundistas* [agriculturalists working very small plots of land]. Localism made it difficult to apply a valid concept derived from the Vietnamese experience—when establishing a guerrilla base, always keep in mind the time to leave; when defending the base, always keep in mind the moment to abandon it.

The revolutionary forces owed their strategic success in overcoming the pitfalls of localism mostly to their work in creating a wider political consciousness. In those cases where they made the mistake of trying to overcome localism by strictly military means (e.g., the forced transfer of combatants to new zones beyond their home areas), they failed completely. The question of encouraging a broad political consciousness is vital to understanding two other issues: how building a flexible restricted rear guard linked deeply to the extended rear guard characterized the Salvadoran revolutionary process; and how the operations of this restricted rear guard proved indispensable in overcoming the contradiction between the country's territorial constraints and its armed struggle. A brief look at the military campaigns of July and August 1981 and of March 28, 1982 will help illustrate this process of construction and consolidation.[13]

The first campaign began on July 19, 1981, with the systematic sabotage of electrical-transmission service. The FMLN blew up fifty-six high-voltage transmission towers in different parts of El Salvador, affecting territory from the Guazapa region in the center to the coastal provinces of the west. This action was accompanied by sabotaging and seizing control of the routes of ground communication, including demolishing four bridges and carrying out seven successful ambushes.

After forty-eight hours of combat, the FMLN occupied the town of Perquín, taking thirty-four prisoners of war and seizing a quantity of arms. From this brief account, the following points emerge as particularly relevant:

- In many cases, the revolutionary forces extended the areas of combat to points far from their traditional zones of control, thus rendering useless the government's military tactic of seige and annihilation.

- Such extension proved vital in overcoming the prevailing localism of the combatants and the mass-political cadres; it contributed to a definitive rupture with the existing limited outlook of the rear guard.

- The rear guard grew deeper and stronger through having eliminated the government forces from positions in settlements within the control zones.

- Circumstances showed the organized masses in the control zones that their safety did not depend on a closed defense of territorial positions or on the existence of topographically impregnable zones. From this moment on, what the new popular Salvadoran revolutionary idiom referred to as *guindas* (the flight of great masses of people, especially women, children, and the old from a zone undergoing an enemy incursion) would gradually change. In short, territorial contraints were overcome once again.

The 1981 campaign took place while the government army was engaged in new offensives in other FMLN zones of control (it had just withdrawn from the Cerros de San Pedro zone, located in the north of San Vicente department, and from Chalatenango). The FMLN thus forced the government to interrupt plans and reorganize forces, causing it to lose the military initiative taken toward the end of August 1981.

During the next offensive, which began in late December 1981 and culminated on the eve of the elections of March 28, 1982, tendencies only nascent in the campaigns of the previous July and August became more pronounced. A central objective was to bring the war to the principal election sites, forcing the army to deploy large numbers of troops in the cities and freeing the revolutionary forces to consolidate and enlarge the two most important zones of the restricted rear guard, Morazán and Chalatenango. It is not my intention to detail the military campaigns of the revolutionary forces, but rather to show how these campaigns helped to consolidate the rear guard and to overcome territorial constraints. In this respect I can note:

- There was a deepening of the tendency begun in the previous campaign to extend the war throughout the entire country by carrying out operations in wider areas ever more distant from the control zones.
- A qualitative leap was made in overcoming localism by taking fighters not only to other rural zones but into the cities as well.
- By fighting battles in urban areas, the revolutionary forces shattered the notion that guerrillas can only fight in the mountains or the jungle; this brought a radical change in the view of the rear guard and of the country's territorial limitations.

By the end of these campaigns, one thing was clear: only the quantitative growth and qualitative development of the armed revolutionary forces permitted the consolidation of the control zones and the expansion of the restricted rear guard, thereby deepening the war of the people. The slogan Resist, Develop, and Advance popularized by the high command of the FMLN had been superseded by the middle of 1981. Yet it remained an accurate reflection of the movement's determination to avoid a passive and defensive posture (even if that stance was intended as a guarantee for the construction of the rearguard) and to employ a strategy of attack to overcome its territorial constraints. Only an essentially offensive military strategy could provide for the self-defense of the masses and for the defense of the rear guard.

After each campaign, the FMLN retreated toward the control zones. There, the rear guard would be positioned in a flexible manner coordinated with the working masses, a tactic that guaranteed the preservation of the political and military initiatives taken. The FMLN made great efforts to consolidate its territorial gains within a framework that was flexible for the rear guard, rather than focusing upon predetermined areas. This strategy doomed the counterinsurgency attempts to "take the fish out of the water," since these attempts assumed that the "pond" had geographical boundaries. Even if aerial bombardments and ground artillery attacks at saturation levels massacred civil populations, such measures could not eliminate the "water," which stetched out on all sides and moved continuously. This constituted an obstacle that in the long run not even a direct and massive intervention by foreign troops could remove.

After the military campaigns of October 1982 and January 1983 (part of the "starting the seizure of strategic initiative" campaign), the control zones were expanded and consolidated at an even faster rate, an indispensable move for advancing the revolutionary war and increasing its intensity. This expansion and consolidation had economic, political, and cultural aspects, not just military ones, and the government army was obliged to cede ample sections of the country's territory. Two fundamental objectives were achieved after October 1982, deepening the military initiative that had been retaken in June and July and developing an adequate framework for a political proposal of dialogue. The government army found itself in almost total retreat, even declaring at one point that it would no longer bother to retake certain settlements "because they have no strategic importance." For example, in Chalatenango it withdrew to the settlements near the hydroelectric dams on the Lempa River, while in Morazán it retreated south of the Torola River.

There was another, perhaps even more substantial, advance for the revolutionaries. They surmounted the relative disconnection between political and military action by establishing the first overall political proposal inside El Salvador since 1981 for resolving the war. Although I shall discuss this subject later, I note here that this quantitative leap forward would lead to a strengthening of the extended rear guard, as General Giap said.

Expanding the Territory under Control

After January 1983 the government army decided upon a defensive deployment in fixed positions. The tactics employed by the FMLN since mid-1982, particularly the ambushes of government troops as they moved from one place to another, had exhausted the army. The revolutionary forces took advantage of this deployment, attacking and dislodging the army from small and medium-sized positions in a gradual process of eradication that expanded the FMLN zones of control. These efforts had a clear impact on broadening political work and consolidating the rear guard. During this period, the revolutionary forces made their most significant gains in the central region, especially in Chalatenango. In the east, their success in gaining control of the important city of Berlin at the beginning of February 1983 reflected their extraordinary capacity for concentration, mobility, and deployment. The FMLN established a connection between control zones in the northern and southern parts of the eastern region.

After the "Comandante Ana María" campaign in April 1983, this pattern became even more pronounced as the revolutionary forces enlarged their theater of operations considerably. The FMLN dislodged government forces from villages located near the Pan American Highway in the departments of San Vicente and Usulután. Government troops proved unable to recapture these areas. The revolutionaries carried out attacks as far as the extreme east of the country, including the border at Amatillo and the important city of Santa Rosa de Lima. They forced the government army from its key positions south of the hydroelectric dams in the province of Cabañas. Finally, they launched attacks in the western zone.

By 1983, the FMLN's rear guard had been formed. Future efforts would deal with the political and military security of the rear guard, with being prepared for a possible massive U.S. military intervention, and with changes in the tactics of government forces. The revolutionaries continued to follow a flexible plan in which territorial limits were not the determining factor. After February 1983 the army tried unsuccessfully to dislodge the revolutionary forces from Guazapa, one of their control zones. In mid-1983, it radically changed tactics in a serious bid to regain the initiative and retake the ground it had lost. The army also, and particularly, sought to resolve its two immediate weak points: a lack of coherent leadership and not having enough troops for the recently expanded military theater. The Salvadoran military found the FMLN expansion particularly threatening since it pointed to a rear guard capable of fulfilling three indispensable functions at this stage of the war: ensuring the minimal safety of the political and military commanders; maintaining and improving morale among fighters; and gradually creating popular local governments, the incipient form assumed by alternative power in the Salvadoran struggle. The outlaw mentality was giving way to a revolutionary legality, won and defended by force of arms, that paralleled the dominant bourgeois legality.

At this point the revolutionary forces were able to achieve another essential component of victory, the development of diverse means of communication. It was impossible to separate the logistical aspects of the war from its political aspects. Both were rooted in the advancement of the social base supporting the revolutionary forces. Throughout the 1980s, the FMLN would continue to expand the territory covered by its military and political operations. Conditions led the revolutionary leadership to observe at the beginning of 1984, "[a]s the

FMLN continues to expand its rearguard, strategic cities and highways are becoming "no man's land."[14]

The course of the war would modify this evaluation over the years, but always within the continuous and changing expansion of the theater of political and military operations of the revolutionary forces. One day, this matter will be the subject of an exhaustive historical analysis. Here, I will simply examine how the prolongation of the war influenced its dynamics.

The War Is Prolonged and Extended

How did the length of the conflict affect the transcending of territorial constraints and the construction of a rear guard?

I must establish at the outset that the nature and characteristics of the revolutionary war changed with its relative duration. Its extension in time implied an ever greater territorial deployment of offensive revolutionary actions. This, in turn, led to the development of an increasingly complex and solid rear guard that bound its restricted and extended dimensions more closely together. Without this, the country's territorial constraints (topography, vegetation, territorial expanse, etc.) would have presented insurmountable difficulties for the development of the revolutionary war. Only the ample and profound political work that the revolutionary forces had carried out earlier throughout almost all of El Salvador allowed them to meet the conditions imposed by the prolongation of the war. By the end of 1983 and the beginning of 1984, the lack of correspondence between the zones of FMLN strategic military operations and the control zones of tactical support had been constantly diminishing. The FMLN thus benefited from the spread of the control zones through their flexible extension and from the growing fusion of the two forms of rear guard. The revolutionary forces succeeded in reducing the time that their units depended upon a fixed base of support. As conditions for a prolonged revolutionary resistance improved, a growing mobility in the implementation of support bases demonstrated that localism had been virtually transcended.

This raises a controversial issue regarding the Salvadoran revolutionary process: the thesis of the "prolonged popular war."[15] At a certain distance from the debate, one can see today why the formulation of the problem of the relative duration of the war was both appropriate and necessary. Its discussion was highly charged, given the emotion inherent in the day-to-day struggle and the predominance of a schematic "principaledness" that has subsequently been overcome. Certainly the discussion and the airing of attitudes about the length of the revolutionary war in El Salvador were indispensable to the formalization of more concrete strategic planning, especially the drafting of appropriate tactics. Related discussions took place about a war of "rapid definition," a general insurrection, the buildup of the rear guard, and the question of territorial constraints. One must remember that if the conditions needed to produce a general insurrection are not present and the correlation of forces is not favorable (as is the case in almost all revolutionary processes), prolonging the popular revolutionary war becomes obligatory. In this way, the war modifies the character and form of both the insurrection and the rear guard.

This point should not lead to a schematic formulation of the thesis of a prolonged popular war, confusing its definition with an extension of the war obliged by the impact of increasing foreign intervention. To do so would be to reject the capacity of revolutionary forces to take advantage of the weaknesses and inconsistencies of their opponents, accelerating the war, radically changing its balance of forces, and thus shortening the interval before victory. This position on the duration of the war carries implications for revolutionary political tactics dealing with such matters as territorial extension and the absence of an external rear guard, that is, a neighboring country with a political regime favorable to the revolutionary forces.

I will first discuss the question of internal territorial extension and its link to the relative duration of the war. Here I return to the essential political-military and popular character of the strategy and tactics of the revolutionary forces in El Salvador. At this stage, the war had spread throughout the country in its armed and unarmed forms. The extension came about through the actions of commando groups and of the masses, through using both violent and nonviolent tactics, through the employment of economic and of cultural methods—the war, in short, had become at once political and military. Thus the problem transcended the strictly military, although military action was the principal and determining form of struggle most of the time, anchored in the breadth of the social forces it incorporated. The war was waged in all possible locales simultaneously, thus preventing it from becoming limited to fixed military fronts. The FMLN had developed an approach to combat characterized by high levels of mobility and flexibility.

Although the popular revolutionary war in El Salvador was waged by five armed revolutionary organizations, and although it exhibited certain important zones of concentration, it did not have either a fixed central point or various central points. The general war command had no permanent base. The boundaries of the control zones varied and had gone on expanding since 1981. The ongoing social and political expansion of the borders of the revolution conquered its territorial constraints, thus providing a serious obstacle to those who supported massive military intervention by foreign forces. Certainly, not having a neighboring "sanctuary" country constituted a particularly difficult limitation for the Salvadoran revolutionaries. Nevertheless, they overcame it through a qualitative development of the internal rear guard, particularly by paying attention to the political-military issue of forging local popular power. I shall now briefly examine its development in connection with the problem of the rear guard.[16]

When the revolutionary forces began withdrawing toward their control zones after January 10, 1981, they encountered a social base organized within a system reflecting conditions antedating the start of the war in its open form. The population had considerable experience in revindicative struggles, most of which had been legal, and some initial experience in armed self-defense. These qualities proved insufficient either to resist the sieges and military offensives launched by the government army or to supply the extra material necessities of the growing contingents of new combatants.

At first, production and defense were organized to meet these newly created conditions, but this only strengthened localism and produced an inadequate defensive posture. Army attacks increasingly took on the character of a regular war, in contrast to the simple repressive control of the security forces. Indeed, the fixed character of this strategy allowed the government forces to destroy the harvests and local infrastructure, prompting the exodus of many families. This period gave rise to the idealistic plan of making each revolutionary soldier half-producer, half-combatant, a scheme that resulted in combat inefficiency and a heightened localist spirit. Little by little, experience created a new system that embodied local popular power in a variety of different forms and names (e.g., councils known as "Consejos Farabundistas"). Organizational structures spread beyond the control zones and their social base, reaching into zones of expansion and the lives of their inhabitants.

Under the impotent gaze of the government army, the organization of local power managed to administer settlements of sometimes thousands of inhabitants, exercising, in fact, an almost complete control over numerous municipalities. It was no longer a question of marginalized population groups confined to control zones from which they had to flee constantly. Through struggle and sacrifice, a new legality emerged that foreshadowed new forms of political and social organization. The positive effects of this popular local power on the construction and consolidation of the rear guard demonstrate how it is possible to overcome territorial constraints, no matter how difficult they may be.

I point out one aspect in which the development of popular local power clearly represented a contribution to the construction of the rear guard: the attention revolutionaries gave to the health care needs of the civilian population while attending to wounded FMLN combatants, a measure that reinforced the social organization of the communities within the control zones.[17]

The development of these alternative forms of power, as partial and disconnected as they may appear at first glance, had a cumulative effect. Research on the repopulated Salvadorans who had lived as refugees in Honduras or who had been displaced to various locations within El Salvador shows the existence of new forms of social organization:

> [T]housands of peasants that fled from their places of origin to other parts of the country or abroad have begun not only to return to their localities but also to construct their communities under a set of new political principles and social relations.
>
> Certainly, within the national geopolitical context these communities constitute a limited base of experience due to their reduced territorial expanse and the predominance of the state administrative-political forms; nevertheless, it must be emphasized that these community self-governments are collective and cooperative experiences that are being conducted outside of the areas of Agrarian Reform and/or the traditional cooperative sector. In addition, these are not clandestine structures created and/or controlled directly by the FMLN as were perhaps some years ago the "Local Popular Powers" constructed by masses in constant mobilization throughout the territory under control.
>
> This leads to the conclusion that although the population has developed a certain level of autonomy with respect to the FMLN, it continues to identify with the struggle of the FMLN at the level of individual political opinion. After all, the FMLN defends their fundamental interests, not the governmental army, which permanently punishes them and places new obstacles to their development.[18]

This source goes on to identify 407 community organizations spread over seven of the country's fourteen departments (represented in the Patronato para el Desarrollo Comunal en El Salvador [PADECOES—Council for Community Development of El Salvador]), five repopulated communities, and seven repatriations in three of the hardest hit departments of the country. This phenomenon has given rise to various organizations like the Comité Cristiano para los Desplazados de El Salvador (CRIPDES—Christian Committee for the Displaced of El Salvador).

Other elements of the expansion and prolongation of the war also demonstrate that the extension of the revolutionary rear guard could not be measured strictly in territorial terms. Indeed, were it not for the success of the rear guard, the transportation shutdowns ordered by the FMLN between 1986 and 1989 would not have lasted as long, nor covered as much of the country, as they did. In like fashion, the rear guard played a fundamental role in wresting political power from the municipalities, which since 1932 have played a key role in the country's repressive governmental system. Furthermore, it helped to wear down the counterinsurgency programs that tried to mobilize support for the government through control of the civilian population—for example, CONARA (National Commission for the Restoration of Areas) in 1984 and "United to Reconstruct" in 1986.[19]

With the FMLN's buildup of the rear guard between 1980 and 1983, the war entered the stage in which the revolutionary forces broke down traditional patterns of territorial control (as had happened in Nicaragua between 1977 and 1979).[20] The Salvadoran case employed different means, with the result that the effects of the breakdown flowed beyond the strictly military and extended into the political sphere as well. In a contradictory way since the beginning of the decade, two state policies have reinforced this breakdown of established patterns of territorial control: first (and the one that I feel is decisive), the implicit classification of the zones of control or influence of the FMLN as war zones; second, the partial implementation of the first and third stages of the agrarian reform decreed in March 1980. (In later chapters, I will further explore the influence of state policies like agrarian reform.)

A thorough survey of the development of the revolutionary rear guard would require a more detailed analysis of the events of the second half of the 1980s. Yet, even from the overview offered here, it is easy to see the extreme weakness of evaluations such as the thesis of "military stalemate" that have been offered as comprehensive explanations of the revolutionary war in El Salvador.

The Formation of the Revolutionary Army

Constructing the rear guard was necessarily intertwined with creating the revolutionary army. Although it is premature to offer a definitive history of the development of that army, a look at some critical aspects of its evolution is vital to a proper understanding of the military dimensions of the Salvadoran war. For this purpose, I will analyze documents and declarations of those in charge of the process of creating the revolutionary army, the leaders of the FMLN. I will rely on their assessments at four key points: the middle of 1981, the beginning of 1984, the beginning of 1986, and the end of 1988.

I begin with the following precise view:

> *Much has been said about the meaning of the actions of January 10 for the development of the struggle of the Salvadoran people, but the majority of the analyses do not begin with the objective impact on the correlation of forces at a military level; instead they provide a political focus with expectations of an immediate resolution of the situation.*
>
> *The actions carried out by the revolutionary forces . . . reflected a substantial change in the correlation of forces at the military level, a result which would not take long to become apparent to everyone.*[21]

This change was reflected in what I have already pointed out: the revolutionary forces supplied themselves with arms, learned to use them, withstood aerial and artillery attacks, carried out tactical maneuvers in different terrains, organized themselves more professionally, adopted modern forms of radio communication, and constructed a restricted rear guard. By mid-1981, only six months after the war had begun in its open military form, the revolutionary army had already established its basic foundations. The official armed forces and their U.S. military advisers were obliged to recognize this fact and to change their strategy and tactics accordingly. The analysis by the FMLN general command at the beginning of 1984 shows how the formation of the revolutionary army accelerated between July 1981 and the end of 1983, frustrating the successive tactical readjustments designed by U.S. advisers:

> *The mastery of terrain, the capture of weapons, and the erosion of the strength of the dictatorship's army all indicate the ad-*

vance of the revolutionary army. In one year of war, from June, 1982 to June, 1983, the FMLN managed to gain control of one fifth of the country and to eliminate almost a third of the Salvadoran army.[22]

Territorial control did not consist of the expansion of an insurrectional offensive. Instead, it was a complex and dynamic process in which the political and military growth of the FMLN combined with a moral weakening and an exhaustion of the enemy forces. Once the notions of an uprising launched at will and of great offensives were overcome, a greater understanding emerged of the characteristics of the revolutionary war in El Salvador.

The fundamental military tactic of the FMLN during this period validated the flexibility shown in the construction of the rear guard. Setting forces into a traditional war of positions was not conducive to the FMLN's step-by-step defense of sites, a fact that would have great offensive value in the struggle in upcoming years. The execution of this tactic was possible thanks to an important strategic change that occurred in October 1982. At that point, the FMLN achieved a substantial gain in the coordination and the simultaneity of the actions of its various forces. These improvements helped it to capture a brigade barracks for the first time and to blow up a number of highly fortified strategic bridges.

The first signs of local popular power manifested themselves at about this same time through production, literacy, health, and other programs that would have a significant impact on the structuring of the revolutionary army. Popular local power served as a way for the revolutionary forces to create new theaters of operation, to establish and evaluate new bases of support, to design new lines of expansion of political work, to incorporate new social elements that differed from those in the rear guard, and to distribute logistical reserves in accordance with new plans. This process of shaping the revolutionary army rested on the following principle: "Combin[e] the military struggle with the political struggle, while treating the former as primary and decisive."[23] Although valid for the moment, this view needed modification later as the war dragged on and, above all, as changes took place in the Salvadoran political system.

The formation of the revolutionary army was tied closely to the strategic perceptions of the revolutionary leadership. For example, although the assessment later proved untenable, early in the war the leadership foresaw direct foreign military intervention as the official army collapsed: "The FMLN intensifies the offensive and begins the struggle for vital zones of the country, thereby increasing the possibility of a second intensification of the revolutionary situation and a yanqui intervention."[24] This consolidation can be observed in the data presented in Table 1.

Following the consolidation of the rear guard and the forging of large military units, one can observe an apparently paradoxical shift as of 1984. The FMLN restructured its military units and extended its operations throughout the entire country, without sacrificing the ability to concentrate forces at specific places and times for large-scale operations. What explains this radical change? In my opinion, there were three contributing factors. The first was the recognition of the constraints of the military factor in a revolutionary war, clearly expressed by one of the FMLN leaders in 1986:

In a popular war, the role of the military component is not absolute; the key for a revolutionary movement is to know if the forces have achieved a sufficient military buildup capable in combination with political factors of changing the correlation of forces. In 1983, despite the fact that the attacks of the FMLN placed the army on the brink of military collapse, the lack of an

Table 1
Military Advances of the FMLN, January 1981–January 1984

Phase III	Arms Recovered (×1,000)	Official Army Losses (×10,000)	Prisoners Taken (×1,000)
I Jan.–July 1981 (7 months)		900	
II July 1981–June 1982 (12 months)	429 rifles, 31 support weapons	3,718	178
III June 1982–Sept. 1983 (16 months)	2,964 rifles, 148 support weapons	6,826	1,134
IV Sept. 1983–Jan. 1984 (5 months)	1,422 rifles, 116 support weapons	3,000	753
Totals	4,815 rifles, 295 support weapons	14,444	2,065

Source: Comandancia General del FMLN, "Situación revolucionaria y esclada intervencionista en la guerra salvadoreña" (México, 1984).

upsurge within the popular movement prevented these military victories from obtaining more significant changes in the correlation of forces.[25]

This true assessment clearly indicated a recuperation of the political dimension of the Salvadoran struggle, a side considered deficient by the revolutionary leadership when it affirmed in 1985 that the 1982–83 strategic-tactical plan exhibited a limited grasp of the concept of "a war of all the people."[26] The rush to create large military units had weakened guerrilla and militia units, raised the need for service personnel, increased expenditures for munitions, facilitated the task of the government's air power, left room for enemy patrols, and generally made it more difficult to maintain continuity in the struggle.

The construction and development of the extended rear guard both permitted and obligated the FMLN to readjust to a strategy capable of utilizing its maximum potential to counteract changing government tactics. The readjustment greatly affected the structuring of the revolutionary forces, allowing the FMLN to lay the foundations for a strategic counteroffensive that would neutralize the growth of the government army:

[T]he correct and well-considered thing to do was for the FMLN to change to a more political strategy that would allow it to coordinate the political struggle with the military struggle. A very important fact should be pointed out. It is not the air war, nor the changes in the army's tactics that force the FMLN to expand the war. Having broken the defense of vital areas, having accumulated military and cadre experience, and enjoying a favorable conjuncture for the popular struggle, it would have been a grave error for the FMLN to pursue the war only on its traditional fronts.[27]

This shift in strategy had important political implications as well. It requires a greater number of political cadres to lead small military units than it does to lead large concentrations of combatants; this fact obliged the FMLN to intensify its political-ideological efforts. In this new context, the significance of weapons necessarily changed. In the continuous consolidation of the people's army, popular weapons such as explosives came to play a key role, as did the constant sabotage of the war economy of the regime. This feature has not been understood fully:

> It is highly simplistic to think that a people like ours with a tradition of struggle is going to determine its attitude and conduct toward the war based solely on the complications of the struggle itself and not on the structural factors that determine the necessity to struggle in the first place. . . .
>
> When talking of advantage or disadvantage, one should analyze what weighs most heavily in the conduct of the people and the understanding they may have of the war and of sabotage. One must ask what has the greatest impact, the sabotage or the economic package.[28]

With respect to one of the major changes in the strategy of the government army—the decision to resort to air power—the FMLN took the position that defeating the government did not require completely destroying its forces. It was only necessary to render them incapable of containing the advance of the revolutionary forces. In an analysis written at the end of the decade, Joaquín Villalobos summarized the progress made by the revolutionary army:

> At this point, the FMLN employs multifaceted military action that has both a military and political impact. Its strength continues to grow with new contingents; under the leadership of experienced forces, these units have over a very short time helped to increase the capacity of attacks, taking advantage of their knowledge of the terrain and their relationship with the masses.[29]

Villalobos went on to emphasize how the expansion of the war throughout the country, including vital areas like the cities, linked the revolutionary military capacity to El Salvador's explosive social situation.

By the end of the 1980s, the revolutionary army was a successful reality that had produced more than 30,000 enemy losses, captured over 2,000 prisoners, recovered more than 10,000 arms, and shot down or destroyed over 60 airplanes or helicopters. All the while, it operated in the principal cities of thirteen of the country's fourteen departments.

Changes in the Official Armed Forces

In a parallel process of day-to-day opposition to the growth of the revolutionary army, the official armed forces underwent a profound transformation. As their membership quintupled between 1979 and 1987, they became an experienced military organization, different from the institution of decades past, which was so docile toward the oligarchy and so repressive toward the people.

This accelerated growth resulted from a counterinsurgency strategy designed abroad, one that did not reflect the needs of the majority of the Salvadoran people. This fact produced contradictions that enormously reduced the effectiveness of U.S. weaponry and military advice; it also increasingly alienated the army as an institution from national interests.

Changes in the government army began very early in the war, during the first half of 1981, when the number of troops grew from ten thousand to twenty thousand as part of a plan intended to reduce FMLN forces to small pockets of resistance that could be isolated through a political strategy.[30] Implicitly, the government had acknowledged that it lacked the means and men necessary for a rapid annihilation of the revolutionary forces. The latter had already forged a restricted rear guard, despite the fact that twenty thousand government troops constituted the equivalent of one man per square kilometer. The core of the government's military plan was to cut off supplies to the revolutionary armed forces, subject them to constant attrition, and attack the civilian population that made up the FMLN's social base of support. This goal of "taking the fish out of the water" would not be reached.

Besides an increase in arms and in troop levels, the official armed forces began building a mobile strategic force on the suggestion of their U.S. advisers. It initially consisted of three battalions charged with annihilating or neutralizing the centers of resistance. This initiative faced enormous difficulties due to time constraints, the lack of trained officers, and contradictions within the government army itself. Nevertheless, the strategic mobile force was created as the vanguard of the new military tactics devised by the U.S. advisers as the way to vanquish the FMLN. Table 2 gives a detailed breakdown of the army's capacity.

Table 2

The Structure of the Salvadoran Armed Forces

	1979	1980	1981	1982	1983	1984	1985	1986	1987
Troops*	10	17	20	24	37	40	44	50	56
Maneuver battalions	13	16	17	22	43	40	41	42	41
Airplanes	28	28	22	21	25	38	42	49	63
Helicopters	5	5	13	17	28	32	47	67	72
Naval units	4	4	4	4	10	12	13	21	33

Source: A.J. Bacevich et al., "American Military Policy in Small Wars: The Case of El Salvador" (Cambridge, Mass.: John F. Kennedy School of Government, Harvard University, March 1988).

*In thousands; includes the security forces.

The New Tactics of the Government Army

By mid-1983, the tactical changes advocated by the U.S. advisers reached their apogee. These had been imposed gradually after January 1981, despite the serious conflicts they engendered within the Salvadoran armed forces.[31]

Revamping the army's traditional tactical planning was certainly necessary, given its unsuitability for the conditions of an irregular revolutionary war. This reform was part of the strategic option chosen by the U.S. advisers once the war entered its protracted form after 1981. Its goal was the annihilation of the revolutionary forces by the Salvadoran government's armed forces without a massive direct intervention by U.S. troops. Despite the enormous political costs such an intervention would entail, it was not absolutely ruled out in case of dire necessity.

This new tactical approach had four elements: modifying weaponry to suit irregular revolutionary war; restructuring troops into new units capable of irregular combat; organizing appropriate leadership for these new units; and changing the essence of tactical operations. During 1981, the first objective was achieved almost completely. The M-16 rifle replaced the G-3, a heavier weapon of higher caliber requiring more maintenance; the M-79 grenade launcher, the portable 90 mm cannon, the light 60 mm mortar, and the light M-60 machine gun were all introduced in quantity; A-37B aircraft, which had proved their efficiency in Vietnam, replaced the Fouga and Ouragan planes, both obsolete and inadequate for combating guerrilla forces.

Restructuring the government troops began in 1981 with the introduction of the first mobile elite battalion, the Atlacatl, followed in 1982 by the Belloso Battalion (trained in the United States), and then by the Bracamonte Battalion. The *cazador* (hunter) battalions also emerged for the first time; these bore the names of the brigades from which they originated. The cazador battalions comprised only about three hundred troops, making them more suitable for irregular warfare. The intent was to create smaller mobile units independent of any particular military draft. Nevertheless, several factors made it difficult for the U.S. military advisers to achieve their second goal: first, increasing the number of troops proved painfully slow, since recruiting for the elite groups could barely keep pace with the enormous number of casualties inflicted by the FMLN; second, the growth in troop strength required more officers, when combat losses were making them scarce; and finally, the changes in military units conflicted with the objective of restructuring the system of command.

A reorganization of the command structure could not take place without grave contradictions, despite its indispensability to the optimum development of the new strategy. Modifying military leadership implied challenging the power and privileges of the *tanda* currently holding the highest positions, thus threatening the ambitions of the upcoming tandas. In El Salvador, the oligarchy never permitted military officers access to ownership of the means of production, limiting them to marginal gains through involvement with contraband and other "dirty" activities. Therefore, the time when a tanda reached the apex of military power was the most opportune moment for its officers to increase their wealth and social status. It was clear to the U.S. advisers that the departmental command posts of the brigades were not up to dealing with the irregularity and mobility of a revolutionary war. The process of restructuring the leadership continued to be full of pitfalls; only seeing that the government was losing the war convinced corrupt and inefficient officers that change was necessary.

The lack of coherent military leadership had roots extending well beyond the tensions among the tandas and among different military groups and beyond the disputes over appropriate military tactics. While these sources of contradiction certainly existed, the fundamental aspect of the situation was the persistent crisis of hegemony within El Salvador's dominant classes. This deep-seated problem of the Salvadoran social formation permeated the entire state apparatus, including the armed forces, and prevented the imposition of a single coherent political project. Given the poor prospects of finding a solution to this crisis, any reorganization of army leadership could offer only a temporary solution to the lack of cohesion.

The fourth element of the new strategy, modifying the essence of tactical operations, depended upon completing at least a major part of the first three elements, as well as upon new training for both troops and officers. As a result, it was not until mid-1983 that efforts were undertaken to put the fourth element into place; even then, the persistent troop shortages made for limited results.

This part of the new strategy had a pronounced impact on the process of constructing the rear guard of the FMLN. One of the principal changes in the government army's new strategy was to increase the duration of its offensives—short, concentrated assaults lasting from eight to twelve days grew into campaigns lasting several months. Another change was to launch more-intense attacks against the zones of revolutionary control using the new cazador battalions, which would then remain on constant patrol. Yet another was to increase the simultaneity of attacks. Finally, the important principle of giving a political content to the army's operations was brought into play. The framework would be unlike either the traditional Plan of Civic Military Action, developed during the 1960s for peacetime use, or the construction of Vietnam-style strategic hamlets, practically impossible in El Salvador given the country's size. Instead, the political content derived from efforts to repopulate abandoned rural areas with political supporters of the regime, to organize them militarily for their partial defense (the cazador battalions were also responsible for defending them), to provide agricultural credit, and to create infrastructure along with health and educational services. The aim, in short, was to modify the social base in zones subject to the control and the influence of the FMLN.

This new strategy failed because of the shortage of operative government troops and especially because of the political and military efforts of the revolutionary forces. It did, however, oblige the FMLN to change its criteria for constructing and consolidating the rear guard, since the government's new approach was more appropriate to the natural territorial constraints that the armed revolutionary struggle faced in El Salvador. Above all, it forced the restricted rear guard to become more flexible and mobile, thus improving its coordination with the extended rear guard. The government army's new military strategy provoked a qualitative leap by the FMLN in its efforts to overcome the territorial limitations of the Salvadoran revolutionary war.

It took the U.S. advisers almost three years to implement the new strategy. Meanwhile, the war dragged on, and many key aspects of the strategy lost their relevance. The revolutionary leadership concluded in 1984:

> *Parallel to the expansion plan, U.S. advisers outlined an offensive design that supposedly would allow the Salvadoran army to keep its forces alive and to protect key zones. But the exhaustion of the army is constantly greater as the presence and activity of the FMLN spreads further in vital areas.*[33]

During this period, more than 80 percent of the government's military capacity was in permanent use. The regime was thus unable to deploy its remaining forces scattered around the country. Faced with the military advance of the FMLN in 1983, the army had to reduce the defense of its minor fixed posts to a minimum and establish more-defensible positions. It began to contest only sites of strategic military, political, or economic importance, giving up territory and establishing a strategy of mobile defense. In other words, the strategy promoted by the U.S. advisers devolved into a retreat by the army into new defensive lines. This outcome contradicted the offensive objectives originally planned in order to separate the masses from the FMLN, isolating the latter in the northern region of the country—and it all stemmed from the mistaken assumption that the revolutionary forces were tied to their control zones. The strategy of "troops without barracks" became a rigid and essentially defensive scheme.[34] Even the massive utilization of air power did not reverse these tendencies. As Villalobos pointed out in 1986,[35] the air war arrived too late. The FMLN had already broken vital defensive lines, increased the territory either under its control or in dispute, and extended the operations of its forces into urban or suburban areas, where the air force could have been used only at a very high political cost.

The profound changes that took place between 1981 and 1984 continue to characterize the official armed forces even today at the end of the decade. The army is no longer the traditionally inefficient and repressive institution of earlier times. It is larger, more modern, and better trained. But it continues to be unable to defeat a revolutionary army that was formed in barely nine years. How can these limitations be explained? Certainly, the fundamental answer must be rooted in the popular character of the struggle facing the government and in the persistence of the structural social, economic, and political causes that gave rise to the conflict. Just the same, it is important to look at the impact of change upon the military from within. For this, I rely on the revealing analysis of four U.S. military officials, A.J. Bacevich, J.D. Hallums, R.H. White, and T.F. Young.[36]

Limitations of the Transformation of the Official Army as Seen by the U.S. Advisers

The premise underlying U.S. strategy remains very clear—to reverse the record of successive U.S. losses in small-scale wars by defeating the Salvadoran insurgents through supplying material support and military assistance to the Salvadoran government without direct combat intervention by U.S. forces. This comprehensive counterinsurgency strategy has conceived of "military policy" as an integration of military measures with political, social, economic, and diplomatic actions, all with the objective of defeating the FMLN. Under the pressure of the military climate in the early years of the war, revolutionary leaders found it difficult to evaluate clearly the real possibility of direct intervention by U.S. troops. No single concrete document existed that articulated the counterinsurgency strategy of the United States. Consequently, in its analysis of the possibilities of U.S. armed intervention the 1984 rebel assessment underemphasized the changes taking place within the government armed forces.[37] It also proved difficult then to comprehend the political reconstitution of the dominant classes in El Salvador, another process that indirectly influenced the United States choice of options at the beginning of the war. (Nevertheless, this confusion did not invalidate the FMLN's decision to carry out a decisive shift after 1984 in its strategy and in its political-military tactics. Observers of the Salvadoran situation have emphasized the military dimension of this change, making it harder to appreciate its political dimension.)

The "almost invisible" means of intervention adopted by U.S. strategists explains the relatively limited number of permanent military advisers in the country (55 at the beginning, 100 toward the end of 1984, a few more than 150 in 1987–88, according to the four U.S. officers). While the strategists did not have a single document that unified the different ways in which the conflict needed to be addressed, three documents issued between 1981 and 1984 together do offer a complete vision of U.S. policy, according to Bacevich, Hallums, White, and Young: the Woerner Report (1981), the National Campaign Plan (1983); and the Kissinger Commission Report (1984).

The Woerner team concentrated on restructuring the government army; quadrupling its forces; providing it with up-to-date equipment; introducing modern tactics; improving its leadership, control, communication, and intelligence; and establishing a new logistical system. It also evaluated the Salvadoran air force and the navy. However, the team did not have enough time to carry out its mission fully. Even more important, I would argue, it lacked the ability to analyze other facets of the counterinsurgency strategy, such as control of the civilian population, economic and political reforms, government programs, civil defense, and psychological operations. Not until the National Campaign Plan of 1983 was there any effort to formulate this counterinsurgency strategy more comprehensively in order to win popular support for the Salvadoran government. However, this new iniative failed, in large part because the genocide of 1980–82 stripped credibility from any administration prior to that of José Napoleón Duarte. Thus, it is no more than a partial truth to claim, as did the four advisers, that the principal reason for their failure was a lack of support from the government and people of the United States.

The objective of the Kissinger Commission Report was to provide a regional vision with a wide-ranging strategic formula for holding back revolutionary movements in Central America and the Caribbean. This report coincided with the accession of Duarte to power, the peak of the counterinsurgency strategy in El Salvador. Thereafter, the strategy slid toward defeat, since it went against the interests of most Salvadoran workers and since it rested upon a crisis of hegemony that still remains unresolved at the end of the 1980s.

I now examine in detail some of the critical evaluations of the new Salvadoran army provided by the four U.S. advisers. One problem concerns the decisions about purchasing military equipment, an issue in which they repeatedly insist that United States input was quite weak. As a result, despite the apparent modernization of the government army and its efforts in most cases to adjust to the exigencies of an irregular war, senseless acquisitions occurred. Communications equipment was purchased for which there were neither Spanish-language manuals nor logistical support within the U.S. army. In like fashion, heavy arms (such as the 105 mm howitzer) were procured that were of little use in irregular combat and that significantly reduced tactical mobility because of their need for mechanical transport.

Analogous contradictions can be found in the case of the air force. At the end of 1987, there were only seventy active pilots to fly 135

planes—in a context marked by poor training and deficient maintenance. As the U.S. advisers revealed, the FMLN's change in strategy reduced the effectiveness of the air force. Its deadly power against the civilian population endured, however, thus posing an interesting paradox:

> *In a war that pays a premium for being* among *the people, the
> UH-1 [helicopter] has made [the] EASF [armed forces of El Sal-
> vador] into an army that spends too much time* above *the people.*[39]

Given the growing number of soliders, preparing new officers and
training operative unit and troop leaders constituted significant problems. Since the expanded army needed a great many new officers, the
time allotted for their preparation was sharply reduced, a factor that
had serious repercussions on the army's levels of training. In addition,
this schooling took place in U.S. academies where instruction pertaining to small counterinsurgency wars was minimal, according to the
four advisers. The limited duration of the tours of duty for advisers
sent to El Salvador and their unequal skills compounded the almost
insurmountable obstacle of the excessive rotation of soldiers. The accumulation of experience in the training of operative and troop leaders was slow. It remained difficult to coordinate the land corps with
the excessively autonomous air force. Nevertheless, the structure of
the army did change in a relatively short time.

The greatest problems appeared among the officers, since the effects
of military reform had political implications transcending the institution
of the armed forces. The four U.S. advisers indicated that the question
was not simply one of training and education. It involved, rather, a military tradition characterized by insubordination toward civilian author-
ities,[40] a lack of respect for human rights, and the logic of the tanda system. Bacevich and his colleagues note that the latter still constitutes the
key barrier to the true professionalization of the officer corps.

The problems generated by these tendencies are complex. They include certain tensions between the new officers who were prepared
rapidly (the "gringos") and those who were matriculated in the traditional way. Many of the former have undergone a strong "denationalization." All these problems lead to the same central question: At
what point might ten years of war, enormous military growth, the har-
rowing risks associated with day-to-day fighting, and the changes in
the country's political system over the decade make the Salvadoran
army as an institution abandon its traditional role as an unconditional
and docile guarantor of the interests of the dominant classes?

One finds various indicators bearing upon the development and resolution of this question in the existing patterns of contradiction within the heart of the army itself, between the army and ARENA, and between the army and the United States. The army cannot forgo U.S. assistance without provoking its own collapse, but at the same time U.S. aid has made the military an increasingly dependent institution. Moveover, the question cannot be separated from the crisis of hegemony within the Salvadoran political system. In this context, the U.S. advisers admitted to being unsure about the future role of the army, even in the case of an FMLN defeat.

It is undeniable that the army's operational capacity has improved, despite various problems, especially the much lower combat morale of soldiers as compared to FMLN fighters. This is a political problem, and its remedy goes beyond the possibilities of foreign aid. Perhaps the greatest change within the Salvadoran army in recent years, aside from its greater size, is the increase in its logistical systems and installations. As Bacevich and the other advisers pointed out, however, the role of high technology in a counterinsurgency war is clearly secondary. Despite the intent of U.S. assistance, the Salvadoran army today still employs conventional tactics in an irregular war, operating with battalions, relying on armored vehicles and helicopters for combat transportation, and depending on a high level of firepower.

The army's growth in manpower has been accompanied by deficient performance in such areas as psychological warfare, military intelligence, and, especially, the formation of civil defense. (In 1987, civil defense was organized in only 240 localities over the country. Chalatenango and Morazán, the departments with the largest FMLN influence, possessed civil defense units in only seven and one localities respectively.) These conditions helped to assure the failure of the army's political plans, including the latest one: United to Reconstruct.[41]

In summary, the assessments of the U.S. advisers reflect the fact that the fighting has entered a set pattern since 1985. Despite its disproportionate numerical inferiority, the FMLN continues as a formidable opponent capable of sustaining the war indefinitely, although the government army has won the initiative in a strict tactical sense. Even with progress toward democratization in the country, the government project is ineffective and the war has become a stalemate.

A year and a half after the document by Bacevich and his colleagues became public, events validate many of its assessments. But the FMLN continues to make headway. In the words of a retired Salvadoran military official:

The Salvadoran crisis cannot be resolved by waging an internal war of annihilation or, put another way, by pursuing a military solution, because that simply does not touch upon the essence of the problem; therefore, a political solution should be pursued.[42]

And one of the more prominent military leaders contends:

The war at present does not have an eminently military solution; it is a question of defeating the prolonged popular war through the use of economic, political, and mass propaganda components in addition to employing the military at the level of terror.[43]

As the FMLN leadership claimed, it is obviously not enough to look at how much the government army has and receives when assessing its transformation and growth. It is even more important to examine the army's real capacity to assimilate voluminous aid and to determine what proportion it could utilize effectively. At the end of the 1980s, while the army high command talked about applying a new strategy (which was strikingly similar to the one that was designed in 1984 but never really applied), the FMLN was developing a different strategic approach:

The new strategy of commandos and irregular warfare, designed by the advisers and proclaimed by Colonel Ponce [René Emilio Ponce, later General and Minister of Defense under the ARENA government of Alfredo Cristiani], intends to disrupt the FMLN within its territories while operational troops win over the population. This turns out to be totally absurd and unrelated to the current conditions as the FMLN has hurled itself in a decisive way to search for the definition of the war in vital areas by mobilizing the people, the one factor that breaks the equilibrium in a total and definitive manner.[44]

On Insurrection

Now, it is time to reconsider a central problem in the Salvadoran revolutionary strategy: the relationship among the territorial constraints, the duration of the war, and insurrection. Many have asked whether the Salvadoran revolutionary process should not have produced a generalized insurrection, given the country's territorial constraints and the important popular mass movement that had developed (principally in the capital) between 1977 and 1980. Revolutionary organizations insistently posed this question in 1980, some more so than others. An analysis of the problem will elucidate the particularities of the popular revolutionary war within El Salvador.

To begin with, the initial disparity of military strength between the revolution and the counterrevolution encouraged the struggle toward a war of "rapid definition." (After all, the victory of the Sandinista revolution was still fresh, and the relatively brief duration of the Cuban revolutionary struggle also seemed to validate this tendency.) The territorial constraints of El Salvador and the expectation of a generalized insurrection reinforced the thesis of quick struggle, since these two factors made it difficult to prolong war indefinitely. This notion was strengthened by the fact that the revolutionary armed struggle appeared at the apogee of the mass struggle, following a rapid development of forms of armed self-defense. Reality, however, proved to be more complex with regard to the insurrection. Let me offer a brief analysis.

Engels points out that insurrection is subject to certain rules that, if overlooked, can bring about the ruin of the revolutionary party.[45] He enumerates them: (1) once decided upon, insurrection must be pursued until the end; (2) once initiated, insurrection must be always pursued offensively; and (3) it is important to maintain the high level of morale achieved by the first victory by surprise in order to attract vacillating elements. Lenin creatively developed these fundamental theses of Marxism on armed insurrection, particularly in his works of 1906 and 1917.[46]

From Engels's first rule, various essential derivations clearly stand out. The moment at which insurrection should be initiated must be calculated exactly, since being too early or too late can lead to the defeat of a movement. Insurrection necessarily assumes a massive and violent character. (It is, after all, the condensed expression of the organized violence of the masses.)

Other important precepts derive from the second rule about a continuous offensive. Insurrection necessarily lasts only a short time. Moreover, the start of the insurrection presupposes previous political and military organizational development. Yet this requirement should not be seen to contradict a necessary measure of revolutionary improvisation. Insurrection is, according to Engels, "an equation with highly undefined magnitudes" whose solution demands an enormous degree of boldness.

There have been many insurrections since Engels wrote in 1852. Most took place in European cities with prominent industrial proletariats. More than a few defeats have been suffered by revolutionary movements in various countries that forgot the basic rules governing this form of struggle. On the side of at least temporary success, perhaps the richest and most instructive case is that of the Paris Commune of 1872, which foreshadowed the definitive seizure of power by the proletariat. Lenin would apply the lessons of the commune to the situations in Moscow and Leningrad in 1905 and 1917, respectively, and add another basic law to all insurrectional movements: to succeed, the struggle must be led by a revolutionary party and be developed within a revolutionary strategy for seizing power. These cases are sufficient to affirm the universal validity of the general laws that govern insurrection as a form of struggle. They also demonstrate the obligation to apply these general laws creatively to each specific situation. In other words, one must discover and apply the particular laws of insurrection to each historical moment and to each concrete social formation.

How do these laws apply in the Latin American countries of today, particularly in El Salvador? Latin America has witnessed two successful revolutions, the Cuban and the Nicaraguan. The latter case showed the importance of insurrection as a form of struggle (to the point of one of the Sandinista groups being labeled "insurrectionalist"). Both were of short duration—they could be classified, with certain reservations in the case of Cuba, as revolutionary wars of "rapid definition." Unlike the case in Cuba, urban insurrectionary movements played a definitive role in Nicaragua.

Particular features characterized the Sandinista revolution. Insurrectional movements were not confined to the principal urban location, the capital city of Managua; at times, they developed simultaneously in various outlying cities where there was virtually no industrial proletariat. Even in the case of Managua, the urban popular masses, in the broadest possible sense, were the participants in insurrectional activities.

The Cuban revolutionaries, however, defeated the dictator Fulgencio Batista's army chiefly in the countryside. This does not imply the absence of significant armed resistance work in the cities (logistical operations for example). But the principal form of armed struggle—the essential characteristic of the Cuban revolutionary process—was the eradication of government mobile units on the highways and in the mountains of the interior. In a strict sense, vast insurrectionalist movements did not emerge in the cities or in the countryside, although the development of urban forms of struggle had an important history that dated back to resistance to the dictatorship of Gerardo Machado in the late 1920s. The Sandinista insurgency of the 1970s would prove that multiple revolutionary roads were open in Latin America. In this case, insurrection was essential and assumed its own forms, an expression of specific conditions. First, the development of the insurrection relied on a previously organized and experienced revolutionary army that had been forged during the uprisings. The insurgents could rely, second, upon rearguard zones (e.g., areas in the mountains controlled by the guerrilla forces) to which it was possible to withdraw; this was so even the case of Masaya, twenty kilometers outside the capital, which served as a place of retreat for the insurrectionist masses of Managua when they could no longer hold out in battle.[47] Third, insurrections developed simultaneously in various cities, together with powerful operations by the revolutionary army in rural zones. Fourth, the clandestine leadership combined the centralized direction of the popular urban mass uprisings with the command of the revolutionary army. Insurrections took place, fifth, within a context of broad, flexible alliances rooted in the revolutionary classes rather than in intrigues; these alliances subordinated national and international bourgeois sectors to the revolutionary project. And finally, although the central spaces for uprisings were in the cities, they spread by way of interurban communications.

To analyze the role of insurrection in the Salvadoran popular war it is necessary to focus on a particular fact of this process: the alternating lack of synchronization over the past decade between the development of the revolutionary mass movement, on the one hand, and the military development of the revolutionary organizations, on the other. This split can be traced over time through the following schema:

- Between 1972 and 1977, from the onset of the urban guerrilla actions to the consolidation of the popular mass organizations whose formation began in 1974. At this incipient stage, the split between the development of the mass movement and the military development of the revolutionary organizations was not terribly acute.
- From 1977 until the beginning of 1980, the necessity of protecting the mass movement was clearly demonstrated; the self-defense militias arose out of this situation, acquiring an impulse equally as strong as the continued growth of the urban and suburban guerrilla units. This split did not reach very acute levels.

- During 1980, however, the split did reach a point powerful enough to mark both the subsequent retreat of the mass movement in the cities and the open popular revolutionary war after January 10, 1981.

A grounding in the events of 1980 is essential for understanding the problematic of insurrection in El Salvador, and I shall now examine them in some detail. During the first third of 1980, the revolutionary mass movement reached its peak after six years of combative growth and development. At this point, the objective and subjective conditions for the insurrection had been created within the popular urban masses, especially in San Salvador. However, the particular characteristics of the revolutionary process required a level of military development that the revolutionary organizations had not yet attained.

Since the end of 1979, all the groups that would later form the FMLN had recognized this necessity. They had begun the task of forging their armed units, starting with the experienced nuclei of guerrilla fighters on whom they could count. This job was accomplished in the face of great difficulties and unexpected sacrifices, but it did not involve much awareness of the work of the masses. Toward the end of 1980, the split between the development of the mass movement and the development of the military structures had not been resolved. Instead, the split was turned on its head: from a condition of insufficient military development relative to the mass movement, the situation became one of a rising military development just as the mass movement fell into retreat.

This explained in part the relative failure of the call to insurrection and general strike launched during 1980. Nevertheless, the events of January 10, 1981, constituted a true series of insurrections in the countryside, indicating the necessity to look for the specific characteristics of insurrection in the Salvadoran revolutionary process. Here I lay out some ideas:

- Insurrection in El Salvador could not be conceived of in classic European urban terms, nor could it be developed in the same fashion as the Sandinista revolution.
- Insurrection could not be the superior form of the armed struggle; nor could it necessarily constitute the final and definitive phase of the popular revolutionary war.
- In the Salvadoran process there have been and will continue to be partial, local insurrections, both urban and rural, that form the concentrated moments of the political-military struggle.

- Of necessity, these uprisings rely on the existence of a strong revolutionary army.
- The uprisings are neither mechanically linked to the development of strike movements nor to particular political conjunctures.

Let me juxtapose these ideas with the position expressed by the leaders of the FMLN regarding this form of struggle. In an early analysis, issued six months after the general offensive of January 10, a member of the FMLN leadership gave the following explanations about the insurrection:

> *Much has . . . been said about why there was no insurrection or general strike. To be able to bring this matter into proper focus we have to analyze two fundamental questions: a) In the Salvadoran case, the insurrectional activity of the masses was present throughout a whole period without enjoying a favorable military correlation; this subjected it to attrition, since the very survival of the struggle was tied to the heroic activities carried on by the masses. The activity of the masses in the countryside and in the city was the center of international attention and the only instrument on which the Salvadoran people could rely in order to give themselves the time and space necessary to develop their military force. This meant that to reach the insurrectional stage, the movement had to go through significant changes in direction at the level of military preparedness; the events of January 10th were the beginning, not the outcome of these changes. b) Other elements entered into play because of the characteristics of El Salvador (density of population, makeup of the urban and suburban areas, the high ratio between the size of the territory and the army forces, etc.). To overcome these factors required a significant qualitative and quantitative military advance of the revolutionary forces, thus moving on to the stage of insurrection and general offensive actions.*[48]

This explication offers a clear view of a particular conception of the insurrection given the peculiarities of the Salvadoran revolutionary process and of the context in which it developed. An affirmation by the same leader five years later confirmed this view.[49] He then argued that the January 10 offensive constituted a large popular insurrection, featuring massive participation by rural workers, principally peasants and agricultural workers, who were joined by various urban sectors. It cannot be denied, however, that various nuanced positions have existed within the core of the FMLN leadership over the concept of insurrection as a form of struggle. In some cases and in some moments, insurrection has been seen as a final, definitive action, essentially urban, and similar in character to the classical historical examples. Nevertheless, there was a constant effort to grasp the peculiarities of the Salvadoran case. Thus we see the FMLN leadership claiming in 1984 that:

> [t]he ideas of willful insurrection and "grand offensive" [have] cease[d] to be elements that govern the FMLN's plans ever since a better understanding developed of the characteristics that had already shaped our revolutionary war.
>
> After January, 1981, the Salvadoran revolutionary phenomenon took a new course of an accumulation of forces; many judged it unfavorably since they had thought for almost two years in terms of an insurrectional perspective derived from the Nicaraguan process. . . .
>
> Stated more clearly, the rich and ascending process of mass struggle in El Salvador provided the foundation permitting adaptation to the new conditions imposed by the masses; these saved the FMLN from its own tardy attempts to apply an insurrectional conception at a moment in which the war had already taken another turn.[50]

Nevertheless, this same document held out the possibility that the Salvadoran revolutionary process would take on an insurrectional expression. There would be a great military battle at the end, whose timing and conditions could not yet be foreseen. Another analysis in 1985 affirmed the main objective of combining the armed struggle and the mass political struggle closely and profoundly.[51] This strategy would accumulate forces and pave the way for combining the strategic military counteroffensive with popular insurrection.

It does not seem fair to criticize the oscillations that may have occurred in the positions expressed by the FMLN leadership at different times. The extreme complexity of the struggle within the country explains these variations. The FMLN held to the underlying correct idea of grasping the unique nature of the Salvadoran case without becoming bound by stereotypical preconceptions. As the dynamics of the conflict began to change again toward the end of the decade, popular insurrection was once more seen as a decisive form of struggle. In a 1989 analysis, Villalobos reviewed the experience of almost a decade in the face of this problematic:

> *When the possibility of a social explosion is posed, it relates not only to the will for action on the part of the FMLN but also to an evident objective reality into which the FMLN inserts itself in accompanying the most logical course of the social struggle in El Salvador. Not to do this would be a strategic error and would leave all the space open to the recuperation of the political-economic model of domination that has generated the war and led to U.S. intervention.*
>
> *Our process has its own particularities, the product of the conditions in which it has developed. It therefore requires the construction of its own concepts for a strategic offensive. Thus, the popular insurrection in El Salvador is not comparable to the almost strictly urban pattern that evolved in Nicaragua. In El Salvador, there is already a process of permanent insurrection within the rural masses that has spread to nearly every part of the country. . . .*
>
> *It is quite evident that the FMLN has developed links with new contingents of masses in vital areas near and within the cities. The density of the Salvadoran population, totally different from that of Nicaragua, provides for different social characteristics. We can predict that the concept of insurrection in the Salvadoran case will have its own particular features due to the different balance between the city and the countryside and between the city and outlying urban areas. In addition, the weight of the military factor and the development of military capacity are also different. It is not a question of a strictly insurrectional phenomenon, like the one that virtually occurred in Nicaragua, but rather a combination of war and popular insurrection in which the concepts of time, partisanship, and the spreading of war and insurrection are different. . . .*
>
> *. . . [T]his insurrection will be the result of multiple factors such as the military offensive of the FMLN, the insurrectional process of the masses in the city and in the countryside, the generalization of repression, the political disintegration of the government and the armed forces, and the weakening of the policy of the U.S. and its instruments in El Salvador. These factors and*

others more are marching on. Their convergent ascending interaction will have a detonating effect.[52]

In 1989, many of these factors are effectively still present, although there are others that have not been developed and new ones that now exist (such as the profound political changes taking place at the level of Central America as a whole). Today there exists, as Villalobos claimed, a unity between the revolutionary forces and their military development that was absent in 1980. For this reason, it is wrong to make a schematic comparison of the current situation, which is one of ascension, with the earlier one of definition. The question of insurrection in the Salvadoran revolutionary process remains open. The discussion among revolutionaries has been sound, and it shows that there cannot be a mechanical application of blueprints with regard to this form of struggle and its role.

To talk of various forms of insurrections relying on the existence of a strong revolutionary army raises the matter of the necessary existence of a solid rear guard. Thus I return to the thread of my earlier exposition.

Returning to the Territorial Constraints

We can affirm that foquismo did not take root in El Salvador for various reasons. Perhaps the most important is that the emergence and development of the revolutionary organizations began when the limitations of the foquista attempts in Latin America and their painful lesson (including its urban versions, if these can be so classified) had been made evident. This fact, more than the matter of territorial constraints, led to the creation of the political-military organizations.

A little later, the similarly painful defeat of the reformist strategy in Chile would further reinforce a sense of certainty about the approach in El Salvador. Popular revolutionary war paved the way with its combination of methods and its seemingly opposing forms of struggle, its integrated vision of the political and military alloy, its moments of offense and retreat, its combination of interior and exterior work, the richness of its different forms of armed organization, and the complexity of its rear guard. Territorial constraints no longer seemed an insuperable obstacle in the path of pushing forward the armed revolutionary struggle.

Throughout the process, the construction of the vanguard was under way at the same time as other elements of building the revolution fell into place: strategy and tactics developed; foundations and logistical networks were created; the movement attained autonomy from necessary conditioning factors abroad; the mass movement reorganized under new forms that respected its autonomy; and, last but not least, the rear guard was constructed. This rich and complex process clearly indicates the linkage between the rear guard and the construction of the revolutionary vanguard. Keep in mind that, after a certain stage in the development of the war, the revolutionary leadership should be located where the strategic forces of the masses and the military are found.

The Salvadoran revolutionary organizations have been building their rear guard, overcoming their territorial constraints, and safeguarding forces in order to increase their offensive capacities. This parallels the actions of the 1970s, when urban guerrillas struggled not just to survive but to accumulate forces that were to be deployed at the right moment. This pattern follows the indications of General Giap that revolutionists should fight at the same time as they construct and develop their forces; they must recognize that maintaining the continuity of the war is more difficult than launching the initial attack—from that point on, the rear guard remains indispensable.

Economy and Population:
The Profound Transformations
of the Decade of the 1980s

An extremely high level of concentration of the means of production has characterized the historical development of the Salvadoran economy ever since the liberal reform period in the last quarter of the nineteenth century. This phenomenon has held true across the board—in industry, in commerce, in finance, as well as in agriculture. Accordingly, many studies have defined both the Salvadoran society and the Salvadoran state as oligarchic. Certainly, the country's economy has become as well known for its centralization as for its dynamic growth from the 1950s to the 1970s.

I will not review the Salvadoran economy before 1980 (although some knowledge of it is indispensable for understanding the events of the 1980s). Instead, I shall begin by examining the overall official data on the behavior of the economy during the 1980s. This will serve as the groundwork for analyzing three key processes that help to explain the political situation: the economic reforms of 1980 and U.S. aid; the profound demographic transformations at work in society and the impact of economic transfers from abroad; and the economic formulations of the ARENA government.

In order to examine the behavior of the economy, I shall rely on the 1988 report of ECLA (United Nations Economic Commission for Latin America). Among its conclusions:

Following the virtual stagnation of the previous year, in 1987 the Salvadoran economy once again began the slow recovery that has characterized its trajectory over the last five years. The real gross domestic product increased almost 3%, but this level was 7% less than that of 1980; the per capita product was equivalent to levels a quarter century ago. The need for additional resources to repair the damage caused by the 1986 earthquake, the prolongation of the armed conflict, and the deterioration in the terms of exchange made the country's dependence on external aid more acute.[1]

Analysis of the data in Table 3 discloses four broad economic tendencies: (1) the constant deterioration of popular living conditions, reflected in increased unemployment and inflation, and in decreased

Table 3
Principal Economic Indicators, 1981–87

Indicators	1981	1982	1983	1984	1985	1986	1987[a]
Basic economic indicators							
GDP at market prices (1980 = 100)	91.6	86.4	86.9	88.9	90.4	90.8	93.2
Gross national income (1980 = 100)	90.0	84.9	83.0	83.3	85.4	90.3	87.5
Population (millions of people)	4.58	4.63	4.66	4.71	4.77	4.85	4.93
Per capita GDP (index 1980 = 100)	90.5	84.6	84.4	85.5	85.9	84.9	85.6
Short-term economic indicators (percentage rates of growth)							
GDP	−8.4	−5.6	0.6	2.3	1.8	0.4	2.6
Per capita GDP	−9.5	−6.5	−0.2	1.4	0.5	−1.1	0.9
Rate of unemployment[b] [c]	21.2	27.4	32.2	32.9	33.0	—	—
Consumer prices (annual variation)	14.7	11.7	13.1	11.7	22.4	31.9	24.9
Real salaries[d]	−7.3	−10.5	−11.6	0.4	−13.8	−13.2	−19.9
Government income flows	6.4	0.6	13.3	22.4	23.7	50.9	−5.5
Total government expenditures	13.3	0.2	45.3	−1.3	4.8	45.0	5.5
Fiscal deficit/total government expenditures[b]	36.4	39.0	54.3	37.9	26.7	23.6	31.6
Fiscal deficit/GDP	7.3	7.9	14.8	8.1	4.9	4.5	5.3
Current export value of goods and services	−23.9	−11.0	6.2	2.3	1.4	13.2	−10.9
Current value of imported goods and services	−0.8	−10.4	1.9	8.7	2.7	−2.7	3.6

Table 3 (*cont.*)
Principal Economic Indicators, 1981–87

Indicators	1981	1982	1983	1984	1985	1986	1987[a]
Relation of price of trade of goods and services	−7.3	1.9	−10.3	−9.7	−0.3	17.8	−19.4
External sector (millions of dollars)							
Trade balance of goods and services	−237	−238	−187	−260	−279	−127	−280
Current account balance	−272	−271	−211	−243	−243	−80	−209
Capital account balance	223	242	235	250	270	155	260
Variation in net international reserves	−43	−27	39	19	30	75	51
Disbursed foreign debt	1471	1710	1890	1949	1980	1928	1876

Source: ECLA, on the basis of official figures.
[a] Preliminary figures.
[b] In percentages.
[c] Refers to the number of people who are openly unemployed or underemployed as percentages of the workforce.
[d] Real minimum wages of industrial and service workers in El Salvador.

real wages; (2) the profound imbalance in international trade and payments (barely ameliorated by the decrease in the foreign debt); (3) the persistence of the fiscal deficit (the financing of which rests principally on U.S. credits); and (4) the maintenance, more than the recuperation, of the economy's productive sectors despite the war. Two extremely important external economic flows fundamentally emerged during the 1980s and made this "stabilization" of the Salvadoran economy possible: remittances from Salvadorans living abroad and the multi-million-dollar program of U.S. aid. I shall return to this topic later. For now, I will look in some detail at the behavior of certain sectors of the economy, presented in Tables 4 through 8.

Although the period in question is relatively short, in the last ten years there has been no sectoral transformation of importance in the Salvadoran economy. Agriculture and manufacturing have retained roughly their same share of the economy. This would indicate that the structural reforms of 1980 have not modified the country's economic panorama, at least at an aggregate level. Two key crops among the chief traditional agricultural exports, still one of the country's economic mainstays, suffered perceptible drops in production: coffee and, most of all, cotton. The war should not shoulder the exclusive re-

Table 4

GDP by Economic Activity at 1980 Market Prices

Economic activity	Index (1980 = 100)		Composition (percent)			Rate of growth (percent)			
	1985	1986	1976	1980	1987	1984	1985	1986	1987
Agriculture[a]	88.3	85.6	87.7	27.8	26.2	3.3	−1.1	−3.1	2.5
Mining	97.3	100.0	112.8	0.1	0.2	2.6	—	2.8	12.8
Manufacturing	87.9	90.1	92.8	15.0	15.0	1.3	3.7	2.5	3.0
Construction	81.6	83.7	95.4	3.4	3.5	−5.7	4.6	2.6	13.9
Electricity, gas, water	106.9	106.9	112.3	2.1	2.6	2.7	5.0	—	5.0
Transportation, warehousing, communications	92.3	92.8	94.4	3.5	3.6	2.7	1.8	0.5	1.8
Other services	92.2	93.8	95.5	48.0	49.1	2.5	2.5	1.7	1.8

Source: ECLA, from official figures recalculated on the basis of constant prices of 1980.

[a] Preliminary figures, including the livestock, forestry, and fishing sectors.

sponsiblity for their declining performance, since trends in the international market were quite influential, determinably so in the case of cotton. Basic grain production remained rather irregular throughout the decade. Although I cannot enter into a detailed explanation, it must be stressed that the changes exhibited in this sector cannot accurately be characterized as a collapse.

While manufacturing shows a decrease compared to the end of the 1970s, it is undergoing a slight but steady recuperation, especially in sectors linked to construction. Another indicator of this modest upswing is the increase in the consumption and production of electricity, even though this is one of the sectors most affected by the war. An examination of exports (destination, value, and composition) reveals a reduction for coffee, the virtual disappearance of cotton, and increases for shrimp and clothing. Of particular importance is the modification of the share of exports to Central America and to the rest of the world. Finally, domestic prices during this period clearly reflect a deteriorating popular standard of living in both urban and rural areas, ameliorated partially by remittances of U.S. dollars coming from Salvadoran emigrants.

Examination of the above data shows a complex evolution that cannot be explained solely from an economic perspective. It is important

Table 5
Indicators of Agricultural and Livestock Production, 1975–87

Product	1975	1980	1985	1986	1987[a]	Rates of growth (percent) 1984	1985	1986	1987[a]
Coffee	163	186	149	136	152	−3.4	−0.3	−8.7	11.8
Cotton	73	61	25	13	11	−22.8	−20.7	−48.0	−15.4
Sugarcane	3,166	2,564	3,455	3,647	3,269	12.8	1.6	5.6	−10.4
Corn	400	528	495	437	578	19.0	−6.1	−11.7	32.2
Beans	38	39	34	50	24	15.4	−29.5	47.1	−52.0
Gold rice	39	39	46	26	23	46.5	8.8	−43.5	−11.5
Cattle[b]	187	185	140	150	152	0.7	−4.6	7.1	1.3
Pigs	115	126	146	155	160	−9.7	—	6.2	3.2
Poultry[c]	—	14	27	29	30	10.5	28.6	7.4	3.4
Milk[d]	253	331	311	311	325	32.2	13.1	—	4.5
Eggs[e]	588	818	880	891	934	0.6	−22.8	1.3	4.8

Source: ECLA, on the basis of figures from the Banco Central de Reserva de El Salvador and the Ministerio de Agricultura y Ganadería (MAG).

[a] Preliminary figures.
[b] Thousands of head.
[c] Thousands of tons.
[d] Millions of bottles.
[e] Millions of units.

to place this information within its social and political context. One must avoid both triumphalist visions (for example, the type indulged in by those ideologues of the dominant classes who contend that defeating the popular revolutionary movement militarily is enough to ensure sustained accumulation of capital) and catastrophic visions (for example, those that focus upon the growing misery of the popular classes almost exclusively without understanding the peculiarities and perspectives of the development of the Salvadoran economy during this decade).

The Economic Reforms of 1980 and U.S. Aid

In 1980, the government announced major reforms in three areas—agrarian policy, international commerce, and banking—that were part of an integral plan of structural changes. From a naïve point of view, they might seem to be measures whose profound impact would frac-

Table 6

Indicators of Manufacturing Production, 1975, and 1984–87

Product	1975	1984	1985	1986	1987[a]	1984	1985	1986	1987[a]
						\multicolumn{4}{}{Rates of growth (percent)}			
Food, drink, tobacco	88.5	90.6	96.6	98.2	100.4	3.4	6.6	1.7	2.2
Textiles, clothing, leather products	118.9	63.3	58.1	61.1	61.7	−0.8	−8.2	5.2	0.9
Wood, paper	76.3	82.4	81.4	79.1	82.6	−8.1	−1.3	−2.8	4.4
Chemicals derived from oil and rubber	137.6	87.2	84.0	86.8	89.7	−1.1	−5.3	1.7	3.4
Nonmetallic mineral products	97.6	80.6	84.6	89.0	102.3	−9.1	5.0	5.2	14.9
Machines and metal products	118.6	67.5	72.7	80.8	82.9	3.1	7.7	11.2	2.6
Industrial electrical consumption[b]	410	499	503	556	614	0.4	3.1	0.8	10.5

Source: ECLA, on the basis of figures of the Banco Central de Reserva de El Salvador.

[a] Preliminary figures.

[b] Millions of kilowatt-hours.

ture the prolonged oligarchic domination of Salvadoran society. But, as events would show, the reforms should not be examined in isolation from either their political context or the problem of political power. In less than a decade, their enormous limitations became dramatically apparent, as I shall now demonstrate by looking at each area of reform in turn.[2]

The agrarian reform consisted of three phases. Phase I affected properties larger than 500 hectares (decree 154 of March 8, 1980); Phase III aimed to transfer agricultural land directly to the cultivators (decree 207 of April 29, 1980). Phase II initially affected properties of between 100 and 500 hectares, but it was revised in 1983 to apply

Table 7
El Salvador: Exports of Goods, FOB, Selected Years, 1975–87

	Millions of dollars			Composition (percent)			Rate of growth (percent)			
	1985	1986	1987a	1975	1980	1987a	1984	1985	1986	1987a
Total	695	755	573	100.0	100.0	100.0	−1.3	−6.5	8.6	−24.1
Central America	96	91	111	27.6	27.5	19.4	−6.3	−39.1	−5.2	22.0
Rest of world	599	664	462	72.4	72.5	80.6	0.2	2.5	10.9	−30.4
Coffee	458	539	347	33.7	60.9	60.6	−0.5	17.5	17.7	−35.6
Cotton	29	5	2	14.9	7.9	0.3	−83.7	218.7	−82.8	−60.0
Sugar	23	25	12	16.0	1.2	2.1	−35.4	−10.4	8.7	−52.0
Shrimp	10	17	21	2.0	1.2	3.7	37.3	−51.5	70.0	23.5
Clothing	3	3	4	2.6	2.9	0.7	−20.8	−63.2	—	33.3

Source: ECLA, on the basis of figures of the Banco Central de Reserva de El Salvador.
a Preliminary figures.

Table 8
El Salvador: Evolution of Domestic Prices, 1980–87

Yearly average index	1980	1981	1982	1983	1984	1985	1986	1987
Consumer price indexa	127.6	146.4	163.6	185.1	206.7	252.9	333.6	416.6
Food	130.3	153.3	169.6	192.3	219.5	261.0	344.0	431.3
Index of wholesale pricesb	132.9	149.5	162.1	175.1	187.5	221.0	226.1	—
Imported products	133.2	144.0	161.3	169.3	178.5	220.5	266.6	
National products	136.7	161.8	173.8	192.0	205.0	224.4	272.9	—

Source: ECLA, on the basis of official figures.
a Base, December 1978 = 100.
b Base, January 1978 = 100 (excludes coffee).

only to properties of between 245 and 500 hectares (article 105 of the 1983 constitution). The execution of Phases I and III involved only 14.1 percent of the agricultural acreage of the country. Of the lands affected, more than half did not produce crops, in most cases because of their extremely poor quality. This explains why land cultivated within the reformed sector accounted for only 7.7 percent of the area dedicated to grains and export products in 1985–86. If the data in Table 9 show a decrease in the relative importance of the reformed sector within El Salvador's cultivated area, the figures in Table 10 demonstrate an even greater decline in the share of overall levels of production. They fell from 14.1 to 10.8 percent, with a particularly dramatic drop in basic grains.

At the root of this situation lie two problems. One is contextual, related to the war and market conditions; the other is internal, related to the process of agrarian reform, technical assistance, commercialization, financing, and the technical training of members of cooperatives. In the 1985–86 growing year, only 65.6 percent of the cooperatives received technical assistance. Marketing was largely under the control of intermediaries. Credit granted to the reformed sector comprised less than 15 percent of the credit extended to agricultural concerns between 1985 and 1987. Only 50 percent of the cooperatives had established literacy programs, and 60 percent lacked access to schools

Table 9

Participation in the Total Cultivated Area of the Reformed Sector, 1979–80 through 1985–86 (in thousands of hectares and in percent)

| | National | | | Reformed Sector | | | | | |
	Export Products	Basic Grains	Total	Exp. Prd.	% of Nat.	Basic Grains	% of Nat.	Total	% of Nat.
1979–80	383.3	470.6	853.9	—	—	—	—	—	—
1980–81	350.5	479.9	830.4	52.0	14.8	29.1	6.1	81.1	9.8
1981–82	351.1	454.8	805.9	44.1	12.6	27.4	6.0	71.5	8.9
1982–83	347.1	423.8	770.9	48.3	13.9	16.2	3.8	64.5	8.4
1983–84	348.5	420.4	768.9	46.5	13.3	13.0	3.1	59.5	7.7
1984–85	378.8	432.0	810.8	49.1	13.0	9.8	2.3	58.9	7.3
1985–86	325.7	432.2	757.9	47.7	14.6	10.8	2.5	58.5	7.7

Source: Calculated on the basis of data from the Ministry of Agriculture and other official sources.

Table 10
Participation in Production by the Reformed Sector, 1979–80 through 1985–86 (in thousands of quintals and in percent)

	National			Reformed Sector					
	Export Products	Basic Grains	Total	Exp. Prd.	% of Nat.	Basic Grains	% of Nat.	Total	% of Nat.
1979–80	12,271	16,684	28,955	—	—	—	—	—	—
1980–81	10,175	16,214	26,389	2,225.8	21.9	1,490.9	9.2	3,716.7	14.1
1981–82	10,493	15,377	25,870	2,173.4	20.7	1,282.1	8.3	3,455.5	13.4
1982–83	11,255	13,043	24,298	2,360.3	21.0	619.7	4.8	2,980.0	12.3
1983–84	9,935	13,811	23,746	2,202.2	22.2	760.0	5.5	2,962.0	12.5
1984–85	11,116	16,471	27,587	2,427.8	21.8	575.9	3.5	3,004.7	10.9
1985–86	9,986	15,406	25,392	2,105.8	21.1	626.7	4.1	2,732.5	10.8

Source: Calculated on the basis of data from the Ministry of Agriculture and other official sources.

during 1985–86. With respect to health and rural housing, the situation was abysmally deficient.

The de facto cancellation of Phase II of the agrarian reform—even the measures approved in the 1983 constitution were not put into practice—left the economic power of the Salvadoran oligarchy untouched. Of the lands expropriated in Phase I, those in coffee cultivation represented only 2.9 percent of the national surface area. Many studies have shown that the most productive coffee-producing properties in the country were those between one hundred and five hundred hectares.[3] At present, as I will point out later, the government of Alfredo Cristiani has begun to adopt measures to reverse even this inconclusive reform.[4]

The key 1980 measure in international commerce reformed coffee exports (decree 75) and created the Instituto del Café (INCAFE, or Coffee Institute). This change was supposed to modify a structure in which large producers and processors controlled all three phases of coffee production: agricultural, agro-industrial, and export. Since it was limited to coffee exports, this measure failed to break up the pattern of internal commercialization. Above all, it left the large producers untouched by agrarian reform. Therefore, the only objective achieved was an increase in taxes collected. This revenue, in turn, went to finance the war and to unleash a pattern of enormous corruption during the government of Napoleón Duarte.

Wages in the coffee sector fell by almost half between 1982 and 1986; by 1988, the salaries of coffee pickers were 32 percent of what they had earned in 1978. Given the importance of the crop in the Salvadoran economy, one can grasp the depth of this crisis. Output per area in cultivation dropped by 25 percent between 1979–80 and 1987–88, while the rate of unused capacity of private coffee processors reached 50 percent.

In this light, one notes an important document presented to the Legislative Assembly by the Asociación Salvadoreña de Beneficiadores y Exportadores de Café (ABECAFE—Salvadoran Association of Coffee Processors and Exporters).[5] Examining various areas (foreign trade, coffee policy, internal commercialization, financial and fiscal effects, and the institutional development of INCAFE) in detail, it affirmed that

> the centralized export system which supposedly would bring benefits in the form of foreign exchange, tax revenues, payments to the producers, the possibility of paying better salaries to the workers, and a strengthening of the economy in general has instead produced a thorough failure in every one of these respects.
>
> It is sad to have to insist that the centralized system of exports has been bleeding the financial system of the country at a time when financial resources to aid economic development and projects of social interest have been so scarce. . . . The country has experienced a fiscal deficit crisis, resulting in an inflationary spiral that hits the popular sectors very hard. The source of this fiscal deficit is the hasty prolongation of a system of commercialization that does not pay taxes. . . . In the meantime, in order to survive, the country has to rely on international donations or compromise the destiny of future generations through growing indebtedness. A system of commercialization of the principal export product is maintained that limits income from foreign exchange.

Beyond the truth of these facts, and the populist and nationalist slant of the document's conclusions, what stands out is the almost complete absence of the war as a determining factor in the crisis of this sector. This crisis will not be solved simply by reprivatizing the commercialization of coffee as proposed by the present ARENA government.

Banking reform, the third major structural change (decree 158 of March 7, 1980), had among its several objectives to end the concentration of credit, channeling it toward sectors that historically had been barred from access, and to do away with the oligarchy's control of ownership in the banking system. As indicated in Table 11, an analysis of credit distribution for the years 1986 and 1987 shows that owners of medium- and large-sized businesses received more than 80 percent of the loans made by the nationalized bank.

Credit assigned to the reformed sector of the agricultural and livestock industry made up less than 15 percent of the total; neither the reformed rural sectors nor urban microenterprises benefited from the banking reform. A partial explanation lies in the new ownership structure of the nationalized bank. According to the law of nationalization, 20 percent of the stocks had to be offered to bank employees and 29 percent to private investors, with the state claiming the remaining 51 percent. By 1987, the government and the Banco Central de Reserva (Central Reserve Bank) owned 90.2 percent of the stock, employees 3.4 percent, and private investors 6.4 percent. Thus, it had become a state bank, leading to the key question of political power: Who holds it and who profits from it? Although the dominant classes no longer own the banking system directly, they maintain economic control of the country and slant the system to benefit their own interests.

Table 11

Nationalized Banks, Structure of the Loan Portfolio by Economic Size of the Users, 1986–87 (in percent)

Users by Assets	1986[a]	1987
Microenterprises (below $20,000)	1.3	2.0
Small ($20,000–$150,000)	14.6	13.3
Medium ($150,000–$400,000)	8.1	7.6
Large (more than $400,000)	77.8	75.3

Source: Banco Central de Reserva, Memoria 1987, 48. Due to rounding, totals do not equal 100.

[a] Revised figures.

I shall dwell on this point a moment longer, given the importance of democratizing the banking system as defined in the reform laws. (Such analysis is usually relegated to a minor plane when studying the granting of credit.) Alberto Benítez, president of the Banco Central de Reserva until March 1987, claimed that the main goal of the reform was the creation of a democratic model of banking administration and not the simple nationalization of the system.[6] To achieve this democratization, in addition to expropriating capital stocks, the top executives and board members of the banks were dismissed and the administrative structures were reorganized.[7]

These actions went beyond state ownership of private banks, yielding in practice an administrative centralization of decision making in the hands of the executive power. As Valdés shows, this was paralleled by a growing centralization in the use of financial resources by the executive branch, as reflected in the rapid increase in the amount of credit granted by the Banco Central de Reserva to state institutions. If one includes the banking sector after 1980, state institutions as a whole received more than 80 percent of the credit granted between 1982 and 1985 (see Table 12).

Almost a decade after 1980, the reforms intended to modify El Salvador's unjust economic and social structure had failed to break the oligarchy's stranglehold. They had, instead, helped to create new contradictions that, after the election of the Cristiani government, merit close attention. A continuing flow of U.S. economic assistance has bolstered the reforms; both the aid and the reforms are integral parts of a counterinsurgency scheme. It is evident that the Salvadoran economy would not have been able, on its own, to sustain the expense of the war, especially in the midst of the contradictions generated by the

Table 12
Loans of the Central Reserve Bank, 1982–85 (in thousands of dollars)

Type of Loan	1982	1983	1984	1985
Public sector	1,060,083	944,644	1,128,143	1,238,398
Banking sector	255,241	315,189	270,807	354,363
Private sector	70,637	67,162	95,126	85,604

Source: Consejo Monetario Centroamericano, *Boletín Estadístico, 1985* (San José, Costa Rica), cited in Mauricio Valdés, "Reformismo y guerra: Una evaluación del la nacionalización bancaria en El Salvador," *Cuadernos de Investigación del CSUCA* (San José), 42 (sept 1988).

Table 13
Composition of U.S. Aid to El Salvador, 1980–89

	1980	1981	1982	1983	1984	1985	1986	1987	1988	1989
In millions of dollars										
I	5.9	35.0	82.0	81.3	196.5	137.7	123.1	112.3	96.5	96.5
II	12.4	68.8	140.3	197.4	216.0	201.2	192.3	211.8	223.9	187.9
III	43.2	19.1	28.1	61.2	72.7	85.2	91.1	104.5	65.8	67.7
IV	3.0	26.6	27.2	39.0	46.0	49.0	48.0	49.9	35.0	9.0
V								129.2		
Total	64.5	149.5	277.6	378.9	531.2	473.1	454.5	607.7	421.2	361.1
Percentages by fiscal year*										
I	9.1	23.4	29.5	21.4	37.0	29.1	27.1	18.5	21.0	25.0
II	19.2	46.0	50.5	52.1	40.0	42.5	42.3	34.9	54.5	49.0
III	67.0	12.8	10.1	16.2	14.0	18.0	20.0	17.2	16.0	17.0
IV	4.6	17.8	9.7	10.3	9.0	10.4	10.6	8.2	8.5	9.0
V								21.3		

I Direct aid for the war; II Indirect aid for the war; III Aid for reforms and development; IV Commercial and food aid; V Aid given for earthquake damage.

Source: Elaborated by INVE: data for 1980, 1988, and 1989 based on PACCA (Policy Alternatives for Central America and the Caribbean) and from US AID, USA Overseas Loans and Grants, 1987; data for 1981–87 taken from INVE, "La ayuda norteamericana a El Salvador: dos presupuestos, un objetivo y tres calamidades," *Boletín El Salvador: Coyuntura Económica* 18 (Feb. 1988), 16.

*Rounded percentages do not equal 100.

reforms of 1980. As the totals in Table 13 indicate, between 1980 and 1988 the economic and military aid authorized through the Agency for International Development (AID) by the U.S. administration reached $3.4 billion.[8]

An analysis of the composition of this aid, made by the Instituto de Investigaciones on the basis of the classification used by the Arms Control and Foreign Policy Caucus of the United States Congress, reveals its true destination:

> *[I]n 1988 three-fourths of the assistance consisted of resources oriented directly and indirectly to the war. . . . Of the total aid, 21% was direct aid for the war, with the most substantial part of this*

*being the Military Assistance Program. . . . Another important
component was the indirect aid to the war (54.5%). . . . This indirect assistance was earmarked for the restoration of public services, the financial support for the government, health and employment services for the displaced, nutritional assistance, etc. . . .*

In 1988, U.S. economic aid amounted to 65 percent of El Salvador's total exports, reflecting the country's extreme degree of dependence on the United States and the fragile environment in which
the Christian Democrats attempted their reforms. The same conditions will influence the attempts of the ARENA government to stim-
ulate the "reactivation" of the economy.

Demographic Changes and the Role of Financial Remittances From Abroad

Quite possibly, the 1980s marked the greatest transformation of El
Salvador's demographic structure in the country's history. The main
cause of these changes was the war and its attendant consequences
(many of them not yet documented). The Salvadoran transformation
is something new. It is not a function of the well-known pattern of
migration from the countryside to the city stemming from the pene-
tration of capitalist production into rural areas and the exhaustion of
the agricultural frontier. Nor is it the result of alterations in the age
makeup of the population due to changes in health conditions. It involves, instead, a new context—one in which the greatest share of the
migrants leave the country. In the meantime, within El Salvador itself,
the conditions of war have assured that young people make up most
of the seventy thousand killed since 1980.

Official figures cannot express this dramatic reality adequately un-
less they are accompanied by explanations of internal displacement,
external and internal migration, and wartime deaths. I will try to address these matters briefly, relying on the research conducted by the
Universidad Centroamericana José Simeón Cañas (UCA).[9]

The studies from the UCA that I have cited, as well as historical
data, affirm that the high level of unemployment in the countryside
has long constituted the fundamental cause of both seasonal and permanent migratory patterns. Between 1930 and 1971, more than half
a million persons left El Salvador, most of them destined for Honduras
and the United States. This number is particularly impressive if one

notes that the official tally put the country's population at about 3.5 million in 1970.

High rates of migration are not a new phenomenon, but the migratory patterns of the 1980s are unprecedented for El Salvador, both qualitatively and quantitatively, as the UCA research shows. As early as 1984, a work by Segundo Montes documented the existence of half a million displaced persons inside the country,[10] a quarter of a million refugees in Central America and Mexico, and almost a quarter of a million immigrants (the majority illegal) in the United States. This added up to 25 percent of El Salvador's population, a figure markedly higher than in migrations of previous decades.

The conclusions of the 1986 UCA study on the internally displaced also shed light on the qualitative aspects of the phenomenon. The study affirms:

> *The primary thing to realize is that the problem of displaced people has a national and structural dimension. So do its possible solutions. This is not just because of the magnitude of the affected population, but because the problem and its solutions must be connected jointly to the country and to the society. . . .*
>
> *It will never be enough to insist that the war is a decisive and determining factor in the whole national problematic and in this point in particular. . . .*
>
> *We are convinced that the displacement from rural zones in conflict toward larger population centers has become a process which is fundamentally irreversible for most migrants.*

The Comisión Nacional de Asistencia a la Población Desplazada (CONADES—National Commission for Assistance to the Displaced) in 1985 offered a figure of 406,936 displaced persons; of these, 43.9 percent came from the eastern part of the country, the region most affected by the war at that time. This represented a drastic change from 1980, when the first displaced persons coming from Las Vueltas, a town in the department of Chalatenango, barely added up to 2,000 people. By the end of 1985, the number of displaced had grown to more than 100,000 in 98 municipalities from all parts of the country.[11] According to official sources, this pattern has continued to increase throughout the decade (See Table 14).

Although the final conclusions of the UCA group could be shaded for political reasons, the internal migratory movement has definitely

Table 14

Displaced Population through February 28, 1987, by Department

Department	Total Municipalities	Municipalities with Displaced Population	Number of Displaced Persons
San Salvador	19	15	71,950
Morazán	26	21	68,933
Usulután	23	18	48,165
San Miguel	20	15	43,061
San Vicente	13	13	38,453
Chalatenango	33	19	29,960
La Paz	22	13	21,605
La Libertad	22	13	18,907
Cabañas	9	7	18,389
Cuscatlán	16	10	16,479
La Unión	18	7	12,600
Sonsonate	16	7	5,217
Ahuachapán	12	3	2,576
Santa Ana	13	1	538
Total	262	162	396,833

Source: CONADES.

transformed the regional and urban map of El Salvador. Any political and economic project will have to take this profound modification of the relationship between territory and population into consideration. The impact of the war on the age structure of the population must also be taken into account. The majority of the people who have died during the decade due to the armed conflict are young, as are the majority of those who have left the country.

Despite the resettlement programs, the number of internally displaced approached 750,000 by the end of the decade. The Fundación Salvadoreña de Vivienda Mínima (Salvadoran Foundation for Low-Cost Housing) showed that 40 percent of the urban population was living in the San Salvador metropolitan area, where 700,000 people lived in 170 shantytowns, 364 illegal colonies, and 55 camps.[12] Exact data on Salvadoran citizens living in the United States is harder to obtain, since there are no reliable registries. Nevertheless, the previously cited work of Segundo Montes states that "despite the suppositions and the limitations of the calculations we have made, it can be sustained that the number of Salvadorans living in the United States is approximately 1,000,000."

I do not plan to detail at length the origin, classification, and other characteristics of this migrant population, as Segundo Montes has done in his work. Two points, however, should be emphasized. First, the volume of the monetary remittances sent by Salvadorans living abroad is critical to explaining the Salvadoran economy's performance in the 1980s; in subsequent years, the volume of remittances will continue to exert a decisive impact. Second, the social and political impact of this phenomenon must be considered. According to the calculations of Montes, the remittances total about $1.4 billion per year, equal to U.S. aid and the country's total export income combined. The remittances are more than double the latter and almost double the annual national budget. Nothing in Salvadoran history can match this stream of money. One cannot ignore the levels of distortion, dependency, and vulnerability that this flow brings to the existing structural problems of the national economy.[13]

The growth of these transfers is presented in Table 15.[14]

Segundo Montes estimates that the monetary remittances made up 47 percent of the total income of the families who received them.[15] Because of these funds, the family units of the popular sectors can maintain their social reproduction in the context of existing income levels. Montes also notes a strange paradox: even as the high-income sectors continue to export their capital, the lowest-income sectors are

Table 15
El Salvador: Transfers from Abroad (in millions of dollars)

Type of transfer	1980	1981	1982	1983	1984	1985	1986	1987
Official unilateral transfers	31	21	119	164	173	194	219	347
Private unilateral transfers	17	39	52	107	134	150	174	198

Source: ECLA, on the basis of preliminary International Monetary Fund figures.

introducing foreign currency into the country, thus sustaining the Salvadoran economy in yet another way.

In his conclusions, Montes addresses a very important yet little-examined issue—the changes in the ideology of the Salvadoran people that this new form of economic dependence promotes. I will come back to this point when considering the strategy and planning of the FMLN leadership in the final years of the war.

The Economic Program of the Current ARENA Government

During the electoral campaign won by ARENA in March 1989 there was a great deal of discussion of proposals that would liberalize the state-dominated Salvadoran economy. According to ARENA, state domination was the principal cause of the country's economic crisis. Nevertheless, a coherent plan was never presented. Speeches of the ARENA candidates gave the impression that the problem of the economy was disassociated from the war within the country.

Once Alfredo Cristiani assumed the presidency, his administration presented the Government Economic Program for June 1989 to December 1990.[16] Its temporary, limited outlook and its weak development of economic policy echo the minimal coherence ARENA showed on economic matters during the campaign. They demonstrate the profound contradictions that exist within the party over concrete economic measures beyond the superficial unanimity of neo-liberal discourse. Cristiani's measures of July 1989 clearly confirmed the view that contradictions exist in the heart of the governing party, greatly weakening its economic and political project in general.

I shall now examine ARENA's economic orientation in four areas: the war, the reforms of 1980, U.S. aid, and the cash remittances coming from the United States.

That ARENA put the war to one side does not imply that the government ignored it; rather, this position simply reflected the belief that a strictly military victory could be won within a short time. For this reason, the Cristiani administration considered it possible to push through a neo-liberal economic plan that would go into effect even as the revolutionary forces were defeated. This extremely erroneous conclusion would make the government's economic goals practically unattainable. The ARENA regime's economic plans hardly differed from the other structural readjustments imposed by the International Monetary Fund in many other Latin American countries. Liberalization and privatization constitute the essence of ARENA's economic policy. The main objective is to break away from state involvement, even though this overlooks the fact that government enterprises account for only 18 percent of the Salvadoran economy, an average below that of many other Latin American countries. Moreover, as is clear from examining the data in Table 16, the government devotes a considerable percentage of its resources to the war.

In the meantime, ARENA has been forced to modify its attack on the 1980 reforms due to underlying contradictions and, especially, the presence of the FMLN. In the realm of agrarian reform, ARENA has switched to a policy of accelerating the provision of land titles; the regime proposes to eliminate state control of the commercialization of coffee but has downplayed its previous idea of privatizing INCAFE. Similarly, ARENA has moved toward permitting private banking as a way to make the state bank competitive, rather than first pursuing outright privatization.

Table 16
Evolution of Public Expenditures, 1979 and 1984–88

Year	Defense and Public Security	Public Debt	Public Health and Social Assistance	Education and Culture	Public Works	Other Expenses	Total
In millions of *colones*							
1979	184.9	62.8	102.1	292.3	223.8	547.4	1,413.3
1984	660.5	725.6	191.5	373.2	200.4	580.5	2,731.7
1985	725.5	313.0	176.5	423.2	189.9	532.1	2,360.2
1986	960.9	741.2	232.3	559.1	263.6	985.1	3,742.2
1987	981.9	580.8	252.7	615.8	280.5	757.4	3,469.1
1988	987.0	634.2	288.9	623.1	296.1	673.6	3,502.9
In percentages							
1979	12.7	4.3	9.8	20.1	15.4	37.7	100.0
1984	24.2	26.6	7.0	13.7	7.3	21.2	100.0
1985	30.7	13.3	7.5	17.9	8.1	22.5	100.0
1986	25.7	19.8	6.2	15.0	7.0	26.3	100.0
1987	28.3	16.7	7.3	17.7	8.2	21.8	100.0
1988	28.2	18.1	8.2	17.8	8.4	19.3	100.0

Source: Ministerio de Hacienda de El Salvador, 1989.

In addition to the absence of any reference to the war situation, the economic plans of the ARENA government also surprisingly fail to mention either the role of U.S. military aid or the importance of cash remittances coming from the United States.

All this reflects the blind ideology of the dominant classes, permitting me to endorse the opinion expressed in the issue of *Proceso* that I cited earlier:

> *The project definitively reflects the interests of the dominant sector in the current government, which is none other than the traditional agro-export oligarchy.*

The initiative of the ARENA government on the agrarian question has privileged individual agricultural property. This policy began to take shape on September 9, 1989, with the transfer of three thousand property titles to an equal number of beneficiaries of decree 207 in the eastern part of the country.[17] The government also requested the dissolution of the Comité de Organizaciones Campesinas (COC—Committee of Peasant Organizations). Clearly, the government agreed with FUSADES that the poor results of the 1980 agrarian reforms stemmed from the creation of cooperatives, a form of organization said to run counter to the tradition and character of Salvadoran peasants. If one looks in detail at levels of production and productivity in the reformed and nonreformed sectors, it is clear that this assertion is false. Such variables as credits and technical assistance do much to explain the prevailing patterns of economic performance. As the September 13, 1989 issue of *Proceso* (cited above) affirms,

> *the Agrarian Reform cooperatives face serious problems. These problems, however, do not derive from the form of property itself. Rather, they result from the particular characteristics that the reform process has assumed in El Salvador, especially the counterinsurgency conception under which it was conceived and the political maneuvers to which it was subjected by Christian Democratic management.*

The government heeded the recommendations of FUSADES,[18] which suggested changes in the finance, economy, planning, and agriculture ministries and in the Banco Central de Reserva. These recommendations reflected two main doctrines: reducing state intervention in the functioning of the economy in all sectors, and opening the economy to foreign trade. The Cristiani government started to dictate laws and take steps toward the denationalization of the financial sector and of foreign trade (measures in addition to the privatizing of the agrarian reform discussed above). Thus, on September 30, 1989, the Supreme Court of El Salvador declared articles 1, 2, and 7 of decree 237 of 1980 unconstitutional; these had created the National Sugar Institute (Instituto Nacional de Azúcar—INAZUCAR). The court thus eliminated the state monopoly of the sugar and sugar derivatives industry, a measure that was similar to the one dictated in August in the case of INCAFE. In the meantime, the president of the Banco Central de Reserva announced plans to begin the first stages of its privatization.[19] This privatizing impetus is the primary feature of the current government's precarious economic strategy. The doctrinal basis for this policy has been amply developed since 1985, when FUSADES first presented it publicly.[20] Further examination is warranted, given the importance of the FUSADES proposal for the future actions of the Cristiani government, especially in the context of the political reconstitution of the dominant classes, the subject of the next chapter of this book.

The formulation presented by FUSADES is not unique. It is the product of realignments in the international division of labor in the wake of the crisis in the world capitalist system. Some of the most acute manifestations of this crisis have appeared in the last decade, revealing phenomena like the "new industrialized countries" (Taiwan, South Korea, etc.). These developments have intrigued many economists and businessmen, among them the members of FUSADES, who observed in their 1985 report that "[t]he experiences of small, recently industrialized countries provide a stimulus for countries such as El Salvador that confront grave financial imbalances limiting their growth."

This model focuses primarily on export-oriented growth and on taking advantage of the abundant labor force that exists in less-developed countries. The attempt to transfer such thinking mechanically to the Latin American context, without regard for the region's unique historical characteristics, has been widely criticized.[21] I am not here rejecting *a priori* a group of economic policies that advocate reallocating resources to labor-intensive activities and modifying the role of the state. The Salvadoran economy will not be able to avoid the historical context in which the country continues to find itself, whatever its model of development. But one clearly must underscore the profoundly anti-popular orientation of schemes like that of FUSADES, which proposes that government participation accommodate itself to the forces of the market.

It is thus not surprising that analyses from this viewpoint of the origins of the economic crisis of El Salvador in the 1980s make no reference to structural causes (the concentration of property in a few hands, the unjust distribution of national income, etc.). These lie at the origin of a crisis whose comprehensiveness goes beyond its economic dimension. Evaluations such as that of FUSADES give an emphasis to key, but only partial, aspects of El Salvador's experience, such as the extreme dependence of the economy on external forces. As the following selections from the 1989 analysis by FUSADES show, there is reason to dispute the capacity of these views to comprehend Salvadoran history fully:

> *[The country's] long-run economic development has been subject to impulses generated from outside, fundamentally through the favorable influence exercised by the export of a few primary products.*
>
> *[T]he pull of the external sector in the country's economy is thus illustrated by the fact that even with the growth observed in industrial exports to the Central American Common Market, the exports of four products (coffee, sugar, cotton, and shrimp) represented around 56% of the total sales abroad.*

This document does recognize the accelerated deterioration of the social situation (unemployment rates greater than 30 percent and inflation oscillating between 12 and 17 percent annually since 1983). It also acknowledges that living conditions for most Salvadorans have not deteriorated further due to funds received from the United States—aid that cannot be counted on indefinitely. Yet, the phenomenon of the war appears as just one more factor in the views of FUSADES—lacking the real weight that it possesses in any effort at stabilization, reactivation, and transformation of the economic model. This, too, is a failure common to the economic discourse of the current ARENA government.

In synthesis, starting with the case of a small and open economy whose development cannot be based on the dynamics of internal demand, the FUSADES model formulates a determining contribution by the external sector, whose key components are the diversification and expansion of exports, the deregulation of the economy, and the drastic reduction of the economic role of the state. The model assumed that

> *at the very least, the military conflict can be reduced, with the objective of economic activities gradually recovering their normal operation, since the costs of economic stabilization and reactivation are greater to the degree that the war persists.*

It went on to state that, given the situation,

> *it will be necessary to adopt some measures that can be separated from the basic objectives of the model, with the understanding that these would have a strictly temporary character.*

The model goes on to detail the principal economic policies to be applied—fiscal, customs, monetary, credit, exchange, prices, labor, education, and training.

This is the foundation that was not applied explicitly either in the economic program of ARENA during the campaign or during the first months of the Cristiani government. The obstacles created by an inefficient and, above all, unjust economic structure have proven insurmountable. The war, whose impact the government tried to underestimate, cannot be resolved by clean elections alone. There are limits that neither the detailed, thought-out model of FUSADES nor the political will of ARENA can overcome in the short or medium term. Therefore, the economic program of the government has begun to clash with the Salvadoran bourgeoisie, so accustomed to profiting in the short run. In mid-September 1989,[22] disputes broke out between the government and industrial sectors centering on the differences over the policies of stabilization and adjustment. These disagreements indicate the profound limitations and ambiguities of this economic project, a fact that cannot be overlooked in assessing the balance of what has occurred in El Salvador during this decade.

The Political Recomposition
of the Dominant Classes

Even a quick glance at the last fifty-nine years of Salvadoran political history conveys an eloquent impression: seven coups (1931, 1944, 1948, 1960, 1961, 1972, and 1979); two significant popular uprisings (the 1932 insurrection and the general civic strike [*huelga de los brazos caídos*, literally, "strike of fallen arms"—Translator] in 1944; three relatively partial and minor popular movements (1960, 1972, and 1977); and five elections in the 1980s. These events all took place within a juridical-political framework guaranteed by five different constitutions promulgated during six decades and, more recently, within a situation of open warfare since 1981.

A Ruling Class without Legitimation

The first impression created by this panorama of conflict is that of a recurrent crisis of hegemony—which constitutes, in fact, the principal question of Salvadoran political power. Intimately tied to this issue is another long-term singular characteristic: the lack of a political party, in its strictest sense, of the bourgeoisie. This trait partially explains the contempt for consensus and the crude manipulation of the electoral process that recur in El Salvador. In the 1980s, these patterns began to change drastically under the force of the revolutionary project of the FMLN-FDR alliance and the political recomposition of the dominant classes. This latter development will be the focus of this chapter.

First, let me detail some of the antecedents to these changes.[1] Before the 1980s, one has to go back to 1931 to find the last time in which there were free elections in the liberal democratic sense in El

Salvador. Labor candidate Arturo Araujo won that year with the backing of popular organizations, including the recently established Communist Party. This occurred during a time that was shaped by a temporary fracture in the hegemony of the oligarchy. The period began in 1927 with the ascent to the presidency of Araujo's predecessor, Pío Romero Bosque; it was ended by the military coup of General Maximiliano Hernández Martínez on December 2, 1931.[2]

In the municipal and legislative elections held on January 5 and 10, 1932, the Communist Party won many predominantly indigenous municipalities in western El Salvador; these elections were quickly annulled by the new dictatorship of Martínez. This constituted the prelude to the armed uprising and the subsequent massacre of peasants and laborers that took place later in January. From this moment on, military dictatorship—under different guises—became the form of government imposed upon the country without interruption for more than fifty years. Successive presidential elections represented merely the necessary mechanisms used from time to time to "legitimize" the military dictatorship of the moment: General Salvador Castañeda Castro in 1945, Colonel Oscar Osorio in 1950, Colonel José María Lemus in 1956, Colonel Julio Rivera in 1962, Colonel Fidel Sánchez in 1967, Colonel Arturo Armando Molina in 1972, and General Carlos Humberto Romero in 1977. At times, the only candidate running was a military officer from the official party.

As I explained in Chapter 1, the military coup of October 1979 marked the beginning of a new political period. This era was characterized by a distinct correlation of forces, as indicated by the rise of the revolutionary movement, and marked the most severe crisis of hegemony of the dominant classes since 1932. I will now briefly examine this crisis.

Let me first make a necessary clarification concerning the analysis. When I refer to a crisis of hegemony, I do so on two levels: first, the crisis of hegemony imposed on the whole of society through consensus or coercion by the dominant classes; second, the crisis of hegemony inside the dominant classes, inside the bloc in power. Although in general terms the first incorporates the second, I will specify which of these two levels I am referring to in each conjuncture under analysis.

Between 1927 and 1932, the two strands of the crisis were joined together; after signs of incubation for several years, the culminating point was reached between December 1931 and January 1932. Once the dominant hegemony was reconstituted at both levels through blood and fire, forty years passed before another serious challenge presented itself. In the presidential election of 1972, a group of reformist petit bourgeois and revolutionary forces with wide popular backing used the electoral process to challenge the existing bourgeois-oligarchic hegemony over the country. It then took another four years for the crisis of hegemony within the dominant bloc to explode over a timid project of agrarian reform in 1976. As a glance at Salvadoran history since 1932 shows, the events of 1972 and 1976 were different in character from the political conflicts of previous decades.

The coups d'etat of 1944, 1948, 1960, and 1961 could all be classified as a particular form of readjusting shares of power within the dominant bloc. None reflected a questioning of the hegemony of the dominant classes within society, or even a real crisis of hegemony within these classes. Such was the case of the civic strike of May 1944 and the later military coup that overthrew the thirteen-year-old dictatorship of Hernández Martínez. These facts of Salvadoran political history, rarely studied until now,[3] demonstrate an absence of any questioning of class power or of any split within the bourgeoisie. Instead, the coup of 1944 expressed a need to replace personal military dictatorship with a new modality reflecting changes in economy and society in the middle of the twentieth century.[4]

Signs of discontent with the dictatorship had begun to manifest themselves around 1940 as the terror that had reigned during the previous decade began to be overcome.[5] The participation of radicalized middle sectors appeared as a new phenomenon in the mass struggles of these years. The political involvement of these groups during the 1920s had not been significant because of their relative weakness within the social fabric. By 1944, however, the participation of these sectors had grown substantially (and paradoxically) due to the important changes in the economy and society that had occurred during the Hernández Martínez dictatorship. In addition, as Parkman confirms, the modest rebirth of labor union activity after 1940 was very important in this context. By January 1944 the Confederación de Sociedades Obreras de El Salvador (Confederation of Workers Societies of El Salvador) had reported the existence of between eighty and ninety union organizations. The dictator tried to co-opt this movement through rhetoric and populist measures in the final years of his rule.

This whole democratizing movement was set against a backdrop of economic growth and a new ideological climate brought on by the impending defeat of the fascists in World War II. The latter was all over the pages of the Salvadoran press, and in 1944 three of the five dailies in the capital (*El Diario Latino, La Prensa Gráfica,* and *El Diario de Hoy*) stood in frank opposition to the regime. This movement never questioned the power of the dominant classes, some key members of which participated actively in overthrowing the Hernández Martínez dictatorship. Two groups particularly distinguished themselves in the opposition struggle: the party Acción Democrática Salvadoreña (Salvadoran Democratic Action), founded in 1941, and the group controlled by the Banco Hipotecario de El Salvador. Most members of these organizations had supported the dictatorship during the 1930s, some even occupying high government positions. Acción Democrática Salvadoreña was mostly made up of large-scale property owners belonging to the Asociación Cafetalera; one of these men, former Auditor General Agustín Alfaro Morán, was the principal actor in the conspiracy to overthrow Hernández Martínez, as Parkman maintains. The group directed by the Banco Hipotecario was controlled almost totally by the Asociación Cafetalera and the Asociación Ganadera. In practice, it had responded more to these associations than to the government, even though it served as a key instrument for agricultural modernization and therefore constituted a pillar of the economic boom experienced under the dictatorship.

Arturo Romero emerged as a leader from within this opposition group of large landowners, government technocrats, professionals of the emerging middle class, artisans, laborers, students, and even a part of the armed forces. Romero was a physician whose charisma and advanced social ideas temporarily gave Salvadoran politics his personal stamp. The size and heterogeneity of the opposition movement showed that it did not question the character of the ruling social and economic structure. The contradictions of different groups within the dominant classes played only a secondary role. The main goal of this opposition was to change the form of government, since personal military dictatorship no longer suited Salvadoran realities. Once Hernández Martínez was overthrown, the country endured four years of instability before a process of readjustment yielded a new government modality: dictatorship in which power was held by a single group within the army. This form prevented personal dominance of any one figure for more than one presidential term. Once satisfied that its power was no longer threatened, the oligarchy abandoned the political scene and withdrew to its economic activities, an error whose high cost could be seen clearly by the 1980s.

The military coup of 1948 marked a realignment of power within the dominant classes and the assignment of a new role to the armed forces. This helped to modernize the state in ways necessary to begin the second half of the century. Although it is not my objective here to offer a detailed analysis of Salvadoran political history,[6] I must point out that the intent of the dominant classes to construct a new hegemonic project underlies all these events. Yet this project was limited by the failure of a fraction of the bourgeoisie, newly empowered by the country's industrial boom, to develop as an economic sector with its own proper stamp.

The military coup of 1961, a distant precursor of the coup of October 1979, was an unusual effort. It attempted to achieve more than a simple readjustment of power, but it was quickly put down because of the insufficient development of its base of political support. Politics lapsed back to the basic pattern created in 1950, one that would not finally be exhausted until the end of the 1970s. Another attempt at modification failed in 1972, when electoral fraud stripped away the triumph of the Duarte-Ungo team and a subsequent coup by dissident officers was aborted.

After 1972, the demonstrated exhaustion of the existing political model and the challenge presented by the coalition of Christian Democracy, Social Democracy, and the Communist Party encouraged an attempt at a new model of political domination, one with four salient characteristics.

First, it represented a radical change in the strategy of capital accumulation, one that again gave priority to the external market for traditional and new export products. This shift was prompted by the evident exhaustion of the Central American Common Market, the looming economic crisis, and the political choice not to carry out reforms that would substantially widen El Salvador's internal market. This last issue was the cornerstone of bourgeois structural economic reform. Serious differences over such economic initiatives persisted between virtually the entire bourgeoisie (except in the case of some powerful groups isolated from it) and the technocrats who managed the state apparatus. The latter were strongly influenced by foreign advisers who saw clearly the extreme short-run fragility of the model of oligarchic domination.

Next, this strategy required the modernization of the productive structure and provision for its growing transnationalization, especially in some sectors of industrial and agro-industrial production. It also implied an increase in the overexploitation of the working classes and, consequently, the control or destruction of existing labor organizations and the creation of obstacles to organization in new sectors.

Third, the new model revealed the necessity of limiting the bourgeois democratic game; this caused the entire formal structure of participation—proportional representation in the Legislative Assembly (which had only been achieved in the preceding decade), municipal autonomy, and so on—to lose its importance. Meanwhile, legal repression increased. (Illegal repression, of course, was a constant for both models of domination; its intensity depended on the degree of strength achieved by the class struggle.)

Finally, a bourgeois ideology was unleashed in which quasi-fascist social and political elements (nationalism, hierarchical order, etc.) clearly dominated; at the same time, attempts were made to create official mass organizations. Both efforts aimed at increasing control of the exploited masses. (Paradoxically, some of the origins of the current Unión Popular Democrática [UPD—Popular Democratic Union], the social and political base of the Duarte government as well as of the death squads, can be found here.)

This model required serious transformations within the state apparatus, thus provoking severe contradictions within the dominant bloc. Changes demanded by the new strategy of accumulation and the new model of domination resulted in the 1976 confrontation over the "agrarian transformation" promoted by the Molina government. This initiative was launched at a time when the class struggle was sharpening, with revolutionary organizations emerging to offer alternatives to the Salvadoran Communist Party. I will try to sketch a hypothetical preliminary analysis of the origin of these contradictions within the dominant classes.

The industrial development of the 1960s spurred by the Central American Common Market had given rise to various bourgeois economic groups with strong ties to the financial-industrial sector associated with imperialist—principally United States—capital. Data from the small amount of research that has been carried out in El Salvador show that the Salvadoran bourgeoisie was not internally differentiated by the sectors in which it invested. In classical economic terms, in other words, there was little differentiation among an agrarian bourgeoisie, an industrial bourgeoisie, a commercial bourgeoisie, a financial bourgeoisie, and so on.

Instead, what emerged was a bourgeoisie whose historical development divided its interests among the various points of capital reproduction. Since surplus value fundamentally derived from the exports of the agricultural and livestock sector, the bourgeoisie first extended its reach into the commercialization of agro-export products, then into the banking sector, and finally into the industrial and financial sector.

The most important groups within the bourgeoisie were thus involved in both the production and realization of surplus value from very early on, creating a small, highly concentrated sector, historically known as the Salvadoran oligarchy, that controlled the whole country.

This situation pertained throughout various expansions and modernizations until it underwent an important change with the creation of the Central American Common Market. This integrationist project forced a change in the oligarchy's traditional strategy of accumulation. From an almost exclusive emphasis on external markets as a way to create profit, El Salvador began to benefit from the internal regional market. The history of the common market has been well documented. Its achievements, its failures, and its structural limitations were, above all, political in nature. It never accomplished the deep reforms in economic structure that most Central American countries needed in order to widen internal markets and to achieve the potential of the integration plan.

During the 1960s, the economic groups of the bourgeoisie that adapted to this new strategy of accumulation differentiated themselves from the others that clung to the old ways. These new groups, the most dynamic sector of the bourgeoisie, were responsible for promoting emerging technocrats to the highest positions within the government apparatus. They began to engender a "modernizing" mentality among army officers in executive posts. A concurrent political tendency argued for structural bourgeois reforms. Paradoxically, this argument was not the direct expression of any predominant faction of the bourgeoisie. Instead, it emerged from the PDC, a party basically composed of petit bourgeois elements. To this day, the Christian Democratic Party has not been able to obtain the support of any important groups from the social class that its political postulates defend.

Founded in November 1960,[7] the PDC has always been led by professionals of the middle classes, although some have had ties to groups of the bourgeoisie as administrators or holders of power of attorney. The eight-member committee that organized the party included five lawyers and two engineers. Throughout its thirty-year existence, two tendencies have struggled to impose their own point of view: on one

side, those fighting to safeguard social-Christian ideological principles, and on the other, those pushing for a "realistic application" of
these ideals.

The PDC clearly favored the middle class and urban sectors, and it
possessed little capacity to establish a base of support among rural
workers until the passage of the 1980 agrarian reform decree. By this
time, however, the revolutionary forces had begun to challenge the
status quo, even as the dominant classes had discovered the need to
constitute their own class party. By the end of the 1980s, the PDC's
trajectory can be classified as a frustrated attempt not only to represent national interests as a whole but also to fashion itself into the
modern party of the Salvadoran bourgeoisie.

The differentiation at the heart of the Salvadoran dominant class
that I have sketched explains this peculiar political situation. There
were two different sectors of the bourgeoisie, each identified according to its strategy of accumulation. The group that in the 1960s
switched its support to a regional market thought only of a market
within Central America, and it created no strategy for the structural reforms needed to develop a wider domestic market within El Salvador.
Therefore, despite a few exceptions, most members of this sector did
not support a reform political option; instead, they attacked it vehe-
mently and constantly. When the common market reached its limits,
this group decided to maintain its traditional strategy of accumulation
through the reorientation of the model of domination after 1972.

However, this process left its marks. In the face of the difficulties
engendered by the proposed new model of domination, desires for
moderate change resurfaced with a timid agrarian reform program in
1976. The "agrarian transformation" advocated by the Molina government had little to do with the actions of reformist petit bourgeois
parties like the Christian Democrats or parties of the Left like the
Communists. The hegemonic crisis within the power bloc came to a
head over this reform effort; and the impact of the division extended
beyond the bourgeoisie. Although reformist groups were fatally lacking in influence within their own class, their dissenting position did
extend qualitatively into other social sectors in the power bloc, particularly the technocrats and the military that had exercised direct control over the state for almost fifty years. This historic blindness of the
bourgeoisie had one fundamental cause: its failure to exercise direct
power, to develop its own class-based parties, and to nurture its own
organic intelligentsia. This pattern brought on a paralysis from which

the Salvadoran bourgeoisie did not begin to recover until 1982, a point at which the revolutionary upsurge had brought bourgeois power to the verge of collapse. Land ownership has been crucial to the history of El Salvador. One can understand the differences between the two tendencies within the Salvadoran bourgeoisie by examining their attitude toward land. Both groups enjoyed representation in nearly all sectors of the economy and depended on agricultural export production as their primary economic base. But the strong links to foreign capital of one group, as well as its success in exploiting the Central American internal market, instilled in it a new concept of land ownership. Now it appreciated that definitive ownership of the land was no longer necessary if it maintained control (as in the case of coffee, for example) of processing and commercialization. Therefore, reformist voices emerged from within this group, although it always remained a the minority within its class. Due to an ancestral fear of Communism, this group never gave its political support to Christian Democracy, which political inexperience kept it from understanding.

When El Salvador reached the state of revolution by the end of the 1970s, it was the military, supported by the Carter and Reagan administrations in the United States, that worked to reclaim the reformist cause in a desperate attempt to moderate the revolutionary fervor of the masses. In this task, the military joined at first with the Social Democratic, Christian Democratic, and Communist reformist sectors, and later with the Christian Democrats alone. Also involved in this frustrated attempt were some representatives of the bourgeois reformist group. Although making up a minority without direct political expression, they adopted the line of moving forward with immediate reforms in the Salvadoran economic structure.

Nevertheless, the dominant classes now confronted a challenge to the very essence of the system, not merely to the form of government. This served as an incentive for them to unite in a process of reconstitution as a political class with its own organic expression, a development that would crystallize by the end of the 1980s. At the root of this reconstitution lies an important fact. Despite the modernizing and reformist voices of its political minority, the monolithic and oligarchic character of this class remained unchanged in economic terms. Studies carried out in the mid-1980s showed that this character had not been reversed by the reforms of 1980; in fact, it had grown stronger.[8]

No fragmentation of the oligarchy took place. Although its political behavior lacked the old cohesiveness, Wim Pelupessy offers some interesting conclusions regarding its historic makeup:

> *Long ago, the Salvadoran oligarchy ceased to be the antiquated landowning class of yesteryear. In the first phase of the industrial diversification of the 1920s, it acquired its true oligarchic character as a result of the conjunction of agrarian, banking, and commercial capital. . . .*
> *This same oligarchic capital in alliance with U.S. financial capital constituted the force behind the subsequent industrial diversifications of the 1950s and the 1960s, with the expansion of the agro-export package of cotton and sugar, and later with import-substitution industrialization at the regional level.*

And referring to the effects of the 1980 reforms, Pelupessy maintains that:

> *[t]he oligarchy's position within the most important industrial enterprises, banking, and other productive sectors strengthens its agro-export interests. The reforms to date have not changed this reality substantially, and in some important respects, they have economically favored the oligarchy.*
> *With a technologically productive base minimally reduced by the war, the oligarchy has not exhibited many symptoms of economic decline.*
> *The alliance with imperialist capital and the skillful management of its interests within the process of productive diversification have not produced the expected economic factionalization. The economic weakness of the oligarchy as a group (evident in the case of nationalization of the coffee export industry) does not necessarily imply its factionalization. On the other hand, this does not preclude possible internal divergencies in the political and ideological terrain.*

This helps to explain, in part, El Salvador's economic performance during this decade of crisis and war, as well as the process of political reconstitution that I have begun to examine. Between the proposed "agrarian transformation" of the Molina government in 1976 and the effectuation of reforms in 1980, there were moments of sharp political difference within the core of the oligarchy, notwithstanding its economically monolithic character. The absence of political practice and of a class-based party were fundamental in generating these political differences.[9]

Past efforts to shape a political instrument of a class character had not been fruitful, especially so in the case of the Partido Popular Salvadoreño (PPS—Salvadoran Popular Party), inaugurated in 1965 by sectors of the bourgeoisie unhappy with the official PCN. The PPS never won the capacity to represent the dominant Salvadoran elites largely because their class power was not in dispute. When their power did come to be challenged in the 1980s, the Salvadoran elites joined around the ARENA party to reconstitute themselves as a political class, a process simultaneous with, while going well beyond, the reconstitution of the political regime.[10]

In my opinion, this final differentiation is very important for visualizing the political future of El Salvador. It requires an analysis of the hegemony within the power bloc, a question that I think has yet to be resolved. The struggle inside the bourgeois elite occurred at the same time as the Salvadoran revolutionary forces were beginning to mold an alternative project for the country, politically and organizationally. They shaped themselves into a force whose defeat became a prerequisite to the selection of bourgeois projects to be followed and to the resolution of the hegemonic crisis within the dominant classes. Such was context in which the political recomposition of the dominant classes occurred. I will examine this phenomenon by analyzing the successive electoral events of the 1980s.

The Elections for the Constituent Assembly of March 1982 and the Presidential Elections of 1984

On March 28, 1982, elections were held to select representatives to the constituent assembly to draft a new political constitution. I submit that the most important conclusion to be drawn from this process is that the elections did not resolve the hegemonic crisis within the dominant bloc. Consequently, the general hegemonic crisis within the Salvadoran social formation was not resolved.[11]

Above all, these elections sought to impose a new hegemony by restructuring the dominant bloc around Christian Democracy as an alternative to the oligarchic hegemony in crisis. For this reason, the elections excluded the Left, despite demagogic calls to democratic and revolutionary groups to participate. The voting could not have a national character; first, the elections had to resolve the power crisis within the dominant bloc. The people's revolutionary war in progress prevented the existence of the most minimal conditions necessary to complete even this limited objective. Officials inflated the total number of votes really cast. Yet holding elections at all, despite the political-military efforts of the FMLN-FDR to hinder them, constituted a first step in the process of reconstituting the dominant classes.

In effect, the most notable characteristic of this election was the support (almost 30 percent of the votes) obtained by ARENA, a rightist party founded on September 30, 1981. El Salvador's political panorama had changed substantially. Between the constituent assembly elections of March 28, 1982, and the presidential elections of March 25 and May 6, 1984, several further changes took place that must be understood. The elections of 1982 not only failed to resolve the hegemonic crisis within the dominant bloc—they exacerbated it through the emergence of a new political formation of the dominant classes not contemplated in the post-1980 counterinsurgency scheme of the United States government.

After May 1982, Alvaro Magaña's so-called government of national unity was plagued by constant infighting unresolved by the interventions of various U.S. ambassadors. The annulment of Phase II of the 1980 agrarian reform constituted one of the most important expressions of the permanent battle between the military–Christian Democratic executive government and the Legislative Assembly, which was dominated by the opposition parties of the Right. These years were characterized by some remarkable changes:

- First, the definitive forging of a true bourgeois political party, the first since the 1920s, in ARENA;
- Second, the recomposition of the old official party of bureaucratic and military cliques, the PCN;
- Third, the advance of the revolutionary war and of the FMLN-FDR alliance, despite the growing intervention of the U.S. government and the position taken by the revolutionary forces toward the 1982 elections.

After two years of intense discord, new elections were held in 1984. Napoleón Duarte assumed the presidency. Subsequent events would underline one of my main arguments: once again, an election failed to resolve differences that existed inside the dominant bloc, and no particular leading group was able to emerge within it. The Duarte government enjoyed only minimal independence. This was the source of its difficulties in holding peace talks with the revolutionary forces, as Duarte had promised during the elections, and of the failure of its vascillating reforms.

One issue remains clear: the solution to the internal contradictions within the dominant classes, as well as the solution to the hegemonic crisis within the bloc, can only be achieved after the Salvadoran revolutionary movement is defeated. This view seems to contradict many historical cases in which a dominant group became more unified as the loss of class power appeared more imminent. While this was partially true for El Salvador, the particular characteristics of the Salvadoran case in the 1980s guaranteed a persistent crisis of hegemony. The political mediations of the Duarte government and its contradictions with almost all of the dominant class provided the appearance of a class division that did not exist. As a matter of class, there was only one common fundamental enemy. In politics, however, a real division did exist within the entire bloc in power, since the bourgeoisie had not exercised direct political power in the past and since it did not control political power in the mid-1980s due to differences in strategy with the United States.

This peculiar fact of the absence of the direct bourgeois control of political power has received the attention of several authors from a variety of ideological orientations. For instance, Enrique Baloyra observes that

> *the fatal flaw of the Salvadoran system inaugurated in 1948 is that in trying to prevent partisan and electoral politics from disrupting the established order, the military precipitated a more direct confrontation between Salvadoran classes.*
>
> *Yet the stubbornness with which the oligarchy resisted the institutionalization of a party system and competitive elections in El Salvador suggests that it clearly understood the socioeconomic implications of such a development.*[12]

Although I do not share the view that Baloyra expresses here, he also mentions the organic crisis of hegemony in El Salvador in his analysis of the critical juncture of 1976, at the time of the Molina government's program of "agrarian transformation."

The tremendous political weakness of the lack of a class-based bourgeois party proved even more noticeable between the military coup of October 15, 1979, and the inception of ARENA in September 1981 (or, more exactly, 1983, when various factions of the dominant classes began to exert direct control over this political party). These were years in which the bourgeoisie examined a variety of alternatives, one example being the formation of the Alianza Productiva, a gathering of the leading economic groups. In analyzing the founding document for the Alianza, Segundo Montes observes:

> *Its principal message to unaffiliated social forces is twofold: an invitation to join them, a promise to respect different ideologies provided they accept the objectives of the Alianza Productiva; and an expression of their own interest in the well-being of the all Salvadorans and their fatherland. The tone of the document is strongly ideological, reflecting a giant effort by "high intellectuals" to reconstruct hegemony and an organic alliance.*[13]

Although they were unknown to Salvadorans under fifty years of age, honest elections came to play a fundamental role in constructing a bourgeois political apparatus and in establishing political hegemony at both of the levels I have mentioned. In the short run, it is clear that the presidential elections of 1984, like the constituent assembly elections of 1982, failed to resolve the hegemonic crisis within the dominant bloc. Nevertheless, both these exercises played their part within a U.S. counterinsurgency strategy for the region in which the establishment of "democratically" elected governments was a key ingredient. Within El Salvador, the voting demonstrated progress in the political recomposition of the dominant classes.

At least three objectives were pursued in the 1982 and 1984 elections: first, to try to resolve the contradictions within the bloc in power (a goal that was not met); second, to establish a "legitimate," "democratically" elected government capable of diminishing the strength and credibility of the revolutionary alternative and of providing a screen for direct and massive intervention, if needed (both objectives achieved in part); and third, to contribute to the reconstitution of U.S. political hegemony in the region.

Even if the first goal was not attained, the attempt to reach it changed the political situation in El Salvador. Toward the end of 1981, there were more than a few who underestimated the significance of Roberto D'Aubuisson and ARENA, dismissing the movement as a fascist group with little potential inside the country. Given the results of the 1982 elections, many were forced to reevaluate their views. What had happened? I suggest one hypothesis: the bourgeoisie recognized that the creation of a political party of fascist tendencies was not the appropriate historical alternative for the moment. Instead, it appreciated the need for a party that could collect the ideas, intentions, and expectations of the broadest range of the Right. The strengthening current in many countries known as neo-conservatism was influential in this political development. Another important factor was the experience acquired in 1976 through the formation of the agrarian-livestock groups known collectively as the Frente de Agricultores de la Región Oriental (FARO—Eastern Farmers Front); these had been organized in numerous departments of El Salvador in order to oppose the Molina government's "agrarian transformation." A source of similar experience was work with such organizations as the "women's front" and the "peace and work crusade."

Another concern at the time was the maintenance of the former official party, the PCN. Many people, prematurely, had assumed its disappearance from the political scene. From numerous accounts in Salvadoran newspapers throughout 1979 and 1980, one can see that a change was under way in the leadership and orientation of the old party. It was led by a group of longtime members from the state and labor union bureaucracies, who had been influenced by their studies in political science at the Catholic University. This renewal of political thought in some sectors of the PCN was reflected in reformist and modernizing formulations. The source of the electoral success of the PCN, especially in 1982, was a combination of these factors and a return to the old political support bases created through years of controlling local governments and the paramilitary group ORDEN. The process of renewal would soon reveal its limits as ARENA grew to become the party of the dominant classes. The decline of the PCN in the elections of 1984 showed that the bourgeoisie had never directly integrated it into its composition and into its leadership. The group was simply a party of the state bureaucracy that represented the interests of the bourgeoisie. The traditional elements of the PCN reclaimed its leadership by the end of 1989, thus foreshadowing the party's final eclipse.[14]

Duarte's first year in office was marked by the continuation of profound, unresolved differences, the greatest expression of which were the discrepancies surrounding the peace talks between the government and the FMLN-FDR in October 1984. Not until the elections of the following year, when the PDC won a majority in the Legislative Assembly, did the constant conflict between the executive and the legislature end.

Let me review briefly the Duarte administration's proposed plan of government.[15] In presenting it, Minister Fidel Chávez Mena pointed out the document's strong ideological-political orientation, deeming it justified by an overall crisis that questioned the fundamental values of Western democracy. Given the persistent crisis of hegemony, the plan emphasized two central elements, the social pact and *concertación* (a process of reaching agreement or harmony through consultation and negotiation, sometimes rendered as "consensus building"— Translator].

Although presented explicitly as a model of a social market economy, the plan of government was intimately linked to the 1980 reforms; it was, as well, being promoted by the PDC, a party that never served as a direct representative of the dominant classes, although it defended their interests. Therefore, the plan played no part in the construction of the new political hegemony. It faded into Salvadoran history as no more than a simple declaration of good intentions, as had so many other development plans of previous governments.[16]

The Elections for the Legislative Assembly of 1985

The PDC won a clear victory in the elections of March 1985. It vaulted from twenty-four to thirty-three seats, giving it a majority in the Legislative Assembly; the Christian Democrats also took control of 75 percent of the mayoralties, including those of the ten most important cities. On the other hand, ARENA suffered an appreciable decline compared to the vote it had received the year before.[17]

However, I am more interested in the question of hegemonic power relations than in a detailed analysis of the electoral process. For the PDC, 1985 marked a high point in consolidating its electoral strength, a fact no doubt related to the expectations of peace generated by the negotiations mentioned earlier. This immediate appearance of power, however, did not reflect the actual correlation of forces. In reality, the almost total control of government by the PDC proved that the party could not, all by itself, successfully implement the counterinsurgency plan begun in 1980. The economic reforms of that year demonstrated a limited ability to dismantle the power of the oligarchy, improve popular living conditions, and contain the revolutionary forces. Thus, a fact emerges that has drastically modified the political map of El Salvador. In contrast with previous decades, a political party forged by the dominant classes exists; these classes, virtually in their entirety, have regrouped themselves politically; in consequence, they now have enormous power. In my opinion, this is the fundamental reason for the decline of the old official party, the PNC, and for the impossibility of any development of other parties of the Right. (My position runs counter to interpretations that attribute the decline of the PNC to contradictions that arose between its old rightist trajectory and the new social democratic vestments with which it has tried to clothe itself in recent years.)

Far from reinforcing the reformist option imposed by the U.S. counterinsurgency strategy, the elections of 1985 contributed to the political reshaping of the dominant classes. The voting did this, however, without resolving the hegemonic crisis within the power bloc. Here I will address a point that has been the source of much discussion over the Salvadoran crisis—the possibility of constituting a political nucleus or a party of the center as an alternative within this extremely polarized political scene. Many (especially those within the PDC) have suggested that this party represented such an alternative. This recurring affirmation was a central idea in Duarte's proposals throughout the decade, but experience has proved it completely false.[18] For a great variety of reasons, Salvadoran Christian Democracy occupied the reformist and would-be centrist political space instead of the local expression of social democracy, the MNR. This state of affairs arose from the conditions associated with the lack of true parties of the dominant classes since the 1920s. The PDC emerged in the 1960s with a double and contradictory mission: to modify the existing oligarchic power structure while simultaneously representing at least the modern sectors of the Salvadoran bourgeoisie, an impossible job given that class's wide-ranging economic interests. This analysis helps to explain the Christian Democrats' vacillating political tendencies, which led to alliances with the Communist Party at one moment and to total acceptance of the U.S. counterinsurgency project at another. The PDC tries to explain this apparent contradiction by reference to the conditions prevalent in different historical conjunctures.

Those who view the PDC as a centrist political option point to the existence of bourgeois economic groups, chiefly industrialists, who lacked political expression during the 1960s and 1970s, and to the emergence of such noncorporate business groupings as FUSADES. But a comparison of the economic policy formulations of the PDC and FUSADES, particularly during the 1987 business strike launched to protest the Duarte administration's economic measures, reveals more differences than similarities. It is more worthwhile to observe the influence of the thought of FUSADES on the business groups linked to ARENA, a point that I discussed in Chapter 3. Nor was it only the Christian Democrats who attempted to construct a "political center." Despite their different content, many of the country's progressive parties talked about constituting a "third force" that would position itself between the two polarized groupings that dominated the political spectrum in El Salvador during the 1980s.

This polemical, but suggestive, idea of developing an intermediary social force is in my opinion unworkable.[19] Instead of the emergence of a "center," the dominant classes reconstituted themselves politically. The supposedly centrist option of the PDC was unable to resolve El Salvador's crisis, despite holding legislative and executive power between 1985 and 1988 and having the full support of the United States. The PDC failed either to defeat the FMLN or to gain the approval of the dominant classes for its contradictory proposals. In the 1988 and 1989 elections, the Christian Democrats were soundly defeated by ARENA, a party that by then truly represented the bourgeoisie and its allies. Transformed beyond the simple dimension of ideological discourse, ARENA constituted proof of the recomposition of the political power of the dominant classes, a power that would have to be taken into consideration in elaborating any future political project.

The Elections of 1988 and 1989

ARENA snatched control of the Legislative Assembly from the PDC in the national vote held in 1988. A year later, it won the presidency for the first time, defeating a worn and divided PDC, as well as other political parties, and winning total control of the government. Since these last two elections constitute part of the same process, I will consider them simultaneously. Tables 17 and 18 summarize the results for both elections.[20] According to *Proceso,* in no election since 1982 had a party won with such a high percentage of votes. The PDC lost even in the national capital of San Salvador, a traditional Christian Democratic bastion, thus leaving ARENA as the undisputed leading elec-

Table 17
Electoral Results by Party, 1982–89

Party	1982	1984 (presidential)	1985	1988	1989 (presidential)
PDC	546,218	549,727	505,338	326,716	338,369
	(40.09)	(43.41)	(52.35)	(35.10)	(36.03)
ARENA	402,304	376,917	286,665	447,696	505,370
	(29.53)	(29.77)	(29.70)	(48.10)	(53.82)
PCN	261,153	244,556	80,730	78,756	38,218
	(19.17)	(19.31)	(8.36)	(8.46)	(4.07)
CD	—	—	—	—	35,642
					(3.80)
AD	43,929	100,586	35,565	16,211	4,368
	(3.22)	(7.94)	(3.68)	(1.74)	(0.47)
MERECEN	—	6,645	689		
		(0.52)	(0.07)		
MAC	—	—	—	—	9,300
					(0.99)
POP	12,574	4,677	836	1,752	—
	(0.92)	(0.37)	(0.09)	(0.19)	
PAISA	—	15,430	33,101	19,609	—
		(1.22)	(3.43)	(2.11)	
PPS	39,504	24,395	16,344	—	—
	(2.90)	(1.93)	(1.69)		
Liberación	—	—	—	34,960	—
				(3.8)	
UP	—	—	—	—	4,609
					(0.49)
PAR	—	—	2,963	5,059	3,207
			(0.31)	(0.54)	(0.34)

Source: Consejo Central de Elecciones (CCE—Central Election Council).

The figures in parentheses refer to the percentages of total valid votes obtained by each party (presented in Table 18). The 1984 data correspond to the first round of voting.

toral force in the country. At the same time, the total number of votes has decreased significantly over the years; of all the estimated eligible voters in 1989, only some 22 percent voted for ARENA.

As the data in Table 18 show, the PDC vote decreased steadily after 1984, even though the party controlled both the presidency and

Table 18
Votes According to Categories, 1982–89

Votes	1982	1984	1985	1988	1989
Valid	1,362,339	1,266,276	965,231	930,749	939,078
Contested	6,412	6,924	4,678	11,388	5,484
Null	131,498	104,557	74,007	107,355	51,182
Abstentions	51,438	41,736	57,690	34,320	7,409
Total	1,551,687	1,419,493	1,101,606	1,083,812	1,003,153

Source: CCE.

the Legislative Assembly in 1984 and 1985. Although ARENA lost votes in these same years, it began to gain substantial ground in 1988. The PCN declined precipitously. Acción Democrática (AD—Democratic Action), which won an important percentage of the vote in 1982 as a supposedly social democratic option of the center, had practically disappeared seven years later. The Convergencia Democrática (CD), a leftist coalition made up of parties from the FDR, the MNR, and the Movimiento Popular Social Cristiano (MPSC—Popular Social Christian Movement), presented itself in the elections for the first time, obtaining a limited number of votes.

In my opinion, the 1982 elections involved three important elements: first, the weight of the PDC's years of accumulated experience as a political opposition force and its importance as a source of support for the U.S. counterinsurgency project; second, the sudden appearance of a party (ARENA) directly representing the dominant classes, despite the fact that elite support was still divided chiefly among the PCN and the AD; and third, the elections, as an important part of the counterinsurgency project in themselves, could not be dismissed, an error made by the FMLN that it later acknowledged.

The relatively minor shifts in the distribution of votes between the elections of 1982 and 1984 showed the persistence of the strong trends first expressed in 1982 and the difficulties inherent in the process of consolidating a party of the dominant classes. The history of the Alvaro Magaña government reflects this clearly, particularly in the Pact of Apaneca, an attempt to establish a party consensus to challenge the important qualitative advances being made by the revolutionary forces.

Nevertheless, the 1985 elections indicated important changes. In general, there was a drastic decline in the number of voters, which affected all the parties. As I explained earlier, ARENA began to make changes in its leadership and strategy at this moment, reflecting the direct control that the bourgeoisie asserted over the party. The 1988 and 1989 elections provided evidence of an important change— right-wing voters shifted to ARENA, leading to the virtual disappearance of the formerly dominant PCN and other rightist parties. As well as marking the end of the PDC's electoral primacy, the elections of the late 1980s also saw leftist parties take part in the country's voting for the first time, despite enormous difficulties and doubts. The evolution went beyond numbers, however. For the first time in more than fifty years, a definitive party of the dominant classes emerged. The presence of an alternative revolutionary organization and project of impressive strength made ARENA an indispensable instrument in the effort to maintain the domination of the bourgeois class in El Salvador.

In my opinion, the most notable result of the elections of the 1980s is the political recomposition of the dominant classes. This process occurred in the middle of the war and coincided with the development of the opposing political pole of the revolutionary project, the latter a phenomenon I will trace in Chapter 5. The changes made by the ARENA leadership between 1984, when Duarte defeated D'Aubuisson in the presidential election, and the 1987 business strike show the transformation that permitted this party to bind together a majority of the dominant classes. To begin with, the creation of an advisory council of prominent business leaders to influence the decisions of the party's executive committee marked an important change in formal structure.[21] It helped make ARENA into a political instrument that allowed the Salvadoran bourgeoisie to resolve its internal differences. Moreover, the party also reached a new height of consolidation with the selection of Alfredo Cristiani (with the support of D'Aubuisson) as president of ARENA. Cristiani had joined the party in 1984. In an interview at the end of 1987, he describes the significance of the recent changes:

> In ARENA's final forum in 1985, it was decided that, in order to consolidate itself, the party needed to include a variety of different political currents without departing from a central ideological framework. Since the ideological framework is not negotiable, one can see [within the party] more radical positions as well as works of a moderate stripe.[22]

These developments allowed more realistic positions to be established within the heart of the party. In the same interview, Cristiani goes on to say:

> *We think that two parallel and complementary strategies need to be developed, one of which is the military part with a "military strategy of victory." Recognizing the fact that it is extremely difficult to end the conflict based on a military strategy alone, it is also necessary to develop a political strategy because we think that this could provide a solution, one that can achieve a consensus around a national proposal for peace.*

These formulations were being developed at the same time as an incomplete proposal for an economic model.[23]

Simultaneously, ARENA began a series of meetings with members of the armed forces high command. This allowed it to smooth over some of the contradictions generated in previous years when party personnel had criticized the "low-intensity war" counterinsurgency military strategy implemented during the decade. ARENA began to establish more flexible relations with the United States through the embassy in San Salvador and through direct lobbying in Washington. Before the electoral triumphs of 1988 and 1989, the most powerful events in the process of politically reconstituting the dominant classes had occurred in the early months of 1987. At that time, three actions combined to produce a clear victory of the rightist opposition over the Duarte government: the parliamentary strike led by ARENA, the decision by the Asociación Nacional de la Empresa Privada (ANEP—National Association of Private Enterprise) to suspend discussions with the government on economic policy, and the business strike decreed by the chamber of commerce in protest against the government's economic measures.

Thereafter, the 1988 election campaign began; in essence, it continued without interruption until the triumph of Cristiani in the presidential elections of March 1989. These elections emphasized ARENA's ability to attract the youth and the middle classes of the country, although the party was not able to establish itself within the workers' organizations. (One important challenge was still to be met: the incorporation of some ultraright business groups [such as that led by Orlando de Sola] and others who had, from time to time, supported the reform politics launched by Christian Democracy [the Poma group particularly]).

Nevertheless, this renovated party faces some other problems. One is the extraordinary weakness of its organic intellectuals. Accustomed during many years to the crudest repression through the use of the docile armed forces at its command, the bourgeoisie never bothered to prepare its intellectuals beyond forming technical-management groups to administer its economic activities.[24] This vacuum, however, is beginning to be filled. The research institutes and the publications that have started to circulate in recent years offer one example. Another problem is the poverty of ideological debate, in part a consequence of the intellectual vacuum; a higher level of discussion is likewise starting to develop within the country. The almost total absence of ideological debate has also been detrimental to the forces on the Left, who had necessarily become accustomed to quick publications and clandestine discussions. However, the most profound impact of the poverty of ideological debate has been upon the process of recomposition that is my focus, particularly in the insufficient development of the political project of the dominant classes beyond the level of general declarations. (This was quite evident in the examination of the economic program of the Cristiani government presented in Chapter 3.) The extraordinary complexity of the current situation in El Salvador, the untried nature of many of its processes, and the challenge of the revolutionary project combine to make these limitations even greater.

Obviously, beyond the consolidation of ARENA, with all its importance, there are other manifestations of the political reconstitution of the dominant classes that must be taken into account. One is the political implications of the strictly economic formulations espoused by people linked to FUSADES. Despite similarities in political and economic policy, this organization cannot be mechanically categorized as a project of ARENA. Rather, FUSADES demonstrates a completely new and modern vein of rightist thought that extends beyond the positions of many of the traditional parties of the bourgeoisie. One representative of this phenomenon is Roberto Murray Meza, who has played an important role in linking El Salvador's problems to the wider Central American context by revitalizing the Federación de Entidades Privadas de Centroamérica y Panamá (FEDEPRICAP—Federation of Private Organizations of Central America and Panama). In his view,

[j]ust as the problems of Central America deepened as the decade of the 1970s reached its end, in the 1980s the idea of giving new life to this Federation emerged, but with two fundamental

> *changes: first, to include Panama in the plan . . . and second, to include the development organizations of the private sector along with the [interest group] associations; they had already sprouted up in all of Central America—in the case of El Salvador: FUSADES. . . .*
>
> *The interesting point about FEDEPRICAP is that it emerges at a time when the entrepreneur understands that the problems of each country are substantially interrelated. That is, the problems of El Salvador can not be solved while the problems of Nicaragua, Guatemala, Honduras, Costa Rica, and Panama remain unsolved.*[25]

Others who share many of ARENA's views have called attention to the new government's obligation to search for national unity.[26] Preliminary social research suggests that there may be a political differentiation in the core of the Salvadoran bourgeoisie resulting from events during the 1980s.[27]

Finally, one issue must remain clear: I believe that the U.S. government, the main author of the Salvadoran counterinsurgency strategy, although initially disconcerted by the ARENA phenomenon, eventually understood the party's irreversible character and its precise class content. This class content overrides the fact that leaders of the death squads hold important positions within ARENA. So long as certain minimal rules of the game are observed, one can expect consistently clearer support for the Cristiani government, and even for the ARENA project, from the current U.S. administration. The emergence of ARENA is the most obvious manifestation of the political recomposition of the Salvadoran dominant classes that has taken place during the 1980s.

This phenomenon has been recognized by many governments,[28] a fact that will inevitably have repercussions in the future for Salvadoran politics. I repeat, however, something that is explicit throughout this book: a permanent political recomposition of the political power of the elite in El Salvador implies a solution of the crisis of hegemony in the dominant bloc; this, in turn, requires the strategic defeat of the revolutionary forces. Thus, the political recomposition of the dominant classes implies many things beyond the recomposition of the political regime, a goal already attained by the presidency of José Napoleón Duarte and subsequently consolidated under ARENA's total control of the government.

The Development of a Popular
and Revolutionary Alternative

5

Just as the decade of the 1970s marked the beginning of the construction of the political-military revolutionary organizations, the decade of the 1980s witnessed their unification, along with the construction and development of a revolutionary alternative of the masses. I will examine the tendencies and basic discrepancies of the initial period in order to understand this process and to see how the popular revolutionary war has permitted overcoming contradictions that would have been difficult to transcend in another political context.

The Construction and Consolidation
of the FMLN

The building of the Farabundo Martí National Liberation Front began in 1970. Ten years later, after innumerable breaks and repairs, there are five organizations united by the same overall strategic, political-military formulation, but distinguished among themselves by a history of different tactical postulates. As they emerged, each of the groups formed its own particular character and developed in ways barely known to the others, a fact that is essential for understanding the process at work. These five organizations covered the full spectrum of revolutionary forces in the country. Nevertheless, their consolidation was already under way by the end of the decade; the process of unification in El Salvador began (in contrast with neighboring Guatemala) without the exclusion of any revolutionary organizations.

The Decade of Initial Construction and Consolidation

The 1970s began with a division in the heart of the Communist Party, an event that had been brewing for a few years because of differences about strategic formulations. These disagreements came to a head over the party's position on the border war between El Salvador and Honduras, provoking the departure of a quantitatively minor but singularly important group. So began a search for alternatives—on the part of this group and others—that would culminate in the construction of revolutionary organizations of a political-military character. Simultaneously, a significant segment of Christian Democratic youth broke away from their party. They had developed a new consciousness produced by changes within the Catholic Church after the conference of Latin American bishops at Medellín in 1968, by knowledge of the role of Christian Democrats in other countries like Chile and Venezuela, and by the party's gradual abandonment of its founding principles (enunciated only ten years earlier).[1]

Many new groups developed between the 1969 Honduran-Salvadoran border war and the fraudulent elections in early 1972. Although these organizations did not derive from previous divisions, they too searched for new alternatives and joined with others in building coalitions.

Although the history of this embryonic process still remains unwritten, Fermán Cienfuegos contributes some important insights:

> All of these factors buffeted the social system and put it to the test. The system of political, economic and military domination of the capitalist regime in El Salvador began to enter in crisis during the years 1960–70.
>
> The internal crises of the Communist party started when it was unable to resolve the problem of putting itself at the head of all sectors in order to lead and direct the mass movement to a higher level. The strategy of peaceful struggle was now exhausted. . . . The PCS entered a period of crisis and began to splinter in 1969. The fundamental point under internal discussion was the question of armed revolution and the incorrect attitude toward the war with Honduras. . . .
>
> A nucleus of the PCS consisting of a sector of young workers and intellectuals, most of them professionals, along with another group from the Juventud Comunista (Communist Youth, during this period called the Unión de Jóvenes Patriotas, or UJP)—

[Union of Patriotic Youth] had been developing the ideological struggle; we formed a faction in order to launch an armed struggle in the country.

A third group, from the Juventud Demócrata Cristiana (Christian Democratic Youth) rather than from the PCS, also decided to begin the armed struggle. This was a new type of Christian group, influenced by the example of Camilo Torres [well-known Columbian guerrilla priest]. It formed the leadership of the Frente Revolucionario de Universitarios Social Cristianos [Revolutionary Front of Social Christian University Students], a university organization of the PDC. Our faction of the Juventud Comunista began to meet with this group to discuss the problematic of the armed struggle.[2]

Over the next decade, different alternative organizations developed out of the components of these three sources. I will now examine the essential features of this complex and contradictory process, first by looking at the original formulations of the groups involved.

From the start, they assumed that the fundamental form of revolutionary struggle in El Salvador was that of war. At the same time, these organizations recognized that the armed struggle must go hand in hand with the political struggle of the masses. They also believed in the wisdom of resorting to warfare from the very beginning of the process. Therefore, there was no need to meet all the objective and subjective conditions traditionally considered essential.

These views constituted nothing new in the history of world revolutionary thinking. They emerged from the criticism of the strategy of "successive periods" (that one should first accumulate forces and then develop the insurrection) that dominated the approach of the PCS and of most Latin American Communist parties. The views also grew out of the initial orientation of the organization that developed the most complete strategic proposals—the Fuerzas Populares de Liberación–Farabundo Martí (FPL–FM—Popular Liberation Forces–Farabundo Martí). These included the need for massive incorporation of the urban and rural population; the prolonged nature of the war; its permanent offensive character on all fronts; and the importance of first developing a worker-peasant alliance, led by the proletariat, to be followed by the creation of a coalition of all popular forces. Even at this moment, the FPL–FM started thinking about diplomatic struggle as an auxiliary strategic tool.

In 1961, after the victory of the Cuban Revolution, the PCS had established the Frente Unido de Acción Revolucionaria (FUAR—United Front of Revolutionary Action). It was a revolutionary paramilitary body formed out of the popular sectors and designed to incorporate the working classes gradually into the armed struggle. The absence of a political-military conception led to the failure of the FUAR. Its organization was largely akin to the traditional "military commissions" of the Communist parties.

The initial bodies that would later constitute the FMLN were the FPL, the "Group" (which, although it lasted only a short time, was of great importance) and the Ejército Revolucionario del Pueblo (the first ERP—People's Revolutionary Army, which later gave rise to other organizations). Each one grew and survived by incorporating dissidents from the PCS, the PDC, and the UJP. Despite the strategic similarities mentioned previously, the new organizations exhibited the influence of the particular mix of elements that formed them. The ERP in its initial form, for example, persistently (although not always explicitly) denied the need for a party. One can see the origins of this position in the critical attitude toward the reformist strategy of the PCS growing out of the predominantly Christian Democratic and independent backgrounds of those who made up the initial ERP. One of the causes can be found here for the subsequent development of a militarist tendency within the ERP, a phenomenon that would produce important divisions later. On the other hand, a vision existed within the FPL from its earliest days that there was a need to construct a new kind of revolutionary party. Although it lacked a name and an explicit definition in the midst of a centralized structure of armed command, this vision should not seem strange, given the importance in the FPL of former PCS militants led by Cayetano Carpio, who had been Secretary General.

The emergence in 1975 of a new organization that had split from the ERP, the Resistencia Nacional (RN—National Resistance), illustrated an advance in the development of the initial strategic formulations. The RN proposed a union between the popular revolutionary war and the insurrection in order to bring about the Salvadoran revolution, thus developing an idea that had been present in other organizations but was not yet systematized. This concept brought about the beginning of the establishment of conditions for a military organization of the masses with insurrectional goals.

The years 1975 to 1980 marked a contradictory advance of the use of combative revolutionary violence by the masses in their revindications, in their self-defense, and in the preparation of conditions for mass insurrection. All this centered on the role of the popular militias. I insist that this highly rich process can ultimately only be analyzed fully by its collective actors. Nevertheless, I will point out the final element that influenced the strategic formulations and the design of specific tactics: the characterization of the prevailing form of state in El Salvador in 1974–75, a controversy over whether the regime of Col. Arturo Molina was fascist in character. The debate, which produced such terms as "fascistoid," and "in fascist escalation," can be found in the exchanges between the dailies *Voz Popular* and *Por la Causa Proletaria*, representing the PCS and the RN, respectively. Despite its limitations, this debate helped to enrich the formulations of the Salvadoran revolutionary organizations. It also deepened their understanding of the need to have a revolutionary party in order to carry the process of popular struggle toward victory. Although difficult disputes and contradictions continued in the second half of the 1970s, the debate generated one of the preconditions for the future process of unification.

If there were numerous common elements at the strategic level, there was also commonality at the internal organizational level as the new revolutionary organizations first began to take shape. Despite the political-military nature of the initial conception and a clear Marxist-Leninist political ideology, discovering what was correct and possible depended upon forming small, clandestine nuclei structured in a military fashion. Their essential objectives were to obtain a minimal level of armaments and initial funds to finance subsequent organizational development.

One must also keep in mind an essential characteristic in the initial proposals of these new revolutionary organizations: a political-ideological independence from the diverse ideologies of the world revolutionary movement. This implied an economic independence from external sources of support. Further on, I will analyze how, through a complicated process of searching, the initial steps were taken toward mass political work starting from the consolidation of small, clandestine political-military nuclei. This took place in a context devoid of possibilities for the development of the Maoist or Trotskyite orientations that were then in vogue in other countries of Latin America. The highly repressive character of the Salvadoran political system resulted in a lack of familiarity with the literature of these positions. Repression left the PCS with minimal polemical and analytic capacity; hence, party figures felt that the teachings of Mao and Trotsky should remain unknown to their militants. The general cultural backwardness of the country and the terror imposed by the highly repressive model of domination that had existed since 1932 fashioned a true "political culture of silence." Limitations imposed by the dominant classes of El Salvador and implicitly endorsed by the Communist Party itself generated an informational wasteland concerning other revolutionary movements of the world. Taken together, these factors, more than any apparent ideological solidity of the Communists, help to explain the noticeable absence of Maoist and Trotskyite influences in El Salvador.

Although surprising to many analysts of revolutionary processes, the ideological independence of the FMLN from the traditional centers of Marxist thought and its extraordinary flexibility in tactics and program are in fact logical. The Salvadoran context allowed the FMLN to adjust its political line to cope with changes in the internal and external situations and with the complexity of the counterinsurgency strategy. During the course of the revolutionary war, the FMLN developed the capacity to draw on the diverse and contradictory experiences of national liberation movements throughout the world:

> We advanced beneath the banner of the changing correlation of forces from the different national revolutions that had broken out since 1979. The view that only the socialist revolutions were revolutions still predominated. . . .
>   Life revealed that there was no exclusively socialist revolution, but rather different types of revolution.
>   The National Liberation Movement showed the possibility for different types of social revolutions of the sort that have arisen in recent decades of this century.[3]

Thus, Maoist and Trotskyite tendencies did not develop in El Salvador. Even though I do not consider these tendencies to be of any benefit to popular armed struggles or to world revolution, it is evident beyond my partisanship that their absence averted unnecessary organic fractionalization during those years of exploration and construction. Let me now analyze how another deviation was avoided that has provoked more than one strategic defeat in this continent: *foquismo*. [see pp. 79–80: trans.].

There are perhaps two basic reasons for this outcome. First, because of the Cuban experience, an automatic association became established between the guerrilla struggle and the mountains. El Salvador seemed to lack the geographical conditions that were supposed to be indispensable to this particular form of military revolutionary action (a conclusion based on false premises, as the struggle of the FMLN during these years has demonstrated). Consequently, those PCS militants in the early 1960s who argued for the privileged role of warfare as the principal form of struggle received little attention. Yet armed struggle constituted a predominant tendency throughout the continent during these years. One could even say that the creation of the FUAR represented an effort by the PCS to combine this trend with its own analysis of the unviability of military struggle in the countryside, thus placing a clear emphasis on urban insurrectional struggle.

The second reason is closely connected to the first. Due to the traumatizing experience of the 1932 peasant insurrection—and, above all, to its own conceptional weaknesses—the PCS had little organizing work taking place in the countryside in the early 1960s. The party could neither understand the peculiarities of this dimension of Salvadoran reality nor appreciate its revolutionary potential.

Ironically, these two deficiencies impeded the emergence of rural-based *foquista* actions (which obviously would have failed). In similar fashion, the history of the Salvadoran revolution avoided the development of what might be called urban *foquismo* because of the relative ideological backwardness of the PCS and the severely limited space of the country's political system. By the time disenchantment with the reformist strategy of the party had provoked an exploration of alternatives, urban guerrilla experiences in other Latin American countries (e.g., the Tupamaros in Uruguay) were already well on the road to disaster. The control of the cities by police during this time made such efforts seem unworkable.[4]

Militarism, however, became the erroneous experience that could not be avoided in El Salvador. The obligatory character of the initial construction of the revolutionary political-military organizations, the ideological weakness of the cadres coming from the PCS, and the Christian Democratic origin of many of the other cadres all provided a foundation for the temporary domination of this deviation. Militarism crystallized principally in the initial ERP. Here, I add an idea that might seem polemical. The militaristic deviation, experienced in varying degrees by most of the organizing efforts of these years, turned out to have a silver lining: the subjective conditions that allowed the masses to advance more rapidly when armed revolutionary struggle took the center of the Salvadoran stage after 1980, and especially in 1981.

When the initial consolidation of these new organizations had been achieved after 1974, work with the masses began, although not in a vacuum. Despite the self-limiting visions of the PCS, there was already a significant level of organization among popular sectors in the Salvadoran countryside. This organizing task had been carried out by social agents of an institution previously above official suspicion: the Catholic Church. The principal agents in this work were the Jesuits and the diocesan clergy of the archbishopric of San Salvador (responsible for attending to the needs of a large region that included Guazapa and Chalatenango). The strategic repercussions of their work radically modified the political map of the country.[5].

I add to these fundamental matters the long organizational and combative history of university students and of the proletariat,[6] as well as the shorter but no less fertile organizational development of the Salvadoran teachers union.[7] Since the 1940s, the main struggle within the union movement had been between workers influenced by the dominant ideology and those led by the PCS; neither group could gain clear predominance. The revolutionary current of the PCS invariably prevailed within the university student movement. Because of grassroots work by the PCS, the positions of greatest responsibility within the teachers union went to leftist leaders independent of the PCS. This enabled the Asociación Nacional de Educadores Salvadoreños (ANDES 29 DE JUNIO—National Association of Salvadoran Teachers, 29th of June) to achieve a national range in its organization. The teachers union earned an enormous amount of legitimacy that made its subsequent repression more difficult (though not impossible). Between 1968 and 1972, it became the social sector that served as the vanguard for popular struggles, a role that had been taken by university students and, to a lesser extent, by workers during preceding years.[8]

If 1974 was important because of the shift toward work with the masses, 1975 was vital for the broadening that went on in the strategic formulations of the revolutionary groups and for their improvement at the organic level.[9] (I have already referred to the incorporation of the role of insurrection in their thinking.) A continuous search for the most competent ways to launch the revolutionary struggle began at the same time as an opening toward work with the masses. Ceaseless debate took place over what tactics were appropriate for each task. It was especially important for the work with the masses to encourage the use of combative violence, to create mechanisms of self-defense, and to develop a self-defense militia.

By the late 1970's, a complicated and difficult process had produced five organizations with high degrees of initial consolidation, common outlooks, and different tactical histories. Although their experiences of organic structuring were so different as to be barely known to one another, the five organizations grew closer day by day. A parallel development toward the same objective was at work, yielding perspectives that constantly became more similar in practice. The crossroads of this process brought contradictions that obliged the organizations to recognize their similarities and to respect each other's roles.

The Beginning of the Unification of the Dispersed Vanguard

Once the shift toward work with the masses began, at least two factors prompted cooperation at the level of the mass organizations: first, many strategic sectors, such as the peasants and teachers (or at least their organizations), did not share a common political tendency; and second, faced with the organizational weakness of the masses at that moment, the certainty grew that the work at this level had to be unified. The perceived need for cooperation did not extend to the level of the partisan core of each political-military revolutionary organization. This situation gave birth in 1974 to the first attempt at unification, the United Popular Action Front.

The assembly that founded FAPU represented four different general types of mass organizations: those with clearly determined political tendencies; those whose views were progressive, even embryonically revolutionary, but who did not subscribe to any organic revolutionary project, (e.g., the peasants); those, like the university students, who were embroiled in disputes over sectoral hegemony; and, finally, those whose leftist-reformist tendencies were incompatible with the strategic orientations of the new revolutionary organizations. Since programmatic work was just beginning to develop, these differences were strongly felt. Deep discrepancies emerged over platforms, especially with regard to the specifics of the struggle and the concrete means of carrying it out. Differences with the left-reform group proved unbridgeable.

The unifying effort was thus converted into an occasion in which the distinct political tendencies tried to impose their own hegemony; given their minimal level of development, this was not feasible. One important lesson remained for each of the groups. Some learned it faster than others, but all eventually learned and solidified it over the course of just three years: each tendency had to construct and aid the development of mass organizations of its own. This was a clear prerequisite to any further attempts at unity or to any imposition of individual formulations. The invaluable lesson imparted by the FAPU experience suggests that this attempt was no failure in the long run. In my view, the establishment of the Revolutionary Coordinator of the Masses (CRM) in 1980 constitutes proof of this.

I have sustained the idea that the objective bases for a unifying process already existed in the strategic formulations of the various revolutionary organizations. Polemics notwithstanding, the establishment of different mass fronts and the adoption of similar platforms and methods of struggle between 1975 and 1979 completed an indispensable foundation. The basis was now laid for a process of gradual but sustained unification, a requirement that became ever more urgent in light of the context of the new political period initiated by the military coup of October 15, 1979.

An overall vision of the movement would permit an additional answer: without any preconceived intent, one can see an extraordinary complementarity in the development of the work with the popular masses by the different revolutionary organizations. This complementarity showed itself within organized social sectors and within their territorial distribution, thus creating an additional foundation for the unification process.

The task was not easy, despite the existence of the minimal necessary objective conditions, the required historical imperatives, and the recent, invaluable example of the unification of the three movements that comprised the Sandinista Front. As the first steps toward unifying the revolutionary organizations were taken in 1979, a new conjuncture was unfolding and a new political period was beginning. Since it was evident that in the months and years to come the armed struggle would move to center stage, the process of unification had to develop against the restrictions of the clock.

Even though this answer is accepted unanimously today, I cannot ignore the fact that the long struggle for hegemony had papered over the development of domineering tendencies (more so in some organizations than in others). Their adherents were not willing to accept the reality of unification and the changes that it implied. Instead, they fought for the predominance of their own individual concepts; the residue of this struggle is still visible today. Nevertheless, I emphasize that unification was the dominant tendency throughout the FMLN, even though the process still had to pass through many difficulties because of subjective and objective historical factors. By the middle of 1981, coinciding with the first phase of the revolutionary popular war, the minimal conditions had already been created to permit a reevaluation of the levels of unity reached. The progress of the war, pessimistic views notwithstanding, reinforced this unification process. Advances were more substantial and rapid than would have been the case had they taken place under less severe conditions of struggle. The situation produced abundant new experiences for revolution in this continent; it surpassed the example of the Sandinista revolution, where unification was less difficult due to the common history of the three tendencies.[10]

The Vanguard Synthesis: A Peculiar Process in Salvadoran Revolutionary History

I argue that the Salvadoran case has almost fully developed a particular quality of most Latin American revolutionary movements: within a contradictory process, a revolutionary vanguard has been constructed from the synthesis of dispersed vanguard nuclei that have emerged and developed historically in a parallel (but separate) way. During this synthesizing stage, which began in El Salvador after 1970 and has continued into the late 1980s, there was no one group whose internal character or external linkages made it the nucleus around which other revolutionary organizations gathered. The role of vanguard was defined, instead, by a long process of synthesis. At any given moment, the vanguard position might be assumed temporarily by that organization whose perception of the situation permitted it to initiate the most appropriate political-military actions. The assumption of this role by different organizations at different moments has become one of the unique traits of the Salvadoran revolutionary struggle. This process of synthesizing the dispersed vanguard does not necessarily have to be completed before the triumph of a democratic-popular revolution, but its solidification at the top levels forms a prerequisite for advancing toward higher stages of the revolutionary process.

I submit that the revolutionary vanguard was formed by synthesizing the scattered vanguard nuclei that had developed historically in a parallel, separate manner in the Salvadoran case. This process originated in the political-military concept of assigning a mass content to the armed struggle as the means to make the revolution, a major contribution of the Central American and Salvadoran revolutionary movements. One cannot fully understand the consolidation of the revolutionary forces without analyzing the development of the union movement in particular, and the popular movement in general, during the 1980s. They both were subjected to one of the most ferocious repressions in Salvadoran history.

The Salvadoran Popular Movement in the 1980s

At the end of the 1980s, after almost a decade of popular revolutionary war, events in El Salvador have modified the analysis of the union movement and the popular movements, each a key element for understanding the development of the revolutionary projects and organizations.[11] The progress of the war and the changes in the Salvadoran political and economic systems are the most fundamental reasons for a distinct evaluation. The political reconstitution of the dominant classes and the consolidation of the revolutionary pole offer additional grounds for such an evaluation. Another, more structural reason lies in the effects on national social structures of the profound transformation taking place in the capitalist economy at the global level.

Some Characteristics of the Popular Movement Before the 1980s

In a work written in 1978,[12] I established four phases in the historical development of the Salvadoran workers movement between 1920 and 1977. The first, extending from 1920 to 1932, was characterized by the emergence of union organizations made up largely of artisans and peasants. Driven by external political factors, this process would not develop under the hegemony of the working classes. During the second phase, between 1944 and 1957–58, described as the formation of the modern Salvadoran workers movement, the relationship between the popular movement and the union movement began gradually to define itself. During this period, encompassing the years 1957–58 to 1969, the workers movement broadened under the industrialization process and the economic integration of Central America. There are no studies of the dynamic relations (during the second or third stages) between the union movement and the general popular movement,[13] primarily because Salvadoran mass struggles found their expression largely within political parties (some of which were ephemeral, even though they had a clearly defined ideology) and the university students associations.[14]

After the 1960s, the situation changed radically. The teachers movement emerged with force; silently, an important movement of rural workers developed that played a prominent role in the 1970s through its decisive involvement in constructing the political-military revolutionary organizations that would make up the FMLN.

In my earlier work focusing on the struggle of the masses in El Salvador, I tried to explore indirectly the relationship between the union movement and the popular movement by analyzing three factors in particular: the fact that at various times different social sectors formed the vanguard of the struggle of the masses; the connection between the mass movement and the political revolutionary organizations within it; and the use of distinct forms of revolutionary violence. From this work, one can observe the growing complexity of the relationship between the union movement and the popular movement as the latter developed new manifestations, especially as of the 1970s. By late in that decade, El Salvador was witness to the ceaseless struggle of one of the most important popular mass movements in Latin America. What was the composition of this movement? How did it advance to this level of development?

To answer these key questions, I point out that after 1977 the social sector at the vanguard of the struggle of the popular movement was the rural workers movement (a necessarily complex mix of small peasants and salaried rural workers, given the weight of the agricultural semi-proletariat in the country). Along with this sector there was the union movement, whose crisis after 1969 perhaps reached its most intense point in 1977.

The Salvadoran union movement can be broken down into the main classical tendencies found in most Central American countries. On one side there are the unions guided by the AFL-CIO, Confederación de Trabajadores de América Latina (CLAT—Confederation of Latin American Workers), and Organización Regional Interamericana de Trabajadores (ORIT—Inter-American Regional Organization of Workers), almost always small and controlled by political parties or groups with clear rightist leanings. On the other side are unions influenced principally by the Communist parties. Salvadoran unionism, which was confined during these years almost entirely to the manufacturing sector, encountered new types of political influences after 1974, when the first revolutionary front of the masses was created.

On the Left, as I have mentioned, the declining influence of the Salvadoran Communist Party did not translate into the spread of those Maoist, Trotskyite, or similar tendencies that have inundated Latin American unions. The revolutionary organizations that consolidated themselves throughout the 1970s and united into the FMLN in 1980 had a different outlook. Despite serious confrontations with the sector of organized labor influenced by the Communist Party, these groups created other poles of the union movement in different forms and in different sectors. The novelty of their type of organization and struggle, and the justice of their revindicative platforms would lay foundations for results that could only be perceived in the current decade.

Let me stop for a moment to look at a self-critical evaluation by the PCS of its work within the masses. It sheds light on some of the reasons for the party's declining influence within the union movement. Referring to the activity of the PCS around the elections of 1972, Shafik Handal, its secretary general, affirms:

> *Within the framework of UNO,[15] the Party played a very important role in the elaboration of its program, in its tactics, and in the application of the line that it followed. As a result of all of this and the great dynamism of the PCS in the electoral campaigns, we generated no small amount of influence on our allies; but also, as the facts demonstrated, our allies generated influence over us.*
>
> *Reformist traits that emerged in the Party led to the abandonment during these 11 years of any efforts by the leadership to develop the revolutionary violence of the masses, in particular their self-defense against repression, and the construction of Party armed forces. Attempts were made to justify this policy with the argument of a "prevention of provocations."*

And later, referring to the agreements of the Fifth Congress of the PCS in 1964, Handal notes:

> *During that period, we saw a contradiction between mass struggle and armed struggle. It is important to remember that within Latin America there was the concept of the foco guerrillero, in which, at least at the start of guerrilla actions, the masses were not needed.[16]*

This led the PCS after 1964 to give almost exclusive priority to class confrontation within the sphere of worker economic revindications. The party thus dedicated itself almost exclusively to political action among the unions until 1967, when it embarked in earnest on its electoral struggle.

Therefore, any look at the unions and at the popular movement in 1979 focusing on that moment would show an image of dispersion and contradiction, making any task of unification unthinkable. Nevertheless, by being connected to the national revolutionary political project as it developed in El Salvador's underground, the union movement and the popular movement began an accelerated process of unity work in 1979 and 1980.

This explains why the union movement regained a protagonistic role within the popular movement in 1980 and why there was the possibility of its reactivation after the end of 1983, in the wake of two years of forced retreat due to the bloody repression that it had undergone. I shall now analyze the crucial general strikes in which the union movements perforce played a central role.

Three general strikes were called between June 1980 and January 1981. Despite its relative success, the first displayed some of the constraints that ultimately led to the failure of the second strike in August 1980 and to that of the third on January 10, 1981. The fundamental limitation derived from the fact that these general strikes, together with urban insurrectional actions and military actions in the countryside, formed an integral part of the revolutionary political plans. Since there was no effort to harmonize the actions (a product of the imbalance between the political and military capacity of the organizations that comprised the FMLN), the calls for a general strike had a limited impact. The leaders of the FMLN themselves have acknowledged this imbalance. The failure of the general strike of January 10, 1981, so costly for the unions, does not counter the fact that the entire assemblage of actions on this date constitutes a victory that would change the course of Salvadoran history.

The widespread FMLN offensive led to a retreat of the union, and of the popular movement in general. Two main factors account for this: first, an escalation of the bloody repression begun at the end of the 1970s; and second, the transfer of many union and popular organization leaders to the recently created rural "battlefronts." As I indicated in a previous work,[17] this retreat was not limited to the cities; it was much more complex than it appeared. To speak simply of a withdrawal led some to expect a resurgence of the union and popular movement under the same forms, and consequently to adopt defeatist attitudes. I think that it is necessary to emphasize again that the demonstration of almost two hundred thousand people in San Salvador on January 22, 1980, marked the culmination of the joining of mass political struggle through open protest with armed defense (through the self-defense militia). Thereafter, it was impossible to repeat this model, as illustrated by the funeral of Monseñor Oscar Romero in March 1980 and by the struggles of the popular masses in the second half of the decade.

The retreat of the revolutionary mass movements between 1981 and 1983 marked the transition (difficult and opaque, like many transitions) toward new forms of struggle. Other modes of organization of mass political activity would be necessary in order to respond to the new conditions of the Salvadoran revolutionary struggle as military action became the principal and determining factor. I do not mean to suggest that there were no errors in the leadership of the union and popular movements—only that, in my opinion, if analysis is not set within an overall framework it becomes difficult to comprehend just how the union and popular movements were reactivated in such a short time.

At the end of 1983, the Movimiento Unitario Sindical y Gremial de El Salvador (MUSYGES—United Union and Guild Movement of El Salvador) was created. It comprised associations and unions fighting for platforms linking economic revindications with national political revindications (for example, a political solution to the war).

Public employees, a new social sector, now began to play a leading role in the Salvadoran political scene. They had long been repressed (even in these years, their unionization was prohibited) or used as a support base and electoral reserve by the successive official political parties through all types of coercive measures. Only the overall context permitted their growing independence and belligerence.

The elections of 1984, which elevated Duarte to the presidency with the support of a meaningful portion of the labor sector, led many to think that this recent resurgence would be easily co-opted or controlled by the new government. Again, Salvadoran history showed the limits of apparent processes. The union and popular movements rapidly turned the political spaces opened by the elections to their advantage; both began to take to the streets once again that year to struggle against a political agenda that failed to meet their interests.

This failure drove the Duarte government and the Reagan administration (through the AFL-CIO) to create the Central de Trabajadores Democráticos (CTD—Democratic Workers Central) at the end of 1984. The resurgence of the struggle of the working classes continued, during the next year, perpetuating earlier tendencies and incorporating new ones.[18] Public employees claimed a primary role, placing fifty thousand people on strike in November while increasing the recovery of public spaces (as evidenced by the growing mobilization in the streets).

New phenomena also appeared, and I will point out three: (1) the willingness of the FMLN to respect the autonomy of workers organizations, a lesson learned from the voluntarist errors mentioned earlier; (2) the emergence within the popular struggle of the cooperativists, a social sector originally created in the wake of the 1980 agrarian reform as an intended social base for the new U.S. counterinsurgency model (the cooperativists of the reformed sector joined with other union and popular organizations after their March 1986 parade involving some twenty-two thousand people; along with the public employees, they became one of the most dynamic sectors within the popular struggle); and (3) the enormous flexibility shown by the FMLN in continuing to adapt its forms of organization to ever changing conditions. I will expand on this last point.

By the end of the 1970s, it became increasingly difficult to distinguish the activity of the union movement from that of the popular movement in general. Although they maintained individual organizational forms, the two forces integrated with each other and acted together. As I have mentioned, MUSYGES, incorporating trade unions and associations, appeared in 1983. By 1985, gains obliged the creation of new forms to permit the incorporation of the social sectors that had emerged in the struggle. This process reached a peak in 1986, but the work in 1985 had already produced the foundation of the Coordinadora de Solidaridad con los Trabajadores (CST—Coordinator of Solidarity with the Workers). As an expression of more advanced development than MUSYGES, the CST incorporated everything from unions to cooperativists, even the Consejo Coordinador de Trabajadores Estatales y Municipales (CCTEM—Coordinating Council of State and Municipal Workers). The Unión Nacional de Trabajadores Salvadoreños (UNTS—National Union of Salvadoran Workers) was formed on February 8, 1986; as I mentioned earlier, UNTS included the organizations of all types of workers, no matter whether urban or rural, production or service, public or private. Even more, UNTS provided a context for organized sectors that transcended the work environment, such as groups made up of people displaced by the war or those victimized by disasters like the earthquake that struck San Salvador in October 1986. Nevertheless, the unions maintained their own organizations, within UNTS, the most notable of which was the Committee of May 1, consisting of the principal unions and union federations from the manufacturing sector.

But the counterrevolutionary project did not lag behind. The Christian Democratic government promoted the formation on March 6, 1986, of the Unión Nacional Obrera y Campesina (UNOC—National Workers and Peasants Union); it included, among other bodies, the Democratic Workers Central created by the AFL-CIO at the end of 1984, within a framework that echoed the basic characteristics of UNTS.

In February 1986 about sixty thousand workers marched in one of the main demonstrations of recent years. A month later, the Coordinador de Trabajadores de Oriente (CTO—Coordinator of Eastern Workers) was formed in an effort to duplicate the experience of UNTS for the eastern region of the country. In July, the Comité de Desempleados y Despedidos (Committee of the Unemployed and Laid Off) was created, followed in October by the Unión Nacional Campesina (UNC—National Peasant Union). In my opinion, 1986 produced an overabundance of organization and struggle, marking both the end of the withdrawal begun in 1981 and the start of new patterns of political struggle (all this despite the inevitable and temporary lull caused by the October 10 earthquake). This year also saw a notable increase in the importance of the role of the union movement, although public employees and cooperativists remained in the vanguard of popular struggles.[19]

These tendencies continued to deepen during 1987. Once the emergency of the 1986 earthquake passed, the inadequacy of the government's plan for the reconstruction of the capital became evident. On March 27, the 1er Congreso de Comunidades Marginales (First Congress of Marginal Communities) took place, with the participation of the Consejo de Comunidades Marginales (CCM—Council of Marginal Communities), the Consejo Coordinador de Comunidades (CCC—Community Coordinating Council), and the Unión Nacional de Damnificados (UNADES—National Union of Disaster Victims). These groups were part of a new organized social sector to whom the "informalization" of the urban economy was highly familiar. It was also in 1987 that organized occupations of urban lands were first undertaken.

At the same time, the dominant classes continued their organizational processes. Through the National Association of Private Enterprise, they conducted a successful industry strike against the economic policy measures decreed by the Duarte government in 1987, managing to mobilize seven thousand businesses and thirty thousand establishments in general (with a predominance of small businesses, a symptom of the polarization in the country).[20]

I emphasize another event in 1987 that decisively marked the tendencies developing in Central America: the signing of the presidential accord known as "Esquipulas II." Although the agreement did not figure directly in the union and popular movements, it cannot be denied that it modified the environment in which they developed. Regardless of the final outcome of the Esquipulas peace process, a study of its influence requires the analysis of consequences that are not yet clearly visible.

In 1987 and 1988, an important debate took place concerning some types of struggle employed by UNTS. There were those who interpreted such actions as burning vehicles, obstructing traffic, painting slogans on walls, and the like as an erroneous return to tactics that had been transcended. This controversial approach provoked tensions within some groups and workers organizations and, along with the failure of a few strikes, led to a virtual reassessment that continues today.[21] The debate gained force with the new calls to insurrection made by the FMLN at the end of the year. The words of Joaquín Villalobos, an important leader of the FMLN, are suggestive of the debate's character.

> *[I]n this sense, it is a mistake to suggest that an ebb has been reached as a result of radicalization and narrowness in the popular struggles. In reality, accompanied by a temporary exhaustion of certain forms of struggle, an advance toward higher methods is taking place through the appearance of more political and radical forms, which have widened the contingent of driving forces. It would be both illogical and suicidal to pretend that under the circumstances of massive layoffs, selective assassinations, and the absence of revindicative victories the masses would continue to opt only for established forms of struggle for the sake of a widening of forces. The move to radicalization comes from the masses themselves; it constitutes a response to the conditions imposed by the regime in its refusal to make concessions and its tendency to repress and to frustrate.[22]*

The end of the 1980s yields a popular movement reconstructed into new forms, one that integrates new actors and that includes a renewed role for the union movement. Only unprogressive opinions unable to understand the Salvadoran political dynamic would characterize this popular movement as a "front" for the FMLN. Undeniably, the movement forms part of the broad and complex development of a popular, revolutionary alternative for El Salvador headed by the FMLN. Yet a brief look at the urban revindicatory movement demonstrates how its rapid development over the last four years cannot be attributed solely to the will of the revolutionary leadership. This movement possesses a significant organizational capacity of its own. To see this, one need only look at examples like the CCM, which unites twenty-five Salvadoran communities; after 1987, it coordinated a series of collective land occupations, an unprecedented occurrence on the Salvadoran political scene. Also worthy of mention are other community organizations like the Consejo de Comunidades de Damnificados, the Unión Comunal de Mesones, and the Unión Comunal de Damnificados de San Salvador (the last drawing members from sixty-five zones in the capital).[23] These groups undertake different forms of struggle, such as parliamentary negotiation or mobilization for de facto actions like illegal occupation of urban lands, public protests, and so on. As Villalobos asserts about the aftermath of the 1986 earthquake in San Salvador,

> *we are organized and we establish greater presence and force in the community organizations; even better, we have a more defined position in terms of solving our problems, carrying out collective mobilizations in the city with the aim of bettering our living conditions.*

This development completes a cycle of profound transformations in the popular mass movement in El Salvador.

The Development of the Project and Political Thought of the FMLN

A definitive account of the evolution of the FMLN is not yet possible; capturing a process of such extreme richness must await future collective work. Nevertheless, one can analyze the recent progress of the movement and understand the extraordinary validity and flexibility that have permitted it to confront one of the most sophisticated counterrevolutionary strategies applied anywhere in the world. To this end, I will base my analysis on the writings of members of the General Command of the FMLN. (And although I consider them fundamental sources, I am not suggesting that the profoundly collective political thought of the FMLN can be equated with these writings alone.) I will analyze the various positions taken over these ten years with regard to five matters: first, the character of the political regimes that the revolutionary forces opposed; the elements of the revolution, why it was fought, and the nature of its program; third, the strategy, tactics, and forms of struggle implemented; the conception of the FMLN as a party—the process of unification of the organizations that compose it, its driving forces, and its politics of alliances; and finally, the external setting and U.S. intervention.

El Salvador since 1932

An overall characterization of the Salvadoran political regimes of the past six decades emerges from a document intended to provide grounding for FMLN proposals at the dialogue and negotation meeting in San José, Costa Rica, on October 16–18, 1989:

> *Throughout its nearly 60-year existence, the military dictatorship which emerged in the wake of the coup of December, 1931 has adapted three fundamental modalities. In its first stage, under the bloody rule of General Maximiliano Hernández Martínez, the dictatorship was structured around the absolute subjugation of the entire state apparatus by force to the personal authority and the total, indefinite monopoly of power of the dictator and his close military leaders.*[24]

This model reached exhaustion by the middle of the 1940s. The coup of December 1948 inaugurated the second modality, which was based on the rotation of political power through the hands of different promotion classes, or *tandas*, of the officer corps:

> *It became clear that the aspiration of those young officers implicitly conveyed their determination for the armed forces to continue as the decisive power within the political system indefinitely. 'Representative democracy' was thus created to serve as the mechanism that assured the rotation in government of successive military cliques. . . .*

> *Electoral fraud became a structural necessity to guarantee*
> *the new model of the military dictatorship, in which the identity*
> *of the President and the Commander in Chief should inevitably*
> *be designated by the military high command.*

This second model lasted until 1979. After 1980, a third modality emerged, based upon a pact among the PDC, the armed forces, and the U.S. government. The new modality combined economic reforms, the cover-up of political repression, and elections that were not fraudulent; however, although the president of the republic was a civilian, the armed forces not only retained but increased their political power:

> *As the third model of military dictatorship, this formula of re-*
> *pression and reforms . . . consummated the division within the*
> *nation, precipitated the evolution of the civil war, and deepened*
> *the involvement of the United States. Its characteristics crystal-*
> *lized with the elections of the Constituent Assembly of 1982 and,*
> *under direct pressure of the military high command and the*
> *Reagan administration, the Assembly's nomination of a provi-*
> *sional 'civilian' government.*

As this FMLN document points out, the third model multiplied the size as well as the political and economic weight of the armed forces. They became the vehicle for surrendering the country's sovereignty and for increasing its dependence on the U.S government. The armed forces emerged as more of an instrument of the United States than of the oligarchy, thus changing a significant characteristic of the Salvadoran political system of the last few decades.

This change is a new and key characteristic of the reconstruction of the political system during a decade of war; it is linked with the political recomposition of the dominant classes and with the formation of its class-based party that I analyzed in Chapter 4. Here is the source of new contradictions within the dominant bloc:

> *ARENA, the party of the oligarchy, from its inception declared*
> *itself fiercely 'nationalistic,' denouncing North American in-*
> *terference as the cause for the inability to defeat the FMLN and*
> *attributing the economic crisis to the reformist policies imposed*
> *by the Yankees. Yet, the dependence of the country and the army*
> *is so crushing that ARENA plunged into a quagmire of depen-*
> *dency once it was in government.*

This model needed the celebration of clean, periodic elections, but the armed forces maintained a veto conditioned by the terms of U.S. aid:

> *In this way, civilian government, decreasing levels of electoral fraud, and the relative opening of political space [go] hand in hand with the most repressive and bloody military authoritarianism. . . .*
>
> *Although it is now more sophisticated, the military dictatorship under this model is more anti-democratic and more anti-national than ever before.*

According to the FMLN, it was clear that this regime in the third phase was a military dictatorship disguised under trappings of great sophistication: efforts at reforms that the bourgeoisie had traditionally opposed, a civilian president, and a very low profile for U.S. intervention. In this nontraditional form, its character as a military dictatorship was rendered hardly perceptible to the Salvadoran masses. These characteristics were apparent in 1984 when Napoleón Duarte, with a government based on the economic reforms decreed in 1980, assumed office as the first elected civilian president of El Salvador since the decade of the 1920s.

The FMLN was obliged to attempt to unmask the true character of the Duarte regime. In 1986, Joaquín Villalobos asserted that the counterinsurgency model of the 1980s could not embody an obvious military dictatorship as if it were 1932.[25] Instead, circumstances required a government with a reformist and democratic appearance. A frankly dictatorial regime would have brought about the possibility of a rapid revolutionary victory. What would have happened, Villalobos asked hypothetically, to a government with a D'Aubuisson in the presidency? In answer, he contended that internal and international isolation would have prevented the regime from staying in power even if it increased the slaughter. Nor could an overtly oligarchic government count on U.S. support for the armed forces. Villalobos went on to claim that Christian Democracy had become the facade for this scheme of military dictatorship. It was a means for achieving a correlation of forces favorable to the anti-national counterrevolutionary strategy. It was, therefore, a mistake to characterize Duarte as the democratizer of El Salvador.

Near the end of Duarte's presidency three years later, while the victory of ARENA in the 1989 elections loomed, the failure of this model and its management of the country was evident. Villalobos identified the great weaknesses of the counterinsurgency project, starting with the fundamental point that if the reformist policies of the Duarte government had succeeded they would have weakened the social base of the FMLN, and the war would have ceased to be a significant problem. He went on to claim that the structural reforms were the product of a political decision of the United States, not of an agreement within El Salvador's dominant classes:

> *The inability of the army to defeat the FMLN militarily is one of the most fundamental elements that created the political crisis apparent within the Christian Democratic model. The persistence of this crisis will end up by disintegrating the army itself, since it is impossible for the army to continue the war without a coherent political component. . . . This is not just rhetoric. One needs only to glance briefly at the current political situation to see profound contradictions within the power bloc and serious shortcomings in its political project.*

And Villalobos foresaw the implications of the changes that were coming:

> *If the correlation of forces changed in favor of the government, the regime would immediately assume its traditional form. Duarte and the Christian Democrats have been a circumstantial but vital component of the low-intensity-war strategy of the United States. The army and the oligarchy continue to be the dominant forces of the society. If they were free of the FMLN threat, both would immediately fill the vacuum of power.[26]*

In February 1989, recalling an interview held days after the FMLN had proposed conditions for its participation in national elections, Villalobos observed that the forces of the Right, who were supposed to have been neutralized by the reformist counterinsurgency model, had instead restructured themselves. The Right controlled the legislature and a good portion of the judiciary, in addition to maintaining its economic power. Even without controlling the executive branch, it had challenged the 1980 reforms, proposing their revocation. Villalobos suggested that

*the old union between the oligarchic power and the army is be-
ginning to be repaired. The components of classical dictatorship
in El Salvador thus start to develop a process of fusion under new
conditions.*[27]

Forming an exact definition of the regime that began to take shape
once ARENA assumed office became a new challenge for the revolutionary forces. This constituted a fundamental question, one that was
not easy to answer—just as in the first half of the decade, when the
holding of scheduled, nonfraudulent elections and the supposed entry of the Right into the political mainstream generated a certain
amount of confusion within the FMLN. The two key processes, parallel but different, that were my subject in Chapter 4—the reconstitution of the political regime and the reconstitution of the bourgeoisie
as a political class—had once more formed a knot.

The Political Development of the FMLN

A second question, the character of the revolution being fought and
the program of the FMLN, had undergone an important evolution
during the ten years of struggle. This has given rise to a great deal of
debate and conflicting interpretations. Clearly there are undeniable differences between the 1980 programmatic platform of the Gobierno
Democrático Revolucionario (GDR—Democratic Revolutionary
Government) and the January 1989 proposal of the FMLN. In my
view, the fundamental question is one of analyzing these programmatic
variations closely in relation to two aspects that determine all revolutionary processes: first, the revolution possible under concrete historical national and international conditions; and second, the problem of
power.

I begin with the second aspect, which I take as the key to understanding this complex question. In 1981, Shafik Handal, a member of
the General Command of the FMLN, asserted that the issue of political power constituted the fundamental problem of the revolutionary
struggle. Abandoning this view, in his opinion, would create reformist
deviations within revolutionary organizations, leading to a split between the democratic anti-imperialist revolution and the socialist revolution. (One must not confuse abandonment with support or criticism of specific economic or political reforms.)

This basic premise explains the radically anti-dogmatic way in
which the issue of the revolutionary program was handled within the

FMLN, pointing up another characteristic of the political thinking of the Salvadoran revolutionaries. Handal expresses this clearly:

> *Another question about this same problem is the exaggerated, sometimes absolutized, role assigned to the Economic-Social Program in the determination of the character of the revolution, the course of the struggle to obtain victory, its defense and consolidation. . . .*
>
> *The history of the world revolution has corroborated this truth over and over: it is not the Economic-Social Program that is central and decisive. The rhythms in which the Social-Economic Program is applied, and the radicality of the economic and social changes depend on the national and international conditions in which each revolution is carried out.*[28]

The development of the thinking of the FMLN goes beyond recognizing the rhythms and conditions of context and proceeds to the content of programmatic proposals. This has provoked more than a few doubts and polemics; the arguments that surrounded the 1984 proposal of a Gobierno de Amplia Participación (GAP—Government of Broad Participation) serve as a good example. Many consider it a negation of the 1980 GDR platform. It could be stated that the GDR formulation was maximalist in 1980, but I do not think so. It reflected the level of the correlation of forces in El Salvador and in Central America as a whole at the time (remember the triumph of the Sandinista revolution in 1979), and, even more, the level of organic development and political thought of the FMLN and the FDR. Because of the broad grounding of the GDR itself, the proposal of a Government of Broad Participation in 1984 generated many apprehensions about its revolutionary character. In an anonymous article of 1984, I tried to get at the true character of this proposal.[29] I will reproduce the main ideas of that article here.

In formulating a revolutionary strategy and in developing tactics, the revolutionary program plays a necessary role, but it cannot play a totally determining one. It undergoes changes along with the other elements of the revolutionary line and action. One is obliged to see the revolutionary program and its role realistically, since popular forces must first conquer political power in order to use that power to transform the social structure.

An opposite point of view would assert that the proposals of the

GAP comprise a replacement for those of the GDR, thereby constituting a regression in the revolutionary struggle. This would be a grave error, one that does not comprehend the need for tactical readjustments that take into account modifications in the correlation of forces. Adjustments aim at the creation of conditions for developing the revolutionary struggle to the best advantage; they cannot be classified simplistically as maneuvers.

When the FMLN–FDR put forth the creation of the GAP, some voices questioned the viability of the proposal, forgetting that any tactical formulation has to be achieved by means of the struggle itself. More radical opinions spoke of the abandonment of the revolutionary struggle, thinking in terms of the mechanical separation of what were traditionally called "minimum" and "maximum" programs.[30]

While it remains preeminent within the revolutionary project, the problem of power has varied in form as it has been adjusted to the changes occurring within El Salvador, Central America, and the world at large. At the beginning of the decade, in affirming that the task at hand was the democratic anti-imperialist revolution, Shafik Handal maintained:

> *If we accept the anti-imperialist democratic revolution as an inseparable part of the socialist revolution, we cannot achieve the latter by taking power peacefully through quotas. One way or another, it will be indispensable to dismantle the state machinery of the capitalists and their imperialist masters and to erect a new power and a new state.[31]*

Handal's statement reflected the conditions of its time and therefore differed from the 1984 proposal for a Government of Broad Participation. By then, the FMLN had advanced considerably in its analysis of the relationship between power and historical conditions. The 1989 proposal was distinct as well; as Joaquín Villalobos stated in his interview:

> *By introducing the proposals, we are obviously playing with a totally new political design, one that constitutes a change from previous formulations for negotiation in which the FMLN had demanded its own positions of power. The FMLN now struggles for a more general demand more deeply felt by all forces: peace and democracy. . . . [Previously], the FMLN demanded territory, military power, a share of political power, etc. . . .*

Now the FMLN sets forth a new strategy in which it works to construct a program with which all the people can identify, and something that also implies a change in the situation.[32]

Does this statement imply a renunciation of the revolutionary struggle? I maintain that it does not; instead, it signifies a mature strategic shift to maintain the force of the revolutionary option in El Salvador in the context of the specific new conditions that have emerged over this decade both within the country and internationally. The formulations for the Democratic Revolutionary Government in 1980 and the Government of Broad Participation in 1984 contributed to the advance of the revolutionary movement in El Salvador. They did not lead to a counterrevolutionary victory, as some contended in 1984–85. By the same token, the January 1989 proposal quickly provoked acute contradictions within the dominant bloc without weakening the FMLN.

This explains why Villalobos in the same interview called for maintaining insurrection as a second alternative. It also explains why the General Command of the FMLN, during the San José meeting of October 1989, proposed breaking up the current repressive military and political structure:

In the nearly sixty years of its existence, the military dictatorship forged an amalgam of army, security forces, and judicial system under a de facto or de jure subordination to the military leadership at all levels. . . .

This is the structure that needs to be broken, disassembled, and purged so that there may be the exercise of sovereignty and democracy in our country.[33]

These statements were made after the negotiators for the FMLN had offered their proposal.

The flexibility and creativity of the FMLN explain some partially developed ideas of Fermán Cienfuegos concerning the form of government being fought for:

Our goal is a self-managing system in which all the popular organizations participate from the base in the political-administrative activity of the state. In addition, diverse sectors (workers, cooperativists, political parties, political fronts, the church, etc.) exercise a permanent oversight within a framework of ideological pluralism. . . . The political and social forces of the mass organizations play an important part in the functioning of the participatory system in addition to their role in local government.[34]

These were polemical ideas, whose public expression demonstrated the opening of the FMLN to the legitimate exploration of alternatives and its permanent break with all types of dogmatism. Although El Salvador offers a panorama of extraordinary complexity and fluidity, it is possible to put into perspective how the FMLN would characterize a truly democratic government. According to Joaquín Villalobos, such a government would consist of the following:

1. In the first place, it is crucial that the revolutionary change have a realistic and true economic starting point. To a large extent, the agrarian reform comprises this starting point, since land is the central factor in the social conflict.

2. There must be an internal political give-and-take combining the representative democracy of elections and parties with the permanent democracy of mass participation in the decisions of political, economical, and social management.

3. The capacity for political debate and reflection by the people constitutes a vital component of a revolution. It is not enough for a revolution to defend itself as just; it should also prove itself to be necessary and possible. The presence of open debate and political confirmation help to reinforce this principle.

4. A one-party system is not appropriate to our reality. The unity of the revolutionary forces in one party should not be confused with a single-party society. The one-party model in classical socialism is the product of a historical reality. Our society has another complexity and social composition.

5. Freedom of expression in a revolutionary model originating in [Salvadoran] conditions . . . is clearly a necessity for internal social equilibrium. If the defense and the security of revolutionary change needs a correlation that assures pluralism, the current context requires a debated political defense and the education of the masses, teaching them to reflect and to defend their historical project. This cannot occur without opposition and without knowing the project that opposes the revolutionary position in order to safeguard against the development of ideological dogmatism and paralysis.

6. An arming to the teeth, military pacts with foreign powers, and the establishment of bases are neither necessary nor realistic. Defense must be rooted within a popular concept. It is enough to be strong by virtue of a popular concept of defense in order to have an acceptable margin of security without the need for numerous, overly armed military forces. In this sense, it is false that a revolution can become a threat to the security of the United States.

7. The Salvadoran revolution is situated within the geopolitical context of Latin America and the United States. On the one hand, this implies a struggle to change the terms of relations with the United States while, on the other, a need to maintain relations with that country. This means a rejection of imperial politics, but an acceptance and understanding of the character of the powerful U.S. nation in its relationships with Latin America.

8. Our culture is a hybrid of our Indian, African, and Spanish races and of the Saxon culture of the north. In addition to their economic value, the nearly million Salvadorans living in the U.S signify a cultural influence on our society that cannot be ignored.

9. The Salvadoran revolutionary process has a social Christian base since a large majority of its combatants are believers. An important number of its cadres are Christians.

10. The FMLN requires a revolutionary change that creates a democratic and pluralistic society, and this change needs a military power that guarantees it. The current army does not guarantee this change. Nevertheless, the FMLN exists. Therefore, it is best to assure a military power that represents a new military correlation within society which neither destroys the current army nor disarms the FMLN.[35]

These principles do not make up a dogmatic set of commandments, but they are the expression of the political project that the FMLN developed collectively through a decade of popular struggle. Despite the debatable character of some of them, the proposals made in the October 1989 meeting carry this effort forward.[36]

The Nature of the Revolution

There exists a third question that has to be examined in order to understand fully the development of this project and its political thought—matters of strategy, tactics, and the forms of struggle launched during the 1980s. Many of these topics have already been addressed: the strategy and its various modifications; changes in military tactics (the fundamental form of struggle used in the early 1980s); the shift after 1984 to giving the political struggle preeminence; and the development of the autonomous popular movement. I will, however, pause briefly to examine two polemical points: the role of dialogue and negotiation, and the FMLN's participation in the electoral process.

In 1985, I wrote that dialogue and negotiation had gained recognition as useful auxiliary instruments in the Salvadoran revolutionary struggle and the strategy that guided its development.[37] They constituted a type of complementary action that the advances of the fundamental form of struggle—armed revolution of a political nature—had wrested from the dominant classes and from imperialism. The means of struggle through dialogue and negotiation could not be mechanically transposed from another revolutionary experience.

I said then that looking at the tactical or strategic character of dialogue and negotiation outside the context of the overall formulations and real actions of the FMLN would only engender sterile discussion. Placing this instrument of struggle in their midst, however, demanded an exhaustive analysis of the possibilities of each concrete conjuncture. It was vital to guarantee that revolutionary strategic and tactical formulations would neither be detracted from nor used by enemy forces. To this day, neither dialogue nor negotiation has run counter to the advancement of the armed revolutionary struggle or to the revival of mass political struggle.

What is the situation at the end of the 1980s?

Here, I will make a brief review of its development. Initially encouraged by external political forces, especially the Socialist International, in December 1980 the recently constituted FMLN made a proposal to the governing junta to discuss the foreseeable U.S. intervention; this proposal culminated in the Franco-Mexican declaration of August 1981. Thereafter, the FMLN's calls for dialogue and negotiation continued, although they received lesser priority until October 1984, when the situation took a dramatic turn. In an address to the United Nations, Duarte offered to undertake discussions with the revolutionary forces. From then on, amid advances and retreats, dialogue and a negotiated political solution to the war would remain essential elements of the popular Salvadoran demands. They were incorporated into the conceptions of the FMLN, since the political struggle had become international as well as national.

In this context, negotiation and dialogue were never conceived of as simple tactical maneuvers, although they were not allowed to impose limitations on the fundamental forms of struggle. For the FMLN, dialogue did not necessarily mean immediate negotiation; it should, rather, lead to it. Both dialogue and negotiation would become more viable to the extent that the armed struggle and the political struggle of the masses advanced. In other words, what was being considered was a continuous process of accumulation of forces.

This conception of dialogue and negotiation has matured within the FMLN, assuming a flexible and audacious development that has allowed the popular movement to maintain the initiative in this field and oblige the government to accept the inextricable link between dialogue and negotiation. That relationship is described in the accord produced during the September 1989 meeting in Mexico as "an effort in appreciation of the value of negotiation to end the armed conflict through political means in the shortest term possible, to advance the democratization of the country, and to re-unify Salvadoran society."[38]

The other point, electoral participation by the FMLN, is a more recent and also more controversial matter, since it implies a drastic shift from the previous position. Speaking about the participation of the PCS in the electoral processes between 1967 and 1977, Shafik Handal claimed that electoral involvement had made possible the political education of the popular masses and served to win over the majority to the side of the democratic cause. At the same time, it allowed the people to recognize the limitations of the electoral process:

> [T]he great masses learned to recognize the true face of the reactionary military dictatorship and its fraudulent game with the elections; they freed themselves from the illusions of the electoral "way" and understood that there was no other road to reach democracy, social justice, and progress in service to the people than through defeating the dictatorship with revolutionary violence.[39]

This position remained unchanged until 1988. The FMLN denounced each election as a mechanism for legitimizing the counterinsurgency project; it also launched military actions to block them, but with little success. An example of this position can be found in the pronouncement made by the General Command on March 30, 1988, with regard to the elections of March 20. It repeated the argument about the significance of abstentions and contrasted the elections with the alternative of establishing a government of broad participation.[40]

On January 23, 1989, the FMLN presented a proposal that marked a diametric shift from its former views. It proposed delaying the 1989 presidential election from March 19 until September 15. The FMLN would respect the electoral process and accept its legitimacy if the following conditions were met: an end to repression; confinement of the army to its quarters on election day; integration of the Convergencia Democrática into the Consejo Central de Elecciones (Central Electoral Council); establishment of an electoral code that reflected a consensus; a guarantee of the vote to Salvadorans living outside the country; and exclusion of the U.S government from the process.[41]

This proposal elicited a controversial series of responses and, in my opinion, generated difficult contradictions within the power bloc. Was this at heart a tactical maneuver by the FMLN, or did it represent a change in its conception of elections? The answer can be found in the declarations of Joaquín Villalobos. In an honest vote, he maintains that the people would choose candidates who stand for a change in the country's critical situation—"This is what causes the FMLN to make a proposal that is not a new tactical one, but rather one with a strategic content."[42]

Under the audacious aspect of the proposal, as Villalobos went on to clarify, the strength that the FMLN had accumulated over ten years would be placed at risk should it lose the election. As to the possible size of the voting population, Villalobos thought that the turnout would surpass 90 percent if the Salvadoran people were convinced that elections would bring peace. He emphasized that a proper understanding of this proposal showed that the FMLN was willing to accept the legitimacy of electoral results if the proposed conditions were respected.

With regard to the problem of power, Villalobos declared that if the Convergence won under these conditions the FMLN would not retain all authority; instead, such a victory would initiate a process of peaceful transition to the structural changes that would resolve the problems of the war and of democracy in the country.

The proposal never became concrete. Elections took place under prevailing conditions, and the Convergencia Democrática obtained a very low percentage of the vote. Months later, the possibility was again posed of a direct participation by the FMLN in electoral processes. An about-face had taken place. To understand its exact terms, it must be placed in a context that would effectuate the preconditions demanded by the FMLN. This requirement is like that contained in the October 1989 proposals for an end to hostilities in which an essential precondition was the modification of the government army through a reduction of its personnel and a purging of its corrupt and abusive elements, just as Joaquín Villalobos declared in the interview cited above.

Even though many questions remain, the FMLN's turn toward involvement in elections will be decisive for the Salvadoran political process in coming years.

The Political Character of the FMLN

The fourth issue involves the conception of the FMLN as a party, the process of unification of its member organizations, and its driving forces and alliances. I have already made some observations about the process of unification and the establishment of the FMLN as a revolutionary party. This rich and unfinished process reveals the constant struggle against dogmatism that has characterized the Salvadoran revolutionaries. Thus, the FMLN leaders can declare openly that their struggle is not a matter of establishing a one-party regime. The Left ranges all the way from the FMLN through the popular movement (with its trade union and political forms) through to the Convergencia Democrática. The revolutionary project seeks to construct a politically pluralistic society, as the development of a popular movement during this decade demonstrates.

Regarding the definition of the driving forces, the FMLN has always sustained the role of vanguard of the workers and the peasants and upheld the strategic character of their alliance. Nevertheless, in this conception it has not dogmatized a reductionist vision of these social classes. Conscious of the growing complexity of the structure of the working classes and of the middle sectors of the country,[43] the FMLN has modified its discourse without modifying the essence of its conception. Fermán Cienfuegos recently affirmed:

> *Reality is one of class struggle, but we can give reality different names. This is the challenge of propaganda, but this does not mean that we renounce the principles of Marxism-Leninism.*

> *However, a basic principle of Marxism is to know reality in or-*
> *der to be able to transform it. Salvadoran reality is very concrete*
> *and changing. It requires a very flexible and concrete lan-*
> *guage.*[44]

It is perhaps in the area of alliances that the FMLN has made some of its greatest contributions to the history of revolutionary politics on this continent, since developing and maintaining a strategic alliance with the parties of the FDR (the MNR and the MPSC) has not been easy and has been subjected to continual sabotage by forces and governments from other points on the political spectrum. Here, I raise a controversial question that is, in my opinion, key to understanding this alliance: neither the MNR nor the MPSC is a political party with a massive social base. (The masses have always—except in the elections in which the Right has been able to manipulate the vote—adhered to the revolutionary political option.) This fact has prevented a contest for the masses between the FMLN and its democratic allies; it has, as well, permitted a correct definition of the parties' respective roles.

But the alliances have not been limited to the level of parties and political organizations. They have developed, at different rhythms and with their own specificities, within the popular movement among organizations that adhere politically and ideologically to the revolutionary project and among others that do not. As a result, during Duarte's presidency, there were moments of alliance between sectors of the popular movement influenced by the FMLN and others influenced by the PDC. After Cristiani's election, there was a growing unity among UNTS, UNOC, and other workers organizations to oppose the oligarchic scheme to revoke the 1980 reforms and to resist increasing repression and a deteriorating standard of living. This dynamic interweaving of alliances has been consistently carried out among popular sectors and workers, without the incorporation of bourgeois groups (as was the case in Nicaragua in the late 1970s). The reasons are clear if one recalls what was said in Chapter 4; this is another unique feature of Salvadoran political history.

El Salvador, Central America, and the United States

The fifth and last point concerns the role of the external context and of U.S. intervention in the political process El Salvador experienced during the 1980s. I will start with the latter, keeping two essential facts in mind: first, unlike Nicaragua, El Salvador had never experienced direct intervention by U.S. troops; second, El Salvador had never had to cope with direct economic intervention by U.S. capital of the type characterized by the banana plantations in Honduras and Costa Rica. Both these factors contributed to the lack of anti-interventionist or anti-U.S. sentiment among Salvadoran popular sectors; I believe that this history with regard to the United States also created the base for a peculiar nationalism among the dominant classes.

After 1980, the situation shifted radically; this change in part explained ARENA's nationalist discourse (stressed more in the early 1980s than later). The political ideology of the FMLN, although cognizant of growing U.S. intervention, had difficulties in taking advantage of the new situation in its propaganda. This context even influenced the exact understanding of the character of the counterinsurgency strategy, in which direct intervention by troops from the United States (or anywhere else) was not contemplated except in an extreme case.

In 1981, Joaquín Villalobos asserted that U.S. intervention would be a matter of last resort because of its high political costs and the unfavorable correlation at the international level.[45] Yet the analysis by the General Command of the FMLN in 1984 devoted considerable space to the escalated intervention of the United States; it became one of the key factors in the strategic readjustment of the revolutionary forces from then on.

This analysis argued that

> *never before as in the present period have we had the necessity to consider the confrontation with the imperialist power so concretely. . . .*
>
> *This escalation can be observed from the last period of the Carter administration, but especially after the 20th of January of 1981, when El Salvador was given priority as a strategic point and Central America as a vital area for the Reagan administration.*

And, referring to U.S. military intervention in Grenada, the analysis stated:

> *Because of this, we must prepare ourselves militarily to confront intervention, and at the same time, to make efforts to impede it*

*through a willingness to dialogue and to accept a dignified po-
litical solution which is just to the interests of our people.*[46]

In 1986, Villalobos postulated that direct intervention had no hope
for success; therefore, the United States would opt instead to increase
constantly its levels of material and advisory assistance. He argued that
a large proportion of the United States military technology would be
underutilized in El Salvador, given the characteristics of the war and
its territorial peculiarities, and that intervention would "Central
Americanize" the conflict:

> *It would become a war that covers the whole region, since an in-
> tervention would force the revolutionaries to develop a regional
> strategy.*[47]

He immediately went on to say that a negotiated political solution was
the best way to end the war. Evidently, between mid-1984 and 1986
there had been a change in the FMLN's perception of the possibilities
of direct intervention of foreign troops in the Salvadoran conflict.

By the end of 1988, it was even more clear that such a direct intervention was extremely unlikely in the view of the FMLN. Again
quoting Villalobos:

> *Without being able to dismiss the possibility of a direct inter-
> vention by U.S. troops, it is beneficial to point out that this al-
> ternative suffers from very complicated margins of decision in
> the U.S.; what's more, it would not be effective, since now, much
> more than before, the U.S. would face an exhaustive war whose
> cost would be very high in North American lives; it would have
> to face a popular resistance and a national unity of great pro-
> portions.*[48]

Although this is true, I believe that there are two additional factors
that contribute to lessening the need for such intervention: on one
side, the reconstitution of the political regime and the political recomposition of the dominant classes; on the other, a change in the regional political situation. Let me analyze this process.

Born out of a colonial political union, and ephemerally joined into
a federal republic in the years after they achieved independence in
1821, the Central American countries have been marked by the con-

tradictions inherent in all processes of political or economic integration.[49] In addition, the location of Central America gives it a key geopolitical position.[50] This well-known feature has resulted in its being known as the 'backyard' of the United States. These realities have produced a permanent interconnection among the struggles and popular revolutionary political movements of Central America.

Thus, for example, one finds the formation of the Confederación Obrera Centroamericana (COCA—Central American Workers Confederation), as well as the participation of many Central Americans in the liberating feats of Augusto César Sandino in the 1920s. During the 1940s, an active link can be observed between the Communist leaders of El Salvador and Guatemala.[51] More recently, the FSLN struggle in Nicaragua and, to a lesser degree, that of the FMLN have offered many examples of solidarity among Central American revolutionaries, with Salvadorans figuring the most prominently.

How has such cooperation influenced the development of the project and political thought of the FMLN? This regional dimension has always been present, even if only one of the member organizations of the FMLN, the Partido Revolucionario de los Trabajadores Centroamericanos (PRTC-Revolutionary Party of Central American Workers), has made attempts to develop it in conceptual, organizational, and programmatic terms. This explains why the regional context, while key, has been viewed predominantly from the angle of its military implications in the declarations and analyses of the FMLN. Thus, official statements such as one made in 1984 present the geopolitical element as the main factor guiding the reasoning:

> *By its continuing on, the Salvadoran revolutionary phenomenon has already surpassed the Cuban and Nicaraguan processes in complexity; as a third revolution, it was obviously bound to confront the experience and the determination of the United States not to permit another in the continent.*[52]

But in 1985, there is a less reactive vision within the leadership of the FMLN. Its analysis of the regional context in which the Salvadoran struggle had developed defined the structural crisis of the country as part of the regional structural crisis. There was, in the view of the FMLN, a regional revolutionary situation, whose peak moments were of unequal maturity. It proposed to work for the unity and coordination of all the revolutionary forces of Central America, since the expanded revolutionary situation in the region could end only in the transcending of the capitalist system.[53] This period witnessed numerous efforts made by the FMLN to encourage the coordination of revolutionary movements in a lucid vision of the need to oppose sophisticated regional counterinsurgency efforts, most notably the Kissinger Plan for the Caribbean Basin. Analyzing the possibilities of massive U.S. military intervention in El Salvador in 1986,[54] Joaquín Villalobos examined the possibilities of a sizable deployment of US. troops. Once again he focused primarily on military matters, although he did link the Salvadoran situation closely with the events occurring in Nicaragua through an underlying vision developed from mutual regional influences.

Later, in 1989, revolutionary analysis broadened this context, ranging beyond regional confines to link regional and global factors with the transformations taking place inside El Salvador during the decade of war. According to Villalobos:

> *Three large aspects form the context and determine the revolutionary model in El Salvador: the weakening of bellicocity in the United States, the geopolitical multipolarity of the current world, and the social composition of the driving forces of change in El Salvador.*[55]

He went on to say that the Salvadoran revolution, lying as it does within the geopolitical context of Latin America and the United States, needs to establish relations of genuine respect with the countries of the continent, independent of their power, level of development, or type of political regime—a policy that is valid for other Central American countries as well. This obviously required rethinking the terms of regional integration in the future, an aspect so far given very little attention by the FMLN.

I have made here a first attempt at describing the evolution of the project and political thought of the FMLN. I have done so by analyzing the documents and official declarations of members of the revolutionary leadership, many of whose writings I have quoted in order to represent their thoughts as accurately as possible. It is obvious that this work should be complemented by exploring the view of reality for which the cadres and militants at different levels struggle. Although I feel that the views expressed by the leaders represent the collective positions of the movement in general, there are important shadings that only a more thorough analysis can reveal.

Though the project and thought of the FMLN are still developing, its hold on reality and its resistance to dogmatism, as well as its extraordinary flexibility and creativity, are acknowledged by one of its principal authors:

> *Analyzing the FMLN's process of development and the construction of its political thought up to now, we can conclude that, throughout its history, the movement has developed an ability to adopt to changing realities; precisely as a result of this, it has been able to resist and to remain at war.*[56]

The general offensive launched on November 11, 1989, coming in the wake of nearly a decade of heroic struggle, was not only a real improvement over its predecessor of January 1981 but proof of Villalobos's affirmation.

Toward the Close of the
Political Period Begun in 1979

The military offensive launched by the FMLN in November 1989 remains highly controversial. It came a few months after ARENA's assumption of the presidency signaled the moment of consolidation of the reconstitution of the bourgeoisie as a political class that had begun in 1982.

November 1989: The FMLN Offensive

A complete evaluation of this crucial action by the revolutionary forces would require consulting different political sectors and numerous elements within civil society. One would want to learn the views of those involved, both positively and negatively, without being limited to analyzing any single opinion or facet—such as military action—in isolation. The observer immediately finds himself faced with a multitude of conflicting evaluations of the offensive. Therefore, I will try to evaluate what I consider the fundamental question, the cause of the action: namely, the need to modify the political and military correlation of forces between the two contending sides in a war that had already lasted nine years.

At that point, all Salvadoran political forces realized that an undeniable situation of military uncertainty was dragging on. Neither the government armed forces nor the FMLN could defeat each other, despite frequent official communiqués to the contrary. The organization of the offensive launched by the FMLN required a great deal of preparation throughout 1989. Its fundamental purpose was not to defeat the official armed forces once and for all. Rather, the uprising sought to provoke a qualitative change in the correlation of forces that would help to restart the stalemated negotiation process for a political solution to the war. Subsequent events, culminating in the signing of the Peace Accords in January 1992, testify to the attainment of this central objective. Nevertheless, some sectors of the FMLN undoubtedly believed that the government army could be decisively defeated through a possible popular insurrection in the capital. Therefore, it is important to examine some conditioning factors and some particular results of this action of the revolutionary forces.

Because the offensive took place in the city of San Salvador, where the war had a relatively low presence despite its proximity, resources of large quantity and high quality were required for its preparation and execution. This had a negative impact on the development of the popular movement, even though that movement did not directly follow the plans and immediate interests of the FMLN and even though it continued to expand, as I shall point out further on. Perhaps the largest human and political cost was incurred as a result of the first three days of the offensive. The decisive action by the FMLN secured important support from the population of the northern and eastern districts of the capital, although the popular insurrection that some had erroneously envisioned did not take place. This support put the official armed forces in check and obliged them to undertake indiscriminate bombing of the areas of the city where the FMLN was powerful. It became evident that neither the insurrectionists nor the people who supported them were prepared to resist a bombardment of this intensity or to sustain the fighting for a prolonged period. The military forces of the FMLN were obliged to retreat because of problems of supply and military sanitation, and particularly because of the suffering of the population.

The events of November 1989 confirmed my earlier evaluation of the role of insurrection in the Salvadoran case, its peculiarities, and its differences from the contemporary experiences of other nearby areas like Nicaragua. Although the FMLN's military offensive constituted the central element in the political juncture that took shape from this point on, the offensive itself was not a popular insurrection. This has not been the preferred form of armed struggle in El Salvador, and it did not shape the definitive phase of the popular war. Instead, partial, local uprisings, mostly by peasants, have seemed to predominate in the history of the country. In urban areas, the principal forms of struggle have been different.

It would be a mistake to conclude that the FMLN offensive constituted a military defeat. Such a claim would overlook the fact that the

FMLN exercised a strategy of a political-military character throughout the entire war, a point that any evaluation of the 1989 offensive must take into account. Although the offensive did not decisively alter the balance of military forces, it certainly demonstrated the capacity and military creativity of the FMLN, thus transforming the correlation of political forces. Hereafter, the hegemonic sector within ARENA became convinced that a military defeat of the FMLN was impossible. In order to institute its economic program, it would have to find a negotiated political solution to the war. One could say that from this moment on the path toward negotiation became unblocked.

In addition, in a desperate moment, part of the high command of the official armed forces decided to assassinate the Jesuit directors of the Universidad Centroamericana José Simeón Cañas (UCA), to whom they mistakenly attributed the intellectual leadership of the revolutionary movement. This massacre led other key actors in the Salvadoran conflict to shift their positions even further. The U.S. administration, pressured by some of its citizens to punish those guilty of the multiple assassinations, removed its unconditional support for a military solution to the war, a policy already under review given the evident failure of the counterinsurgency strategy undertaken since the early 1980s.

In short, the significance of the military offensive launched by the FMLN lies in its modification of the correlation of forces. This change was not so much between the two principal contending blocs as among the various tendencies within them, favoring those on each side who argued for a negotiated political solution to the conflict. Let me expand on this.

The results of the offensive exercised a powerful impact upon the political forces of the Right, grouped principally within ARENA and its complete control of the government. Modernized sectors that supported both a political solution to the war and the consolidation of a restricted democratic regime—they viewed both as indispensable to fulfilling their neo-liberal economic plans—finally prevailed over the ultra-rightist sectors. Although the latter were only a minority of the government bloc, they argued strongly for a military annihilation of the revolutionary forces.

Within the government armed forces, the scope of the FMLN's military action and the response it received must have produced a profound questioning that weakened these hardline sectors. Furthermore, the armed forces lost considerable prestige once it was revealed that the assassins of the Jesuit priests were members of the elite Atlacatl Battalion acting on the orders of a high-ranking officer. Changes within the government armed forces—evident in the shift of attitude toward negotiations following the FMLN offensive—grew out of structural factors associated with the organizational and functional changes within the military over the 1980s that I discussed in Chapter 2. They also stemmed from a phenomenon that must be studied because of its significance for the country's political future: the shift in the mentality of Salvadoran military officers produced by the war and by the profound transformations taking place within El Salvador's society and economy.

With regard to the revolutionary forces, the offensive reinforced a tendency dominant in the member organizations since the founding of the FMLN: to view the military struggle as subordinate to the political struggle. While the war represented an inevitable course of action, its negotiated political solution constituted a central element in the political strategy of the FMLN, not just a tactical component. Those who thought otherwise were clearly a minority within the revolutionary organizations. The force of reality itself obliged them to accept that their ideas were mistaken. Such views stemmed more from the weakness of their political education than from any highly elaborated doctrinal positions.

As for the U.S. administration, it labored under the failure of its counterinsurgency strategy and the growth of its internal contradictions that I previously noted. New global developments now added additional profound changes. The end of the bipolarity of the Cold War sapped the strength of arguments that fundamentally attributed the Salvadoran conflict to external causes. In the midst of notable contradictions and great efforts, those members of the Bush administration who supported a political solution to the war gained the upper hand in the formulation of U.S. policy toward El Salvador. Changes in Central America in the wake of the Esquipulas Accords, signed by the five Central American presidents in 1987, and the electoral defeat of the Sandinistas in February 1990 also exercised a strong influence on U.S. policy.

The Expansion of the Popular Movement and the Objectives of Its Struggle

The creation of a broad popular movement is indispensable for the development of a popular alternative project. Moreover, that movement itself must continue to develop during the further evolution of the alternative project. Thus, one can speak of processes of construction that are permanent and parallel.

Two issues, apparently accepted but generally overlooked, form the base of the preceding premise. First, a popular movement constructs and reconstructs itself in a perpetually open-ended process. Once it attains the capacity to play a role in the construction of a new society it does not become an organizational structure set in concrete. Second, a popular alternative project does not constitute an ideal model for society that can be achieved simply by decree. Instead, it expresses a true dialectical transcendence of contradictions: progress toward the alternative project develops through struggle and through the conquest of spaces of political power.

Many contradictions envelop the relationship between the constitution of a broad-based movement and the building of a popular project. Particularly salient is the overall issue of democracy, a subject highly involved in the internal structure and operations of the popular movement and in the content of the popular alternative project. The question of democracy is highly relevant to specific problem areas, such as the relationship between the popular movement and the FMLN, and to matters of common historical elements, shared visions, methods of struggle, and so on. Although I will examine these issues later, I must outline here a few points about the problem of democracy as they relate to the Salvadoran political process of the 1980s.

As in many countries of the capitalist periphery, the absence of a democratic political system in El Salvador is not the product of fate or culture.[1] The explanation, instead, lies in how the Salvadoran economy and society were structured after 1880, the decisive moment of El Salvador's entry into the world capitalist system. The establishment of an oligarchic regime of exclusionary political, social, and economic characteristics proved indispensable for the country's insertion into the world economy. In El Salvador, as in the majority of the countries in the periphery, the characteristic features of the bourgeois liberal democracies remained absent until practically the final decades of this century.

Today, the new international division of labor assigns another role to the economies of the peripheral countries, and by the same token demands a change in the traditionally repressive and dictatorial governments that dominated until recently. The result has been a process of democratization generally limited to the political realm, principally the election of representatives through nonfraudulent voting processes.

Democracy should not be limited to the political arena alone. Even there, it should go beyond representation to include the effective participation of the citizenry at all levels of decision within society. Moreover, democracy implies much more than discussing the processes needed to make it concrete. True democracy requires addressing the question of content; in the case of elections, for example, democratization should proceed beyond simple representation to effective participation, beyond the integrity of the process to its programmatic content.

Hence, democracy should extend further than the political arena into productive contexts (factories, agrarian and livestock units, etc.), domestic realms (in the struggle to abolish patriarchal domination), and international relations (combating unequal exchange, for example).[2] In summary, democracy is a process of permanent construction that assumes specific forms according to each concrete case in a process of permanent expansion.

With these comments in mind, let me briefly survey the principal actions of the popular movement before November 1989.[3] That year began with the encircling of the Salvadoran University, alleged to be a terrorist sanctuary, and with expressions of popular support elicited by the daring proposal of the FMLN on the conditions of its electoral participation. The proposal, in fact, produced a closer association between UNTS and UNOC with regard to the peace process. Nevertheless, the regime and the rightist forces hardened their positions, as indicated by the expulsion of the workers of Pesca, S.A., who had been on strike since 1987, and by the placement of a bomb in the office of FENASTRAS on February 22.

Positions polarized following ARENA's electoral victory in March. After the government's May 1 demonstration drew only about fifteen hundred people, pressure increased from some sectors of the official party for more firings and for a more repressive policy toward the popular movement. Two events exemplified these tendencies: the dislodging of striking workers from the INSINCA factory on the outskirts of San Salvador, and the brutal bomb attack on FENASTRAS headquarters on October 31 (the latter killing important union leaders). The year ended dramatically with the assassination of the Jesuits at the Universidad Centroamericana.

My previous discussion of the trajectory of the Salvadoran popular movement from 1983 to 1989 showed that the tendencies of the late 1970s—its broadening and growing heterogeneity and a constant search for new forms of struggle—continued over the next ten years.

Other tendencies also developed that today are considered fundamental for any struggle and process of social transformation, particularly the gradual independence of the revolutionary organizations and the political parties as well as the emergence of the struggle for democracy (with all its potentiality, ambiguity, and danger) within their revindicative platforms.

In addition, after 1983 we find another extraordinarily important feature within the popular movement that relates to El Salvador's complex political changes of the 1980s: the legal character of the organizations and of most of their struggles. I shall touch on this matter before describing the expansion and status of the popular movement after November 1989.

While the growth of the popular movement consistently intensified from the early 1970s onward, this expansion assumed different forms. In the early years, popular mobilization appeared as a broad movement of the masses organized into separate groupings of separate organizations, the most notable of which were the Bloque Popular Revolucionario (BPR—Revolutionary Popular Bloc), the FAPU, and the Ligas Populares 28 de Febrero (LP–28—Popular Leagues–28th February). Subsequent expansion produced a large number of different organizations within the popular movement. Although they were united around broad demands, such as a negotiated solution to the war, these organizations did not always act in the same fashion as earlier groups.

Does this imply that the current popular movement is no longer a mass movement? I do not think so, since I believe that the movement and the struggle of the masses remain a constant feature of the Salvadoran political scene. They simply assume distinct forms in different periods of history.[4] For this reason, as I said earlier, massive demonstrations such as the one held on January 22, 1980, cannot be repeated at will. I do not mean to suggest that the popular organizations will not be able to generate massive popular actions in the future—only that the expansion of the popular movement in the 1980s and early 1990s exhibited a different pattern, that of the growing incorporation of new popular social sectors in a constantly increasing number of new organizations. This subject inevitably brings me to the issue of the ever greater structural heterogeneity of the Salvadoran social movement.

More than a decade of war has radically changed El Salvador's society and economy. Although the country has maintained its principal pre-war characteristics, its labor structure today possesses, in contrast to that of earlier years, an important cooperative sector in the countryside and an impressive range of informal economic activities in the cities. To these we can add a relative increase in the level of public employment derived from the policies of the Christian Democratic governments. The demographic structure of El Salvador has undergone significant changes due to internal displacements and migrations abroad, principally to the United States. The cash remittances of Salvadorans residing abroad and voluminous U.S. aid have brought about serious distortions in the productive structure, whose consequences are beginning to gain some attention.

The construction of a new political system means incorporating new practices and actors, integrating the distinct expressions of the popular movement and the nongovernmental organizations that support them, whatever countless contradictions this may involve. Underlying the new reality is the altered social-class structure that has grown up in El Salvador over the past decade. The increasing heterogeneity of the Salvadoran popular movement derives from these changes in social structure. For example, the emergence, development, and active mobilization of cooperativists could not have occurred before the agrarian reform of 1980 (regardless of the judgments that one might make about that reform). By the same token, the growing urban communal movement can be attributed in part to the expansion of the informal market. The revindicative actions of public employees reflect their increased numbers and the political importance they gained during the first five or six years of the 1980s. All these activities and struggles have taken place in spite of the repression that the popular movement faces. Although lessened, that repression still continues. All of this popular activism could not have occurred without the political opening—however limited—that the struggle of the FMLN and of the political parties has made possible.

The increasing heterogeneity of the popular movement will undoubtedly intensify, aided by the economic restructuring that the current ARENA government has undertaken within the framework of the changing world economy and by the political spaces that a negotiated solution to the war opens. This heterogeneity is a structural feature of the Salvadoran reality. It must be taken into account when envisioning the role of the popular movement in the construction of an alternative Salvadoran development model.

I have argued that the implementation of new forms of struggle characterized the popular movement during the 1970s and 1980s. I must go on to point out a key difference between the two periods: the revindicative actions and the movements that supported them were largely illegal in the 1970s; those of the 1980s, however, were legal for the most part. In order to try to explain this change and its consequences for the Salvadoran popular movement, I must clarify some additional matters. First comes the issue of what one should consider legal or illegal for the struggles of the popular movement. Strictly judicial criteria are not enough. Laws have imposed enormous restrictions on the organization and activities of Salvadoran popular sectors throughout the twentieth century, thereby making most of their forms of expression judicially illegal. This cannot be disregarded. Nevertheless, an organization and some of its actions may fall within the area of legality if there is a sufficient insertion into the political arena. Under these conditions, it cannot be prohibited even if it is not recognized legally. This situation would also prevail when the political cost of prohibition is so high that the opposition confers social legitimacy on its actions by default. This process implies winning and building spaces of political power. The popular movement has creatively taken advantage of this tactic during the last several years. In some cases, its efforts have culminated with juridical recognition for organizations and their forms of action. Until 1970, this process was limited to manufacturing unions and their strikes. Nevertheless, the activities of the teachers movement in the late 1960s and early 1970s marked a new stage in a process that subsequently accelerated in the 1980s.

Let me look further at the question of historical antecedents. It could be said that the organization and the struggles of the popular movement as of the 1960s had sought a means to insert themselves within the country's legal framework. In many cases, this strategy followed the political orientation of the Communist Party, the only revolutionary organization that existed in El Salvador during these years. The party had been decisively influenced by its experience of permanent illegality and constant repression since the 1932 insurrection. After 1970, the emerging political-military revolutionary organizations made an about-face from this tendency. They instituted new forms of organization and struggle among the popular sectors with the main goal of obtaining political recognition, not legal status. Although they did not consciously seek illegality, they did not reject it, either.

The gradual but dramatic changes in the system and in political practices during the 1980s proved decisive in altering this orientation once again. The new developments in the Salvadoran political system emerged with the imposition of nonfraudulent elections, the reconstitution of the bourgeoisie as a political class, and the organization of a true party of the dominant classes that began to control the government apparatus directly. Limited spaces developed for the participation and expression of opposition parties and political forces. All of this essentially worked to widen the legal arena, a development that both allowed and obliged the popular movement to thrust itself into the new area of political legality.

The popular movement has been frequently criticized for its use of violence as a form of struggle. Seen in the abstract, its violent actions could appear reprehensible. Using historical analysis, however, one can see that the maintenance of brutal official repression in El Salvador since the nineteenth century has often necessitated a violent response. At some moments of political confrontation, repression has actually reached the level of massacre. One can, therefore, explain violent actions by the popular movement in some cases. Nevertheless, a perceptible decline in the use of violence constitutes another reflection of the changes that have occurred in the Salvadoran political context over the last few years. During the 1980s, the ability of the popular movement to respond to and resist the official forces, the presence of the FMLN, and external pressure have all brought about a partial end to death squad activities and the placement of official repression under relative control, especially in the second half of the decade. This improved context has allowed the popular movement gradually to attenuate its violent forms of struggle. This does not mean that violence cannot reoccur under certain conditions of struggle and at particular junctures; nor does it mean that violence should be condemned *a priori*. And not all forms of confrontational struggle should be labeled as violence. For example, land occupations in the countryside during 1991 certainly operated outside contemporary juridical standards (whose justice and impartiality are highly suspect), but they should not be characterized as a form of violent struggle.

The recent development and growth of the popular movement reflects a constant renewal of the forms of its political activity. This fact is intimately connected with one of its principal characteristics since 1984, the substantial expansion of the content of its revindications. The struggle for democracy, as I noted above, now occupies a central role, a matter that I will discuss further here.

The years before 1980 showed a relatively modest injection of political content into the economic and social revindications of the trade unions and the various sectors of the popular movement. Political demands were limited in range (for example, the demand to free a certain captured leader or that the army withdraw from occupied work centers); rarely did they transcend conjunctural and particular needs. After 1984, however, the popular movement began to incorporate a more general revindication—that the war be resolved through dialogue and negotiation. This demand has remained a permanent objective of its struggles to this day, thus acquiring a structural character within the agenda of the popular movement.

This achievement constituted a qualitative leap that has continued to expand in recent years. Little by little, a negotiated solution has imposed itself; a military solution has proved impossible, and it is clear that the majority of Salvadorans desires peace. The popular movement has come to demand an active participation in the struggle for peace, particularly through the creation of the Comité Permanente del Debate Nacional (CPDN—Permanent Committee of the National Debate), which has carried out numerous revindicatory activities.[5]

Parallel to the establishment of the CPDN, the question of democracy has become an overall revindication of the popular movement, another example of the broadening of the content of revindications after 1984. With this development, the movement was no longer limited to demanding a negotiated solution to the Salvadoran war and its own participation in that solution. It now started to elaborate proposals for the process of democratization and the characteristics of the democratic system that should be constructed in the country. One manifestation of this was the first congress of the Consejo Coordinador de Instituciones Privadas de Promoción Humana de El Salvador (CIPHES—Coordinating Council of Private Institutions of Human Betterment of El Salvador), held in April 1991.[6]

In the early 1990s, one can thus observe an extraordinarily heterogeneous popular movement, one that has expanded substantially, one whose massive character finds expression in a multitude of organizational forms and diversity of actions. Its revindications have reached levels of comprehensiveness and depth previously unattained. This popular movement has earned a legitimacy to go along with the legality that it has won. With each passing day, it acquires more autonomy.

It is vital to ask whether the tendency toward atomization inherent in this type of movement will permit an optimistic vision, or whether the tendency will undermine the victories achieved thus far. Certainly the latter danger exists. Mentioning this problem logically brings me to the controversial issue of the relationship between the popular movement and the political parties, especially the FMLN.

Most of the organizations within the popular movement have sought a transformation of the existing social system of El Salvador. Until 1970, they depended on the only revolutionary political organization then in existence, the Communist Party of El Salvador, although their dependence was not absolute. A few of the popular organizations remained independent, while those in favor of the status quo supported rightist parties. As I have indicated, this situation changed drastically during the 1970s. New elements emerged in the popular movement with strength; for example, the organizations of teachers and of rural workers showed an undeniable growth as independent groups. At the same time, revolutionary political-military organizations were developing, groups that would become part of the FMLN early in the next decade. Throughout the 1970s, the constantly broadening popular movement and the constantly consolidating revolutionary political-military organizations established a close relationship within a common historical framework. Although they were engaged in different patterns of struggle, they shared a vision of a social transformation that they considered essential for the country. If one steps outside the historical context of the time, looking at the formation of the mass fronts of these years can lead to erroneous interpretations concerning the relationship between the revolutionary organizations and the popular movement. I believe that this close relationship reflected a proper course of action at the time. Despite differences over the implementation of a common political project, differences that produced harsh confrontations at times, the relationship was an absolutely necessary one. It permitted reaching the level of development and power required in order to have a decisive impact on the Salvadoran political struggle. This type of relationship culminated in 1980 with the establishment of the FMLN-FDR alliance.

Subsequent years required the creation of another form of relationship among the FMLN, the political parties, and the popular movement. Although each element was differentiated by its specific role, the shared idea of the need for a social transformation produced a joint effort to construct an alternative model for the development of a popular and democratic El Salvador. That shared vision of change endures, even as the common history of struggle now operates under new forms. The independence of the organizations and efforts of the popular movement has constituted an indispensable prerequisite since the middle of the 1980s for the movement to play its specific role.

It would be totally erroneous to characterize the organizations of the Salvadoran popular movement as fronts for the FMLN and thus invalidate their struggles and revindications. Accusations to that effect, which seek an *a priori* justification for repressive actions, simply reflect the fear of the dominant powers in the face of a double challenge. Organizations of the popular movement that shared political positions and ideologies with the Christian Democrats exhibited this same independence of thought and action; they too became the object of accusations and threats, and for the same reason.

With these observations in mind, let me now analyze the status of the popular movement in mid-1991.[7]

The FMLN military offensive of November 1989 and the subsequent government repression forced the popular movement into a temporary retreat, which lasted until April 1990. Following a wave of public sector layoffs (for example, the dismissal of 861 employees of the Ministry of Agriculture and Livestock), the popular movement launched a series of actions oriented toward the search for new lines of struggle and the unification of its organizations. Despite having encountered difficulties at the beginning of the year, on February 22, 1990, UNTS celebrated its fourth anniversary by presenting a proposal for the pacification of the country based on the demilitarization of Salvadoran society. Days before, on the fifteenth, the Asociación Democrática Campesina (ADC—Democratic Peasant Association) was founded. The group included the principal peasant organizations: UCS, FESACORA, ANTA, ACOPAI, Cooperativea 'El Espino,' COACES, FENACOA, SITAS, ANCE, FEDECOOPADES, CCS, and ASID. Its purpose was to fight for agrarian democratization, to facilitate the obtaining of credit, and to continue the development of cooperatives.

In mid-1990, the Frente Magisterial Salvadoreño (FMS—Salvadoran Teachers Front) was formed, including among its members ANDES, UNES, ASTC, ADUES, SGEEPES, CODINES, and MMDC. At the same time, the collection of popular movements raised the banner of the struggle against repression. They actively collaborated with the CPDN, which organized a march on September 15 to insist on the demilitarization of Salvadoran society and to demand democracy. The latter months of 1990 demonstrated that the popular movement had begun to regain its power of mobilization, which had been declining since 1987–88; this period marked a moment of observable radicalization and return to older forms of struggle. The government now clearly found it difficult to confront a renewed popular movement.

The following year began with the popular movement adopting positions on the legislative elections of March, while laborers at ASTEL, the state telecommunications enterprise, and members of the FMS conducted work stoppages. Immediately after the elections, employees belonging to AGEMHA at the Ministry of Finance went on strike, leading to the military takeover of this government institution. In April, there was an intense mobilization of the workforce; most notable were the conflicts involving the construction sector (COGEFAR), municipal employees (AMTRAM), public banking (SITRABHIP), the Ministry of Agriculture and Livestock (ANTMAG), and the private sector (SALVAMEX and FOREMOST). During the preceding month, the Unión Nacional de Asociaciones de Empleados del Estado, Municipios e Instituciones Autónomas (UNASTEMA—National Union of the Associations of Employees of the State, Municipalities, and Autonomous Institutions) estimated that twenty-five hundred persons had lost their jobs due to privatization. As part of its economic program, the government proceeded in May 1991 to privatize INCAFE, the Institute of Housing and Urbanization, and the state bank. The effects of the economic liberalization were soon apparent; indicators showed that employment levels among the economically active population in the informal urban sector rose from 32.5 percent in 1988 to 52.4 percent in 1990.

But the most notable aspect of the popular movement's struggles in 1991 were the rural land occupations led by ANTA, the ANC, the ADC, and CONFRAS. Of the forty-nine that occurred between February and June, seventeen were in the western and middle zones of the country. The actions were similar to those of the 1970s, although they were fewer in number and somewhat different in nature. They led to sharp tensions between the government and the army on the one hand and the popular movement on the other. Meanwhile, threats of violent eviction by the ultra-rightists became ever more frequent. However, the organizations of rural workers had attained a level of power and legitimacy that forced the government to reach a pact with the popular movement, which was formalized in the agreement signed on July 3, 1991, between the popular movement and the ministers of agriculture and defense. Data published by the ADC indicate that forty-three rural properties were at issue, totaling an extension of 17,276 *manzanas* and affecting 2,782 families.[8] In the urban arena, events occurred differently; on June 30, the army ejected the people who had taken over land in the colonia San Luis in San Salvador.

Given the importance of the cooperative sector within the present Salvadoran popular movement, I shall give some data on its development and composition.[9] In 1979, there were 526 cooperatives, incorporating 19,896 founding members. In 1989, the number had jumped to 2,021 cooperatives, with 94,812 members; this indirectly implied that 514,321 people (almost 10 percent of the population of the country) were organized within this economic structure. The most important aspect of the movement was the change in the type of cooperatives in operation: in 1979, 48.2 percent were savings and credit organizations; in 1989, 71 percent were production cooperatives. Some 73.7 percent of the latter undertook agricultural and fishing activities.

The cooperatives have had high level of membership for a number of years. The Asociación de Cooperativas de Producción Integradas (ACO-PAI—Association of Integrated Production Cooperatives) was founded in 1978; the Federación de Asociaciones Cooperativas de Producción Agropecuaria de El Salvador (FEDECOPADES—Federation of Associations of Agricultural and Livestock Cooperatives of El Salvador) in 1979; the Federación de Cooperativas de la Reforma Agraria (FESACORA—Federation of Agrarian Reform Cooperatives) in 1982; and the Federación Nacional de Asociaciones Cooperativas Agropecuarias (FENACOA—National Federation of Agricultural and Livestock Cooperative Associations) in 1984. The Confederación de Asociaciones Cooperativas de El Salvador (COACES—Confederation of Cooperative Assocations of El Salvador) was founded in this same year. It included federations of cooperatives involved in savings and loans, transportation, consumption, and agriculture and livestock; it also included the Asociación Nacional Campesina (ANC—National Peasant Association). The Confederación de Federaciones de Cooperativas del Sector Agrario Reformado (CONFRAS—Confederation of Cooperative Federations of the Reformed Agricultural Sector) was organized at the same time.

In short, if one observes the popular movement in general, the complexity of its composition immediately becomes evident. Table 19 lists the social sectors that compose the popular movement, although it does not provide details on the name and number of the organizations within each one of them.

To the panorama of Table 19, one should add specific organizations like the CPDN, and also bear in mind the support that many nongovernmental groups have provided for the popular organizations.

Now I will return to the discussion of some of the key characteristics of the popular movement at the beginning of the 1990s, a movement in a process of continual expansion. In my view, there are two historical periods in the recent development of the Salvadoran popular movement. The first, between 1983 and 1989, was characterized by

Table 19

Social Sectors Composing the Popular Movement

Sector	Types and levels of organization
Peasant workers	Associations and unions (comprehensive)
Cooperatives	Associations, federations, and confederations of cooperatives (sectoral and territorial)
Industrial workers in manufacturing and private services	Unions and federations (by sectors)
Public employees	Unions and associations (by sector and institution)
Teachers	Associations
Students	Associations
Communal groups (includes those injured in natural disasters)	Community councils and associations of development and communal improvement (territorial and sectoral)
Those repopulated and displaced by war	Associations (territorial)
Others (human rights, political prisoners, Christian base communities, etc.)	Associations

irregular growth and a constant search for new forms of organization and struggle; the second continues onward from 1990. The military offensive launched by the FMLN in November 1989 forms the dividing line between the two phases. Since the second period has just started, it is difficult to establish its characteristics, although I will try to do so with the support of Table 20.

A slowdown of the rhythm of growth can be observed within sectors and organizations of the popular movement in 1990 and 1991. Since it seems that almost all popular social sectors are now included in the popular movement, future growth will thus depend to a great extent upon successfully incorporating larger numbers of people. The profound economic and social transformations resulting from more than a decade of war and the medium-term effects of ARENA's plan for restructuring the economy will bring forward new social elements. They, too, will have to be incorporated into the popular movement, accentuating its structural heterogeneity even more.

The analysis must also consider the thesis of those who contend that the international division of labor is currently being restructured

Table 20
The Development of the Salvadoran Popular Movement

Characteristics	1968–80	1983–89	1990–91
1. Growth	Incorporation of new sectors	Continuation of the preceding	Continuation of the preceding at a slower pace
2. Composition	Increase of heterogeneity	Deepening of heterogeneity	Continuation of the preceding
3. Forms of organization and struggle	Creation of fundamental illegal forms with mass participation and a lessening of mass participation	Development of legal forms with scarce resources, of illegal forms, but with social legitimacy	Within the preceding, the use of illegal forms reoccurs
4. Revindicative platforms	Specific revindications within an ascription to universal programs or projects of the political parties of revolutionary organizations	Specific revindications and incorporation of universal revindications (e.g., the negotiated solution of the war), in relation to the changing political programs, especially that of the FMLN	Specific and universal revindications within a new vision of participation in the formation of society
5. Relations with political parties and revolutionary organizations	Pronounced, though not absolute, dependency	Changing relation between dependency and autonomy	Growing autonomy within a shared political option

at a global level. Such a position holds that the reserve army of labor is located largely in peripheral countries.[10] At the same time, deregulation and informalization of productive activities within those countries has created the illusion that workers can assume control of their economic tasks. Societies like El Salvador face a growing structural heterogeneity of their working classes. This phenomenon will ultimately exercise a significant impact on the composition of the popular movement, its perceptions, and its political behavior.[11]

The specific forms of organization and struggle of the Salvadoran— popular movement will probably exhibit contradictory tendencies— between the legal and the illegal, the old and the new, massive growth and selective sectoral growth. Necessarily, the tension between the legal and the illegal will continue for a long time. It must be borne in mind that the initial phases of democratization of the political system in the country have just started; for this reason, the popular movement will have to endure different types of defamatory accusations and repressive actions. It is necessary, therefore, to insist that the limitations of democracy within El Salvador will oblige the popular movement to use certain forms of illegal action, including a dose of violence in some cases. The land occupations by peasants and rural workers during 1991 must be understood in this context.

But perhaps an even more important challenge for the popular movement, in terms of organization, will be the choice that it will have to make between deepening the movement or expanding it. One of these two options, without excluding the other, must receive priority. The earlier evolution outlined in Table 21 shows a tendency toward a growing amplification of the popular movement through the incorporation of new social sectors. Although the richness of this process must be maintained, it must be complemented, in turn, by an intensification of the work of each sector already incorporated into the struggle. The proper combination of both of these processes can help to pave the way for consolidating the broad base that has just begun to be built.

A twofold shift in direction has taken place during the last few years in the revindications of the popular movement. The first is a trend from specific revindications by each sector toward more comprehensive ones. I consider this a transcending change, vital as a defense against the atomization of popular revindications; political factions from the dominant classes would like to push the movement toward fragmentation under the guises of decentralization and the reinforcement of grassroots organizations. (At times, the work of certain nongovernmental groups has unwittingly contributed to this process). Decentralization is important, of course, but it only contributes to the construction of democracy if it occurs within a process of genuine social and economic democratization. Decentralization must also be supported by expressions of local power; these are not limited to local governments, but include other actions arising from distinct local groups. As I have pointed out elsewhere, launching broad, universal revindications that transcend sectoral interests can avoid the atomization of popular revindications without opposing the necessary autonomy of each social sector within the whole popular movement.[12]

The second change has been a shift from supporting the programs or projects of political parties or revolutionary organizations (e.g., the project of the Christian Democratic Party, or the platform of the FMLN-FDR in the early 1980s) to emphasizing the need for the popular movement to take part in the process of building a model of alternative social development for El Salvador. In other words, the popular movement wants to participate actively in transforming the structures of Salvadoran society. This second shift, which I consider fundamental, implies a radical change in the role of the popular movement in the process of social transformation, thus posing numerous unknowns and challenges. I stress that this path offers the opportunity to break with the reform/revolution dichotomy that has produced negative consequences for the struggles of popular movements all over the world throughout the twentieth century. This shift implies a wholly new relationship among the popular movement, the political parties, and the revolutionary organizations.

The popular movement has, in fact, turned away from its accentuated dependency of the 1970s on different political parties (from the rightist PNC to the leftist PCS). During the 1980s, it developed an evolving relationship of dependence and autonomy. Ultimately, in the early 1990s, the forms of organization and struggle of the popular movement have established a growing autonomy from the political parties and the FMLN. Naturally, there remains a shared option in favor of one or another project for the social development of El Salvador. This evolution is crucial for comprehending the current relationship between the popular movement and the FMLN. I shall take a moment here to refute the simplistic allegations that have labeled the popular organizations as no more than fronts for the FMLN.

As mentioned earlier, the history of the popular movement and the Salvadoran revolutionary organizations have innumerable aspects in common, reflected in their shared vision of the structural changes essential for forging a society that is truly democratic and popular. This common history has led to the frequent accusation that the popular movement simply uses the same forms of struggle as the revolutionary organizations. However, a look at the actions that they have undertaken during recent years reveals the specific qualities of each without denying their mutual influences, support, and protection. But for the strength of arms of the FMLN, repression might well have destroyed the popular organizations as it did in earlier decades, foreclosing their conquest of the still incipient democratic spaces in El Salvador.

On the other hand, the FMLN guerrilla forces would not have been able to resist and develop without the support they received from the broad popular masses.

This dynamic has consequently developed a double challenge—to the highly repressive political system of domination that has persisted for the last sixty years in El Salvador, and to the structure of economic exploitation that has produced the enormous inequality for which the country is noted. This double challenge and the relationship between the popular movement and the FMLN—characterized by the growing autonomy of the former with regard to the latter—constitute keys for future Salvadoran political development. The connection between the popular movement and the FMLN can impede the atomization and fragmentation of popular revindications and thus permit their articulation within the struggle for the construction of a new model of development.

The End of a Long Effort: The Negotiated Political Solution to the War

The negotiations that led to the signing of the Peace Accord on January 16, 1992, have a stormy history that spans all of the previous decade. A detailed study of this process must await the future. Of its many features, I will emphasize but one: the role of the process as a space where the correlation of political forces could find expression and where the highest decisions could be made, ultimately modifying El Salvador's current institutional framework of classical liberalism and extending democracy within the country.

I will begin with a brief outline of the negotiating process. Three distinct phases involving the forces and their correlations can be identified: May 1981 to October 1984, when the FMLN-FDR took the initiative for negotiations; October 1984 to October 1987, when the Christian Democratic government of Duarte took the initiative, although the FMLN-FDR maintained an active participation; and February 1989 to January 1992, when the negotiating process accelerated, with the principal actors being the FMLN and the ARENA government, the latter under the leadership of Alfredo Cristiani after mid-1989.

I will describe the main events of these three phases in detail, proposing interpretations that will help to explain their origins, their limitations, and their culmination at the end of the third phase.[13]

First Phase

1981   On May 22, the Political-Diplomatic Commission of the FMLN-FDR proposed dialogue for the first time as a way to find a political solution to the armed conflict. The government rejected this proposal.

On October 4, the Coordinator of the Government Junta of Nicaragua, Daniel Ortega, brought the FMLN-FDR's formulation for peace talks before the General Assembly of the United Nations.

1982   On October 26, the FMLN-FDR proposed a plan for dialogue to the government, the Legislative Assembly, and the armed forces in order to explore the possibility for a negotiated solution.

1983   On July 18, a "Peace Commission" created by the government of Alvaro Magaña agreed to a confer with the representatives of the guerrilla forces; a meeting took place in Bogotá on August 29.

1984   On January 31, the FMLN-FDR proposed a national dialogue for the consolidation of a "Provisional Government of Broad Participation" that would take charge of creating the conditions for a solution to the war.

On May 18, the FMLN-FDR sent this proposal to president-elect Duarte.

Up to this point, the initiative belonged to the FMLN-FDR. Since their creation in the 1970s, the Salvadoran revolutionary forces principally conceived of military actions as tactics imposed by the totally repressive model of government that had existed since the beginning of the 1930s. Military efforts constituted only a means of support for the political struggle. This political understanding of the war clearly distinguished the FMLN from other Latin American guerrilla organizations.[14] The revolutionary forces did take the position that elections, even if they were not fraudulent, were not the appropriate mechanism for ending the war and bringing about the structural changes that the country required. Other forces of the democratic Left, the Social Democrats and the Social Christians, shared this view.

This position was not the product of any political or military weakness of the FMLN-FDR, as the government, the right-wing parties, and the Reagan administration thought. This erroneous assumption led them to believe they could defeat the revolutionary forces militarily and isolate them politically. All to the contrary—remember that these were the years that witnessed an impressive military strengthening of the FMLN, resulting in an expansion and consolidation of the rural fronts of the war. Recognition of this reality developed abroad, starting with the Franco-Mexican declaration of May 22, 1981, that recognized the FMLN-FDR as a "political representative force" of the Salvadoran people. This declaration afforded the necessary political cover for the FMLN-FDR to move forward with its diplomatic actions. A little more than a year later, on July 31, 1983, Richard Stone, the U.S. special ambassador for Central America, met with a member of the FDR in Bogotá. This event, mediated by the Colombian president, marked the beginning of the recognition of the new Salvadoran reality by the United States. On August 30, Stone met with Guillermo Ungo, the coordinator of the Political Diplomatic Commission of the FMLN-FDR, in San José, Costa Rica.

During this first phase, the conditions for carrying on negotiations did not exist. Nevertheless, the initiatives of the FMLN-FDR have demonstrated their enormous value today; they ultimately resulted in the political recognition of these organizations and in the introduction of a negotiated solution to the war into the political debate in El Salvador. From his own perspective, Duarte took over this initiative in October 1984, thus setting the second phase in motion.

Second Phase

1984   On October 8, in a speech before the General Assembly of the United Nations, President Duarte invited the FMLN-FDR to participate in a dialogue on October 15 in La Palma, Chalatenango.

On October 15, with mediation by the church, the La Palma talks take place, committing each side to studying the formulations of the other in order to achieve peace and to humanize the war.

On November 30, in Ayagualo, near San Salvador, a second meeting was held between the FMLN-FDR and the Christian Democratic government; the FDR presented a "Plan Global" for a political solution to the conflict and the institution of democracy. The government called on the FMLN to lay down its arms and incorporate itself within the national political life. At the suggestion of the government, a "Special Commission" to negotiate the peace was created.

1987   On October 4 and 5, a third meeting was held in the Catholic nunciature in El Salvador; no agreement was reached.

During this second phase, there were several substantive changes. The Salvadoran government and a sector of the U.S. administration began to acknowledge the representative validity and political legitimacy of the FMLN-FDR and the impossibility of achieving a military victory in the war. However, the armed forces and the political parties of the Right refused to recognize these realities and continued blocking the negotiation process.

Nevertheless, the consciousness that the idea of a military solution was untenable grew. The political transformations within the dominant classes led to the political reconstruction of the Salvadoran bourgeoisie as a class and to the confirmation of ARENA as its authentic organic party. The forces of ARENA then won control of the government, first through obtaining a majority in the Legislative Assembly and later by electing Alfredo Cristiani to the presidency of the republic. Cristiani represented the most modern and politically mature sector of the dominant classes. These factors permitted a drastic shift of the perceptions and positions of the bourgeoisie toward negotiations. Here I reiterate that the Christian Democratic Party has never directly represented the dominant classes in El Salvador, although it did defend their interests. The bourgeoisie, however, has always viewed the Christian Democrats as embodying a populist slant and statist, Communist tendencies thought to threaten the interests of free enterprise.

At the same time, one could perceive a growing development of the political conceptions of the FMLN and a precise understanding of the changes taking place in the world situation. It should not be forgotten that the revolutionary forces emerged and developed with a high degree of economic independence and ideological autonomy from the international Communist movement. Their tactical, strategic, and programmatic formulations possessed a deep national content due to their relationship with the Salvadoran working masses. Other political parties also perceived the changes under way and began to incorporate themselves into the negotiation process through a new organizational space: the *interpartidaria,* or "interparty group". Members of this new organization included Social Democrats, Social Christians, and the Unión Democrática Nacionalista (UDN—Nationalist Democratic Union). Another key player, the United States, did not begin to support negotiation until late 1990, a shift connected to the end of the Cold War and the dissolution of the Socialist bloc.

Third Phase

1989   A meeting is held in Oaxtepec, Mexico, on February 20 and 21 between the FMLN and the interpartidaria in which the FMLN elaborated on its January 23 public proposal. This had called for a postponement of the presidential elections slated for March and for the naming of a provisional president by the Legislative Assembly (in order to permit the incorporation of the FMLN into the electoral process following the negotiation of a cease-fire), as well as for reforms in the constitution and the electoral code. The government rejected the proposal.

Between September 13 and 15, representatives of the new Cristiani government and the FMLN met in Mexico. They agreed to reopen negotiations and invited the secretary general of the United Nations to send a representative to serve as a "witness."

On October 16 and 17, the second meeting of this phase occurred in San José, Costa Rica, with the participation of the United Nations.

1990   On April 4, a framework agreement was signed in Geneva that delineated the steps to be taken in the negotiation and in which the participants committed themselves to not abandon the talks unilaterally.

On May 21, the FMLN and the government agreed in Caracas on an agenda and a schedule, which included the issues of the armed forces, human rights, the judicial and electoral systems, constitutional reform, social and economic problems, U.N. verification, and guarantees for incorporating the FMLN into national political life.

On July 26, in San José, Costa Rica, the FMLN and the government signed an accord on human rights, to be verified by the United Nations in El Salvador and taking effect immediately.

1991   In April, an agreement was reached in Mexico on several important constitutional reforms dealing with the armed forces, the judicial system, the electoral system, and human rights; the Legislative Assembly approved the agreement on April 30.

Between September 16 and the twenty-fifth, in New York, with the direct mediation of the Secretary General of the United Nations, a "condensed agenda" was agreed upon in order to accelerate the process of negotiations.

On November 16, the guerrilla forces declared an indefinite cease-fire during a meeting in Mexico.

In December, uninterrupted negotiations took place in San Miguel Allende, Mexico, and in New York. President Alfredo Cristiani attended the New York negotiations, where the most controversial issues were discussed: the reduction and purging of the armed forces, the creation of a new civilian police, and the demobilization of the FMLN. Agreements were made that were to be signed in Mexico on January 16, 1992; the cease-fire was set for February 1, 1992.

During the part of the third phase beginning in 1990, one finds agreements clearly revealing that the negotiation table—along with parallel processes like the interpartidaria and its discussions with the FMLN—were the spaces in which the real correlation of political forces in El Salvador was demonstrated. Here the decisive agreements were made over issues that generally correspond to legislative, executive, or judicial institutions in a classical liberal democracy. The negotiation process created the agreement on human rights in 1990, and on constitutional changes and the creation of the COPAZ in 1991. An analysis of the significance of the September 1991 New York Accords, which created COPAZ, permits one to understand the role of the negotiations in the construction of democracy in El Salvador.

The Results of Negotiation: Toward an Expansion of Democracy?

The New York Accords, signed in September 1991, transcended the limits of the institutional order that prevailed in the country by making decisions on issues that belonged to the organs of the central government: the structure, function, and doctrine of the Armed Forces; the creation of the national civil police; land ownership; and, principally, the establishment of COPAZ. I do not believe, as many ultrarightists have contended, that the violation of the constitution by the accords amounted to a violent assault upon the country's institutional order and legal norms. To the contrary, I believe that the New York Accords led to an expansion of democracy and its practices in El Salvador, and that they reflected an appropriate response to contemporary historical conditions. The special *concertación* [negotiation and reconciliation—trans.] mechanism established in Nicaragua between the Frente Sandinista de Liberación Nacional (FSLN—Sandinista National Liberation Front) and the government of Violeta Chamorro offers a similar example.[15]

Some have suggested that COPAZ represents the start of a truly democratic and modern institutionality in El Salvador through the transfer of the responsibility for supervision and verification of the peace accords to the broadest representation of civil society.[16] The commission consists of two government representatives (including an official of the armed forces), two FMLN members, and one representative from each of the parties or coalitions in the Legislative Assembly. The archbishopric of San Salvador and a delegate from the United Nations verification team (ONUSAL) participate as observers.

For the first time, the political opposition has within its grasp the opportunity to guarantee its existence and to institutionalize an important and effective share of control over the ruling party. It can thus avoid becoming either an appendage of the governing party or a useless opposition, since the conclusions and recommendations of COPAZ about the execution of the peace accords can be made public and since both the FMLN and the government have committed themselves to the agreements.[17]

An FMLN delegate to COPAZ has described that body as a new type of mechanism, the product of a unique process of political negotiation. It embodies the most pluralistic expression of civil society, making COPAZ a particularly suitable instrument for El Salvador at this time and giving the commission the possibility of exercising a permanent political control over all aspects of the peace accords, including the elimination of military predominance over civil society.[18] At the end of January 1992 COPAZ faced its first test: to reach agreement on an amnesty that would serve as a precondition for the February 1 cease-fire. A heated debate took place between the rightist political parties and the armed forces, on one side, and the FMLN, the centrist and leftist parties, the Catholic Church, and the great majority of the organizations of civil society, on the other. The former wanted a general amnesty. The latter proposed the exclusion of certain crimes of a totally unjustifiable character (the assassination of Monseñor Romero in 1980, the murders of the Jesuits in 1989, the Sumpul River and El Mozote massacres, etc.). This latter view suggested that a pardon might be feasible, but only after the trials of the guilty had been concluded. Although reaching a consensus in the Legislative Assembly initially appeared impossible, one was achieved after a COPAZ meeting in Mexico on January 23 agreed to a general amnesty with exceptions. On the same day, the Legislative Assembly approved this formula by a unanimous vote.

As in Eastern Europe, the demand for democracy in El Salvador has been so profound that the meaning of democracy itself has expanded. It now must be extended beyond matters of parliamentary political democracy and state economic policies to include the democratization of civil society itself.[19] By emphasizing "process," the democratization of civil society can help avoid the excessive formalization of democracy that often results from the tension between "content" and "process."

The theme of the limits of the present process of democratization in El Salvador raises some significant questions. Are the calls for constructing a democratic order in the limited sense of classical liberal democracy related to the requirements of the dominant neo-liberal economic model? If so, are they thus the product of a certain degree of imposition from forces outside the country? Or is the demand for democracy in El Salvador, above all, an achievement of popular struggles? The answer contains elements of both approaches. On the one hand, the spread of democracy throughout the world is clearly related to the needs of the new international division of labor to transnationalize the markets of additional areas; on the other hand, the reestablishment and expansion of democratic regimes permit the construction of political space for alternative projects. Popular struggles have made possible the emergence of genuinely liberating projects with the potential to transform the existing conditions of economy and society.

All liberal democratic regimes have exhibited certain uniform features—the individual election of representatives, a search for consensus, the formal equality of political rights among the citizenry, and so on. Yet there is no truly universal pattern of democracy. The model of classical liberal democracy, as a political expression of capitalism, has had to adapt to the individual traits of each country and to combine with different forms of economic and social organization. It does not constitute a universal, permanent model. The unending process of historical transformation has produced other models, and it will continue to do so.

As indispensable as a discussion at a strictly conceptual level might be, I prefer to analyze the democratic practices that have developed in El Salvador in the 1980s, the construction of new spaces and organizational forms suggesting a particular form of democracy that can transcend the traditional liberal model. The situation in El Salvador is hardly one of perfecting an existing democratic system. Such a position offers only a static vision that reduces democracy to an effort to achieve its classical liberal form.

This model limits democracy to the political-institutional sphere— it lacks an integrated social dimension. It rests upon the foundations of an existing value system that guides the organization of the economy and society. It gives precedence to the will of the majority, expressed almost exclusively through elections, over negotiated solutions in matters of conflict and consensus building. It avoids negotiation in favor of the imposition of majority will, in spite of the fact that democracy implies rules (not all of which are necessarily norms that one is obligated to obey) for resolving conflicts within society without resorting to force.[20] This model privileges representation over participation.[21]

I must carry my criticism of this liberal model of democracy further. It is useful to observe the relationship between subjectivity and citizenship, on the one hand; emancipation and regulation, on the other; and the connections between the two.[22] In traditional liberal theory, the principle of *citizenship* refers exclusively to civil and political citizenship; its exercise resides exclusively in the individual vote. Therefore, the principle of community and the formation of a collective will are given only marginal importance. Civil society is conceived of as a complete unit that lies within the domain of the private sphere.

The principle of *subjectivity* is broader than that of citizenship. It is there that the supposed "equality of the citizenry" collides with the differences implied by the principle of subjectivity. The principle of citizenship fulfills, directly and indirectly, a *regulating* and normative function whose predominance over *emancipation* characterizes the liberal conception of democracy. Within this system of regulation, the market predominates over the state, and both predominate over the community. Obviously, social and political struggles have taken some ground from this classical liberal conception of democracy. The welfare state implied the passage from civic and political citizenship to social citizenship—that is, the conquest of social rights within the relations of work, health, education, housing, and so on—even though this achievement meant integrating the working classes into the capitalist economy. That integration, of course, has heightened regulation to the detriment of emancipation, thus intensifying the tension between subjectivity and citizenship.[23]

I do not think it makes any sense to limit analysis to the existence or nonexistence in El Salvador of the classical institutions of liberal Western democracy, such as parliament, electoral processes, or political parties. One must examine the political practices that have developed in the midst of the violent conflict that has defined the country's political struggles during the 1980s. One can thus uncover the central problem of power, since social relations are structured around power, not just around the principle of citizenship or the construction of identity (however important both are). As has been painfully demonstrated by the recent history of the former Socialist bloc countries, the problem of power is not foreign to the principles of subjectivity and emancipation.

Democratic political practices have developed beyond the sphere of the political system. They have exercised an impact on the production and distribution of material and cultural goods and have even modified the symbolic world. They constitute the keys to changing the power relations among the different social classes. Furthermore, they have emerged within a changing national and international economic context. Growing internationalization and interconnectedness, although they must be examined critically, have led humanity over the past decade to discover itself as an indivisible world. This change in consciousness is a product of, among other things, the technological revolution and the globalization of the systems of production, finance, and commercialization. None of this, however, implies the existence of a model of society—and consequently of democracy—capable of being universalized. Nor should it be used to deny the presence of a crisis, not only of distribution and equity but also of values and perspectives, whose most obvious expression is the growing poverty and inequality of opportunity among countries, social classes, and genders.[24] Therefore, democracy must be understood as an ongoing process of construction that assumes specific forms in each concrete case, within a continual movement of expansion and re-creation. Its analysis must go beyond classic liberal institutionalism.

Let me return to the principles of regulation, emancipation, subjectivity, and citizenship to which I referred previously. From the point of view of emancipation, it is possible to think of new forms of citizenship—collective and not individual—that derive to a greater extent from forms of participation within a more balanced relationship with subjectivity than from the normative criteria of rights and responsibilities.[25] Renewing democracy implies a new theory that permits the reconstruction of the concepts of citizenship, subjecthood, and emancipation. Within this new theory would also lie a new vision of representative and participatory democracy and of politics and its practices.[26]

I will add here a few ideas about the process of democratization and the construction of an alternative model of development, a problematic corresponding to the Forum of Economic and Social Cooperation created by the New York Accords. First, one may consider the question of how the distribution of national wealth can be democratized. Arguments about property have oscillated between those who postulate state property and absolute collectivism and those who defend the unrestricted market. History has shown not only the error but the inviability of both positions, but it has also shown that it is insufficient to talk of a mixed economy in general terms. It is not enough simply to establish different forms of property; a real democratization of production and the distribution of wealth demands a popular participation in all the key mechanisms and circuits that govern the economy. The relations between the macro- and microeconomic levels, the regulated and the unregulated, the public and the private, the national and the international factors bearing on the country's development— all of these are central issues that must be discussed in order to define the state's just role in regulation and redistribution, and to avoid leaving civil society with the task of simply managing today's unequal distribution of wealth.

Second, although the themes of citizenship and citizen rights have predominated in political debate in the last few years, and have an undeniable validity and legitimacy, the basic question of justice has frequently been forgotten. The same thing has happened with the predominance of representation over political participation. A truly democratic political culture must create links between the practices of political society and the practices of civil society. To think about either one of them in isolation only aids in promoting the fragmentation that characterizes the neo-liberal and postmodernist thought in vogue today.[27]

Third, an alternative option must take advantage of the fact that the cultural realm is a less directly problematic area than economics and politics. Nevertheless, it is vital to recognize that there exists little access to the systems of mass communication that, together with the educational apparatus, set the framework for the dominant cultural concepts.[28]

The construction of a popular project, a model of alternative development strongly linked to the process of democratization, must recover the socialist values of justice and equity. It must be conceived of as a permanent process whose key objectives are conquering and building spaces with which to modify the relations of power, and constructing a new form of organization and distribution of political power. An alternative project that aims at resolving the structural causes of economic inequality and injustice and responds to accumulated social and political demands must overcome the historical exploitation of labor, nature, and sovereignty.[29]

The spaces for negotiation, *concertación,* and alliances can have a structural significance if they are inscribed within an overall project. If this project responds to the interests of the popular majorities that have historically been exploited and subordinated, then the creation and consolidation of these negotiation spaces, and the new organizational forms and political practices that negotiation generates will signify an expansion of democracy.

The questions for El Salvador in the 1990s do not involve trying to recover or reconstruct a lost democracy, since democracy never existed. We are trying to *build* a democratic society through a process of permanent expansion of democracy. In this effort, new political practices, spaces, and organizations are fundamental and must be developed continuously. Negotiation will play a key role. Only in this way will it be possible to overcome the two main obstacles to the democratization of the country: the militarization of the state and society and the unjust distribution of wealth.

Undoubtedly, the long process that culminated in a negotiated political solution to the war in El Salvador bears close relation to changes in the Central American regional context, especially after the signing of the Esquipulas Accords by the region's presidents in 1987. One could say that, even before the end of Cold War bipolarity and the collapse of the regimes of "real socialism," internal Central American political factors had already given a strong push to the negotiating process in El Salvador.

Central American processes have a historic foundation that I cannot develop here adequately. It extends from the common colonial and postindependence past to the creation of the Central American Common Market in the 1960s. In the course of their historical development, the countries of the region forged multiple, sometimes contradictory links among themselves. By the end of the 1980s, the persistence of the Salvadoran conflict had become an obstacle to the development of the rest of the region. Despite the political and ideological discrepancies among them, the Central American countries agreed that this obstacle had to be removed.

Since the economies of these countries are extremely small and weak, any option for growth and development must rest on close collaboration among them, no matter whether economic policies are derived from a neo-liberal orientation or some other option. An important recent work on the future of Central America states that the development of each of the countries in the 1990s will be affected by the regional situation as much as by the international climate.[30] Without peace, there will be few opportunities for development at the regional level, since plans for investment and public spending would continue to be determined by the demands of a war economy.

Referring to the postwar reconstruction in Central America, another source points to the multiple relations between countries in the region.[31] In contrast to the Marshall Plan, intended to reinforce an existing peace accord in Europe after World War II, plans for reconstruction in Central America must contribute to the achievement of peace. In the Salvadoran case, it is possible to say that the Plan of National Reconstruction must go even beyond this aim and become an instrument for the expansion of El Salvador's incipient democracy.

Epilogue: Reviewing
the Initial Formulations

A central thesis runs through the first five chapters of this book, written near the end of 1989. Posed in the first chapter in a discussion of the thought of Ignacio Ellacuría, the thesis argues that the political period opened in 1979 could only conclude with either the victory or the strategic defeat of the FMLN. The fact is, however, that the Chapultepec Peace Accords, signed in the first days of 1992 by the FMLN and the ARENA government, closed this political period without either the victory or strategic defeat of the revolutionary forces. A new historical period of unpredictable characteristics has begun. Does this imply that my central thesis was false? I think it does. The richness of El Salvador's reality and the complexity of its historical evolution suggest the danger of broaching conclusions that are too sharply defined. I have had to rethink some of my ideas. Yet, the events of the last two years have, on the whole, confirmed some of my other positions, especially those concerned with the political recomposition of the dominant classes and the transformations in the thought and political action of the FMLN.[1]

I wrote this epilogue in 1992, three months after the signing of the peace accords, seeking to revise the initial assertions of the book in light of the processes generated by the accords and the Plan of National Reconstruction. Without attempting an exhaustive analysis of either, I focus on the questions and the potentialities that these processes contain.

When I discussed the modifications that the war had introduced within the official armed forces, I did not explore one question that has proven to be as essential as the transformations in the military's structure and functioning. The war contributed to a new mentality within the officer corps by altering the two basic functions that the armed forces had performed since 1931: the military no longer occupied political office, and its repressive police control of the population turned into carrying out daily combat functions during the 1980s.

This new mentality is evident among the majority of the officers; it has unknown aspects that will influence the future behavior of the armed forces. Signs of these changes appear in two recent newspaper articles written by key representatives of the high command. Even before the signing of the Peace Accords, the current minister of defense discussed the relations between the people and the armed forces within the context of the end of the war in El Salvador:

> *Civilians and the military share a common challenge for the consolidation of the democracy: the adoption of new roles within society . . . [and] the subordination of the institution of the military to civilian political power. . . .*
>
> *New relationships will also have to be shaped between the armed forces and the rest of the society. One undeniable concept is that the armed forces have to be preoccupied with what happens in the society as a whole, adding themselves to the common effort to solve society's problems by assuming a guided role appropriate to the task, not a haughty and monopolizing one. . . .*
>
> *The shift in mentality on the part of the armed forces has been given concrete form in their acceptance of and solidarity with the changes that have taken place. The different mentality has materialized in an institutionalized form with the constitutional reforms of last April, . . . [both] specific constitutional reform, and other significant changes like the creation of the national civil police subordinated to the President of the Republic, . . . the creation of a state intelligence service independent of the Armed Forces, . . . and the redefinition of military justice.[2]*

Another high official, chief of staff during several years of the war, linked public security with social problems:

> *The roles and responsibilities in this period of democratic transition are shared. All of us want to live in a democracy, but it is very difficult to promote it and to preserve it on an empty stomach. We have to combat poverty head-on.[3]*

Obviously, these views yield nothing more than a preliminary sketch of the new military mentality formed during the years of war. Nevertheless, they do not represent isolated or individual opinions. They reflect changes whose significance and depth must be analyzed. In an earlier chapter, I discussed the profound demographic and economic changes that have taken place in El Salvador. I emphasized the role of U.S. assistance, the remittances in dollars from Salvadorans living abroad (especially those in the United States), and the limitations of the economic plan of the ARENA government that assumed executive power in June 1989. After 1990, in El Salvador as in other Latin American countries, changes were begun at the level of microeconomic policy directed at satisfying the new tendencies toward export. During 1990, relative stabilization was achieved, and a process of recuperation developed. As indicated in Table 21, there was an increase of the gross domestic product of 3.4 percent; this was the highest gain in twelve years and a dramatic contrast with 1980, when the GDP decreased by 8.7 percent. However, as in other countries, the beginning of this process of adjustment has been accompanied by a deterioration in the living conditions of the lowest income sectors, as is shown by the consumer price index, which rose 24 percent in 1990.[4] An analysis carried out during the third trimester of 1991 (see Table 22) indicated that the economic recovery begun in 1990 was continuing to accelerate on the basis of a broader foundation as sectors of the construction industry and small and microbusinesses became incorporated into it.[5]

Table 21
Evolution of Some Recent Economic Indicators

Indicator	1988	1989	1990
GDP[a]	1.62%	1.05%	3.4%
Total exports[b]	608.8	497.5	580.2
Nontraditional exports[b]	215.3	244.7	285.4
Balance of trade[b]	−398.1	−663.8	−682.2
Balance of payments[b]	−91.2	−32.7	259.9
Price index[c]	19.8	17.6	24.0

Source: Central Reserve Bank of El Salvador.

[a] Constant percent.

[b] Millions of U.S. dollars.

[c] Average annual variation. Base: 1978 = 100.

Table 22

**Some Economic Indicators of the Current Conjuncture:
Variation between the Second Trimester 1990 and the
Second Trimester 1991**

Current Economic Indicators	Percent Variation (Second Trimesters 1990 and 1991)
Sales of comestibles	+ 14.0
Electric energy production	+ 5.1
Cement production	+ 10.3
Cement consumption	+ 12.3
Creation of new firms	+ 46.5
Import of consumer goods	+ 26.9
Import of capital goods	+ 66.9
Export of nontraditional products	+ 4.5
Credit granted to private sector	+ 3.8

Source: FUSADES, "Informe trimestral de coyuntura" (San Salvador, 1991).

The dominant classes ultimately inclined toward finding a negotiated solution to the war under the undoubted influence of the climate of stabilization, the start of economic reactivation, and the signs that continued improvement in the economy required the removal of the obstacle of the war (along with other factors that I have already mentioned). As noted in Chapter 4, the Salvadoran bourgeoisie had sustained a transformation in its political thought that permitted its reconstitution as a political class. A recent work on ARENA by a researcher from the United States confirms this process.[6]

The investigation revealed that over the course of ARENA's ten-year existence there has been a promotion to leadership positions of a group of modern business people, both male and female. Their economic interests lie more in industry and commerce than in agriculture; they are oriented more toward international than internal markets; and they tend to advocate a decrease in the level of state economic intervention. As a result, these relative newcomers are more inclined to be flexible in their political views. In addition, engaging in debate with leftist representatives in the Legislative Assembly has heightened their consciousness of the costs and benefits of the war, orienting them toward the search for a negotiated solution. The more conservative forces who would like to return to the original intransigent positions of ARENA, and those who support the reemergence of the death squads, do not have the capacity to dominate the party. They are now one of four minority tendencies within ARENA.

Remember that the political inexperience of the Salvadoran bourgeoisie over the course of fifty years gave its position at the beginning of the 1980s a highly confrontational character. Cooperative attitudes only surfaced after it became clear that a military defeat of the FMLN was not possible. This realization first developed at the local rather than at the overall political level, which undoubtedly had an impact on the change in political mentality of many ARENA members. (Interesting examples for study exist in the *micro-concertaciones* that took place in areas under the influence or control of the FMLN.)

Finally, one should bear in mind that ARENA's strength lies in its unity; any tendency that attempts to separate itself from the party by disagreeing with the pragmatic orientation of its present leaders has no hope of growing in the current Salvadoran political space, especially as the decisive general elections of March 1994 are drawing near. This same modernization of the bourgeoisie as a political class has caused it to assume positions against the constitution of the military as an economic group with possibilities of unlimited accumulation. Another issue that will be key to the construction of democracy in El Salvador arises here: not only is it essential to establish a new relationship between the civilians and the military, in which the latter are subject to the political power of the former; there must also be a revamping of the traditional relationship between the military and the bourgeoisie, one whose characteristics remain to be seen.

President Cristiani in his Chapultepec address during the signing of the Peace Accords best summarized this change of mentality within the dominant classes:

> *What is now beginning to happen in El Salvador is not the reestablishment of an existing peace, but the inauguration of an authentic peace based on social consensus . . . and the conception of the country as a whole without exclusions. . . .*
>
> *. . . The crisis in which the Salvadoran nation has been enmeshed during the past decade did not arise out of nothing nor was it the product of isolated wills. This extremely painful and tragic crisis has ancient and profound social, political, economic, and cultural roots. . . .*

> ... *[T]o the FMLN we say with respectful conviction that its contribution is needed for the development within El Salvador of a stable and consistent democracy; in the new stage that we have begun, we are sure that all of the political and social forces can work together.*[7]

With reference to the FMLN, in Chapter 5 I discussed the evolution of its thought and programmatic formulations, an evolution in which its disengagement from dogmatism, its capacity for perceiving change within the national reality, and its creativity are constants that have been reaffirmed during the months following the signing of the peace accords. Although there is no single, completely worked-out formulation of FMLN views, I can point out some important elements. In the first place, there is an accurate understanding of the revolutionaries' influence and role within the range of political forces in the country. This makes respect for the specific conditions and actions of other political forces possible. Second, the FMLN has made a decision—not in an explicit fashion, but evident nonetheless—to respect the development and the positions of each of its five component organizations. This is not a matter of creating a single party, an approach whose negative consequences history has demonstrated in other countries, but one of converting the FMLN into a "party-front," deeply anchored in the popular sectors but respectful of their individual organizational forms. One example of the new way in which the revolutionary organizations do politics was the first assembly of party cadres to be held since the signing of the Chapultepec Accords. The ERP organized this meeting, held in the Department of Morazán in eastern El Salvador on March 23, 1992. The assembly produced a communiqué whose title indicates its content: "The peace of the rich is over; the people's war has begun, 1972.—The people's war has ended; the peace of all Salvadorans has been won, 1992."

Some 155 militants participated in this assembly, among them military leaders, political organizers, cadres in financial, medical, and communications work, and overseas representatives. Women composed 27 percent of the assembly. Its conclusions were of great significance, especially the defense of the accords, the commitment to reconciliation with all political sectors in the country, and the reaffirmation of the FMLN as the historical representative of the Salvadoran revolutionaries. The statements of intent following constitute a new political example for the Left of many Latin American countries.

> *To correct all of the defects and errors that the internal demo-*
> *cratic functioning of our ogranization suffers from as a conse-*
> *quence of being at war.*
>
> *To prompt the democratization of the entire FMLN in order*
> *to convert it into a democratic party whose internal tendencies*
> *will debate and create positions that derive from its community*
> *purposes and ideological definition. To this end to introduce, in*
> *the future, the principles of rotation in office and secret ballot-*
> *ing for leadership positions.*
>
> *To align ourselves ideologically with Democratic Socialism in*
> *a way based on our own Salvadoran reality. This implies fight-*
> *ing to extend and strengthen the social property of the workers,*
> *understanding it to be a type of property which is independent*
> *of the State.*[8]

Obviously, this last statement will be the subject of an extensive discussion within the FMLN. It is not necessarily supported by all. Will
this lead to a split among the revolutionaries? I think not. Paradoxically, for both the FMLN and ARENA, the possibility of launching
their respective projects is founded on the preservation of unity, in
spite of the internal contradictions and the tendencies within the ranks
of each. This feature of Salvadoran political development will have a
great impact on the country's future.

The peace accords are framed within this changing context. Their
implementation, however, is not guaranteed. Already, two problems
have arisen and caused a suspension of the timetable agreed upon. The
first is the resistance of the government armed forces to the effective
dissolution of the principal bodies in charge of the repressive police
control of the population, the National Guard and the Treasury Police. The second is the opposition of powerful elements within the Salvadoran business sector to solving the problems of rural land ownership in the zones of greatest conflict during the war. These areas make
up the social base for the FMLN. The controversy that has developed
over these two questions (as well as lesser ones) darkens the optimistic
environment generated by the signing of the accords.

At the root of these two central disagreements lie issues that go, at
times, beyond the political will of the signatories of the Chapultepec
Accords. I suggest the following hypothesis that would partially explain these discrepancies. I think that the extreme rightist groups
within ARENA and the armed forces that are opposed to the political

solution of the war, although in the minority, have the capacity to destabilize the Cristiani government and to continue placing obstacles in the way of the process of implementing the accords. This would explain the continual emergence of problems that have hindered the execution of the accords. Although they are not serious enough to subvert the peace plan, overcoming these problems will require a high degree of patience. External influences and pressures, not in the form of intervention but rather in collaboration, could be decisive in promoting the creation of a consensus.

Like the Chapultepec Accords, the establishment of a coordinated Plan of National Reconstruction (PRN) has been subject to multiple pressures of different kinds. The PRN has evolved considerably between the first version issued unilaterally by the Ministry of Planning in October 1991 (a sign that the Cristiani government was definitely inclined toward the idea of a negotiated political solution to the war) and the fifth version, agreed upon by the FMLN and the government and presented to the World Bank in late March 1992.

The historical changes in the Plan of National Reconstruction are significant. The first version gave preference to reconstructing the energy system and the rest of the infrastructure damaged by the war, while investment in social programs clearly had secondary importance. In the fifth version, the investment assigned to social programs has grown substantially, a shift toward justice for the popular sectors affected by the war, although it is clearly indicated that the PRN does not contemplate the resolution of all the country's economic or social problems.[9] The plan aims to benefit nearly a fifth of the Salvadoran people, who live in a number of critical areas making up almost half of the country's municipalities. Its implementation will be the responsibility of public sector institutions (mainly local governments), private nongovernmental institutions, and community associations. The National Reconstruction Secretariat, an office that reports directly to the president, is in charge of coordinating these groups. The PRN estimates the investment at $1.5 billion, with the first $800 million authorized during the meeting at the World Bank in March.

Without attempting to analyze either the PRN or the mechanisms set up for its implementation, one notes that both will have an impact on the political projects of El Salvador in the postwar period. On the one hand, the ARENA government has declared on various occasions that the PRN will not affect the direction of the national development strategy (of a clearly neo-liberal bent) that the Cristiani government laid out after assuming office in 1989. Moreover, it maintains that the PRN complements its own plan for economic and social development. A quick glance shows that, by its scope and political impact, if the PRN does not definitely alter the direction of the restructuring of the economy and the state, it will at least introduce substantial modifications in the rhythm of the restructuring that is under way. I could also suggest that if ARENA's electoral possibilities for 1994 are seriously affected by what happens within the next few months there may be a freeze in restructuring, except in macroeconomic policies. In other words, the basis exists for the development of new tensions within the dominant bloc.

One example may be the changes that could take place in the program of social compensation, implemented through the Social Investment Fund (FIS). This program has been designed within the social area of the short-term phase of structural reform, together with the Plan of Emergency Urban Community Development and the Construction of Labor-Intensive Community Infrastructure. It has the objective of providing compensation to the population living in poverty because of the effects of structural adjustment, giving attention to the most vulnerable groups and to the stimulation of individual and community participation in the resolution of problems.[10] Intended to operate over four years, the FIS has already been affected by the PRN.

By way of conclusion, I readdress the central idea of this epilogue: the ending of the political era opened in 1979. The richness and complexity of this period has engaged the attention of numerous researchers and political analysts.[11] Such attention is not gratuitous. There is a close connection between analysis of this period and the political practice of the forces that fight for social transformation in El Salvador, a connection that broadens the meaning of works such as this one. Hence, in rethinking the thesis presented at the beginning of this book, I would say that a substantial alteration of the correlation of political and social forces brings on a change of political period. Such an alteration emerges out of a continual process of struggle, from profound transformations that occur in the sectors that make up these forces. While the internal factors are decisive, they do bear some relation to changes in the external context. In this way realignments and new political alliances are made possible, ones that can reorient the development of the economy, the society, and the state. This seems to be what happened in El Salvador in October 1979 and again in January 1992. The dates symbolically frame a political period in Salvadoran history whose characteristics will make it difficult for the country to return to the unjust situation of the past. After an arduous and lengthy war, a new period opens—one charged with doubts and hopes.

Glossary
The Most Important Salvadoran Acronyms

ANDES	Asociación Nacional de Educadores Salvadoreños 29 de Junio/ National Association of Salvadoran Teachers 29th of June.
ANEP	Asociación Nacional de la Empresa Privada/National Association of Private Enterprise.
ARENA	Alianza Republicana Nacionalista/Nationalist Republican Alliance.
BPR	Bloque Popular Revolucionario/Popular Revolutionary Bloc.
CD	Convergencia Democrática/Democratic Convergence.
CONADES	Comisión Nacional de Asistencia a la Población Desplazada/ National Commission for Assistance to the Diplaced.
COPAZ	Comisión para la Consolidación de la Paz/Commission for the Consolidation of Peace.
CPDN	Comité Permanente del Debate Nacional/Permanent Comittee of the National Debate.
CRIPDES	Comité Cristiano para los Desplazados de El Salvador/Christian Committee for the Displaced of El Salvador.
CRM	Coordinadora Revolucionaria de Masas/Revolutionary Coordinator of the Masses.
ERP	Ejército Revolucionario del Pueblo/Revolutionary Army of the People.
FAL	Fuerzas Armadas de Liberación/Armed Forces of Liberation.
FAPU	Frente de Acción Popular Unificada/United Popular Action Front.
FARN	Fuerzas Armadas de Resistencia Nacional/Armed Forces of National Resistencia.
FDR	Frente Democrático Revolucionario/Democratic Revolutionary Front.
FENASTRAS	Federación Nacional Sindical de Trabajadores Salvadoreños/ National Trade Union Federation of Salvadoran Workers.

FMLN	Frente Farabundo Martí para la Liberación Nacional/Farabundo Martí National Liberation Front.
FPL	Fuerzas Populares de Liberación/Popular Liberation Forces.
FUSADES	Fundación Salvadoreña para el Desarrollo Económico y Social/Salvadoran Foundation for Economic and Social Development.
LP-28	Ligas Populares-28 de Febrero/28th of February Popular Leagues.
MLP	Movimiento de Liberación Popular/Popular Liberation Movement.
MNR	Movimiento Nacional Revolucionario/National Revolutionary Movement.
MPSC	Movimiento Popular Social Cristiano/Popular Social Christian Movement.
ORDEN	Organización Democrática Nacionalista/Democratic Nationalist Organization.
PADECOES	Patronato para el Desarrollo Comunal en El Salvador/Council for Community Development of El Salvador.
PCN	Partido de Conciliación Nacional/Party of National Conciliation.
PCS	Partido Comunista de El Salvador/Salvadoran Communist Party.
PDC	Partido Demócrata Cristiano/Christian Democratic Party.
PNC	Policia Nacional Civil/National Civilian Police.
PRS	Partido de la Revolución Salvadoreña/Party of the Salvadoran Revolution.
PRTC	Partido Revolucionario de los Trabajadores Centroamericanos/Revolutionary Party of Central American Workers.
RN	Resistencia Nacional/National Resistance.
UCA	Universidad Centroamericana José Simeón Cañas.
UDN	Unión Democrática Nacionalista/Nationalist Democratic Union.
UNO	Unión Nacional Opositora/National Opposition Union.
UNOC	Unión Nacional Obrera y Campesina/National Workers and Peasants Union.
UNTS	Unión Nacional de Trabajadores Salvadoreños/National Union of Salvadoran Workers.

Notes

CHAPTER 1

1. Ignacio Ellacuría, "Una nueva fase en el proceso salvadoreño," *ECA: Estudios Centroamericanos* (Revista de extensión cultural de la Universidad Centroamericana José Simeón Cañas, San Salvador), 485 (marzo 1989).

CHAPTER 2

1. For example, A. J. Bacevich et al., *American Military Policy in Small Wars: The Case of El Salvador* (Cambridge, Mass.: John F. Kennedy School of Government, Harvard University, March 1988); John D. Waghelstein, "Post Vietnam Counterinsurgency Doctrine," *Military Review* (Fort Leavenworth, Kan.) 65, no.5 (1985).
2. "Esta guerra no tiene una solución militar. Entrevista al colonel Mauricio Vargas," *Pensamiento Propio* (Managua), 51 (junio 1988); Mariano Castro Morán, "Visión político militar de la guerra: Caso El Salvador," *Presencia* (San Salvador), 3 (oct–dic 1988); Adolfo Arnoldo Majano, "Las fuerzas armadas en Centroamérica," *Presencia*, 3 (oct–dic 1988).
3. In his various works on the war of liberation in Vietnam.
4. The outline of these phases can be found in a book based upon the analysis made by the leadership of the FMLN. See Mario Lungo, *El Salvador, 1981–1984: La dimensión política de la guerra* (San Salvador: UCA Editores, 1985).
5. Here my account is based on various analyses and declarations of FMLN leaders. See Joaquín Villalobos, "Acerca de la situación militar en El Salvador," *Cuadernos Políticos* (México), 30 (oct–dic 1981); Comandancia General del FMLN, "Situación revolucionaria y esclada intervencionista en la guerra salvadoreña," *Ediciones Sistema Radio Venceremos* (México), 1984; Joaquín Villalobos, "El estado de la guerra y sus perspectivas," *ECA*, 449 (marzo 1986).
6. Villalobos, "Acerca de la situación militar."
7. Comandancia General del FMLN, "Situación revolucionaria y esclada intervencionista."

8. Villalobos, "Acerca de la situación militar."
9. See Rafael Cabarrús, *Génesis de una revolución* (México: Ediciones de La Casa Chata, 1983); Napoleón Alvarado and Octavio Cruz, "Conciencia y cambio social en la hacienda Tres Ceibas: El Salvador, 1955–1976," Licentiate thesis in sociology, Universidad de Costa Rica, 1978; Walter Guerra, "Las asociaciones comunitarias en el área rural de El Salvador en la década de 1960 a 1970," Licentiate thesis in sociology, Universidad de Costa Rica, 1978.
10. See María López Vigil, *Muerte y vida en Morazán* (San Salvador: UCA Editores, 1987), and, by the same author, *Don lito de El Salvador* (San Salvador: UCA Editores, 1987).
11. See América Rodríquez Herrera, "La canción campesina de contenido político en El Salvador, 1980–1985," master's thesis in sociology, Universidad de Costa Rica, 1988.
12. Ibid.
13. Analysis derived from FMLN reports and from newspapers of the period.
14. Comandancia General del FMLN, "Situación revolucionaria y esclada intervencionista."
15. It is no secret that this question was the subject of serious contradictions within the revolutionary forces well into the 1980s.
16. A good account of the accomplishments in this aspect during the first years of the 1980s can be found in Jenny Pearce, *Promised Land: Peasant Rebellion in Chalatenango, El Salvador* (London: Latin America Bureau, 1986).
17. See Charles Clemens, *Guazapa* (San Salvador: UCA Editores, 1986) (first published as *Witness to War: An American Doctor in El Salvador* [New York: Bantam Books, 1984]), and Francisco Metzi, *Por los Caminos de Chalatenango* (San Salvador: UCA Editores, 1988).
18. Citations taken from Francisco Alvarez, "Poder contra poder: Un proceso irreversible" (San Salvador, March 1989, mimeographed).
19. See Pablo Castro, "Municipios y territorios en transición: Nueva problemática urbana-regional en El Salvador, 1986–1988" (prepared for the Consejo Latinoamericano de Ciencias Sociales [CLACSO], San Salvador, April 1989, mimeographed).
20. See Mario Lungo, "La guerra revolucionaria y los cambios en la estructura regional," *Geoistmo* (San Salvador) 1, no.2 (1987).
21. Villalobos, "Acerca de la situación militar."
22. Comandancia General del FMLN, "Situación revolucionaria y esclada intervencionista."
23. Ibid.
24. Ibid.
25. Villalobos, "El estado de la guerra."
26. In an unpublished assessment made by the Comandancia General del FMLN in July 1985.
27. Villalobos, "El estado de la guerra."
28. Ibid.
29. Joaquín Villalobos, "Perspectivas de victoria y proyecto revolucionario," *ECA*, 483–84 (ene–feb 1989).
30. Villalobos, "Acerca de la situación militar."
31. See Mario Lungo, "Las nuevas Fuerzas Armadas Salvadoreñas, un obstáculo para la democratización," *Nueva Sociedad* (Caracas), 81 (ene–feb 1986).

32. A *tanda* in the Salvadoran armed forces is a group of officers who were promoted at the same time.
33. Comandancia General del FMLN, "Situación revolucionaria y esclada intervencionista."
34. Comandancia General del FMLN, unpublished assessment of July 1985.
35. Villalobos, "El estado de la guerra."
36. Bacevich et al., *American Military Policy.*
37. Comandancia General del FMLN, "Situación revolucionaria y esclada intervencionista."
38. In addition, although this counterinsurgency strategy was envisioned as making up a whole, a congressional mandate for El Salvador required that military aid and development aid be kept separate.
39. Bacevich et al., *American Military Policy.*
40. This does not deny the role of guardian of the interests of the oligarchic power structure. Historically, the military never had access to these interests, either by accumulating capital or establishing family relationships. Insubordination to civil authority was possible because military officials were representatives of the oligarchy. With ARENA's rise to political power, this situation has changed drastically.
41. An interesting analysis of this last point can be found in Ivonne Melgar, "El Salvador, 1986: De las cenizas a los escombros," Licentiate thesis in communication sciences, Facultad de Ciencias Políticas y Sociales, UNAM, México, 1988.
42. Mariano Castro Morán, "Visión político militar de la guerra: Caso El Salvador."
43. "Esta guerra no tiene una solución militar. Entrevista al colonel Mauricio Vargas."
44. Villalobos, "Perspectivas de victoria."
45. Federico Engels, *Revolución y contrarevolución en Alemania* (various eds.; Moscú: Editorial Progreso).
46. Vladimir Lenin, *Las enseñanzas de la insurrección de Moscú* and *El marxismo y la insurrección* (various eds.; Moscú: Editorial Progreso).
47. Pablo Emilio Barreto, *El repliegue de Managua a Masaya* (México: Editorial, Cartago, 1980), and Carlos Nuñez, *Un pueblo en armas* (report of the Frente Interno) (Managua: Secretaría de Prensa y Propaganda del FSLN, 1980).
48. Villalobos, "Acerca de la situación militar."
49. Villalobos, "El estado de la guerra."
50. Comandancia General del FMLN, "Situación revolucionaria y esclada intervencionista."
51. Comandancia General del FMLN, internal document, mid-1985.
52. Villalobos, "Perspectivas de victoria."

CHAPTER 3

1. ECLA, *Estudio económico de América Latina y El Caribe, 1987: El Salvador,* LC/L.463/add.12 (sept 1988).
2. See the report of the Instituto de Investigaciones Económicas (INVE), Universidad de El Salvador, in *Coyuntura Económica,* 23 (ene–feb 1989).

3. There are numerous analyses of this agrarian reform. Many of them are derived from positions that are not necessarily critical—see, for example, Oscar Morales Velado, "La estructura productiva agraria antes y después de la reforma," *Presencia* (San Salvador), 4 (marzo 1989).

4. The *New York Times* published articles on the subject between July 16 and July 22, 1989.

5. ABECAFE, "El fracaso del INCAFE," *La Prensa Gráfica* (San Salvador), sept 21, 1988.

6. Cited in Mauricio Valdés, "Reformismo y guerra: Una evaluación del la nacionalización bancaria en El Salvador," *Cuadernos de Investigación del CSUCA* (San José), 42 (sept 1988).

7. Ibid.

8. Instituto de Investigaciones Económicas, "La ayuda económica y militar de los Estados Unidos," *Conyuntura Económica,* 24 (mar–abr 1989), from which my data and tables are taken.

9. See *El Salvador, 1985: Desplazados y refugiados* and *El Salvador, 1986: Salvadoreños refugiados en Estados Unidos,* the work of Segundo Montes and a team from the Instituto de Investigaciones de la Universidad Centroamericana José Simeón Cañas, published by the university, 1985–87.

10. Segundo Montes, "La situación de los deplazados y refugiados salvadoreños," *ECA,* 434 (dic 1984).

11. Ad hoc group of the Ministerio de Planificación de El Salvador, "La Población desplazada, 1980/87," *Presencia* (San Salvador), 1 (abr–jun 1988).

12. Published in local newspapers on May 22, 1989.

13. An exception to this situation would seem to be the application of the Simpson-Rodino Act, which regulates the stay of persons who enter the United States illegally. Nonetheless, the complex economic situation in El Salvador has made the law ineffective in stemming the flow of illegal immigrants into the United States.

14. Taken from ECLA, *Las remesas, la economía familiar y el papel de la mujer: El caso de El Salvador* (México, sept 1988).

15. Segundo Montes, "Impacto de la migración de salvadoreños a los Estados Unidos: El envío de remesas y consecuencias en la estructura familiar y el papel de la mujer," document prepared for ECLA's Mexico office, July 1988.

16. A preliminary analysis appeared in *Proceso* (Universidad Centroamericana José Simeón Cañas, San Salvador), 391 (julio 5, 1989).

17. *Proceso,* 400 (sept 13, 1989).

18. FUSADES, "Marco institucional para el desarrollo económico (sugerencias de reorganización institucional)," *Boletín Económico y Social* (San Salvador), 43 (mayo–jun 1989).

19. *Proceso,* 403 (oct 4, 1989).

20. FUSADES, *La necesidad de un nuevo model económico para El Salvador* (San Salvador, 1985).

21. For the Salvadoran case, see the article by Luis René Cáceres, "Será El Salvador otra Corea del Sur?" *ECA,* 457–58 (nov–dic 1986).

22. *Proceso,* 401 (sept 20, 1989).

CHAPTER 4

1. See Mario Lungo, "Las elecciones que significarían la paz en El Salvador," *Diálogo Social* (Panamá) (marzo 1985).

2. An analysis of this period can be found in Rafael Guido Véjar, *El ascenso del militarismo en El Salvador* (San Salvador: UCA Editores, 1976).

3. For documented analysis, see Patricia Parkman, *Nonviolent Insurrection in El Salvador: The Fall of Maximiliano Hernández Martínez* (Tucson: University of Arizona Press, 1988). The information that follows is taken from this book, although I do not agree with all of Parkman's evaluations.

4. A polemical contemporary appraisal of the variations of military dictatorship as a form of government can be found in a document of the Comandancia General del FMLN, "El único camino para construir la democracia en El Salvador" (proposal presented in San José on October 16, 1989).

5. Mario Lungo, *La lucha de las masas en El Salvador* (San Salvador: UCA Editores, 1987), chapter 3.

6. See the essay by Jorge Cáceres, "La revolución salvadoreña de 1948: Un estudio sobre el transformismo," in *El Salvador: Una historia sin lecciones,* ed. Jorge Cáceres, Rafael Menjívar, and Rafael Guido Véjar (San José: FLACSO, 1988).

7. For detailed description of the history of the PDC, see Stephen Webre, *José Napoleón Duarte y el partido demócrata cristiano* (San Salvador: UCA Editores, 1985) (first published as *José Napoleón Duarte and the Christian Democratic Party in Salvadoran Politics, 1960–1972* [Baton Rouge: Louisiana State University Press, 1979]).

8. Wim Pelupessy, "El sector agro-exportador de El Salvador, la base económica de una oligarquía no fraccionada," *Boletín de Estudios Latinoamericanos y del Caribe* (CEDLA, Amsterdam), 43 (dic 1987).

9. This process is analyzed in detail in Sara Gordon, *Crisis política y guerra en El Salvador* (México: Siglo XXI Editores, 1989).

10. Sara Gordon, "Las vías de reconstitución del régimen salvadoreño," *Cuadernos de investigación del CSUCA* (San José), 15 (ago 1987).

11. Mario Lungo, *El Salvador, 1981–1984: La dimensión política de la guerra* (San Salvador: UCA Editores, 1985).

12. Enrique Baloyra, *El Salvador en transición* (San Salvador: UCA Editores, 1986). The quotation is from the original, *El Salvador in Transition* (Chapel Hill: University of North Carolina Press, 1982), 33–34.

13. Segundo Montes, *El Salvador: Las fuerzas sociales en la presente coyuntura (enero de 1980 a diciembre de 1983)* (San Salvador: Depto. de Sociología y Ciencias Políticas, UCA, 1984).

14. *Proceso,* 404 (oct 11, 1989).

15. Ministerio de Planificación y Coordinación del Desarrollo Económico y Social, *El Camino hacia la paz: Plan General del gobierno* (San Salvador, 1985).

16. This plan, containing a number of internal inconsistencies that invalidated it from the beginning, was based upon an erroneous evaluation of the country's reality.

17. Segundo Montes, "Las elecciones del 31 marzo," *ECA,* 438 (abr 1985).

18. CINAS, "El Salvador: ¿Es la democracia cristiana un partido de centro?" *Cuaderno de Divulgación* (México), 3 (ago 1987).

19. I have criticized these proposals at length in "Democratización, poder político y crisis del Estado en El Salvador," *Polémica* (San José), 2d ser., 3 (sept–dic 1987).
20. *Proceso*, 377 (mar 29, 1989), and *Proceso*, 378 (abr 5, 1989).
21. Sara Miles and Bob Ostertag, "The Rise of the Reebok Right," in NACLA, *Report on the Americas* 23, no.2 (July 1989).
22. Interview with Alfredo Cristiani, in *Analisis* (Universidad Nueva San Salvador), 1–2 (ene–feb 1988).
23. Expressed in August 1988 at a conference held at the Colegio de Economistas and published in *El Salvador: En construcción* (San Salvador), 4 (abr 1989).
24. One example is the effort devoted to creating the Instituto Centroamericano de Administración de Empresas (INCAE) in association with North American universities. No similar effort in the field of politics and ideology is known, although the work of certain types of private universities (such as the José Matías Delgado) tend to fill this void.
25. Roberto Murray Meza, "Vocación Política, vocación empresarial (entrevista)," *El Salvador: En construcción*, 5 (ago 1989).
26. Héctor Vidal, "La complicada agenda del futuro gobierno," *El Salvador: En construcción*, 4 (abr 1989).
27. Carlos Vásquez, "El Salvador: Burguesía, proyecto revolucionario y reconstrucción nacional" (manuscript, San Salvador, June 1989).
28. One proof of the foregoing is the meeting of Central American presidents in Tela, Honduras, in September 1989. During the same month, the Soviet Union gave official declarations to Costa Rican newspapers saying that the Cristiani government is legitimate since it is the product of the electoral process.

CHAPTER 5

1. Fermán Cienfuegos, *Veredas de audacia: Apuntes para la historia del FMLN* (México and Managua: Ediciones Roque Dalton, 1989).
2. *Ibid.*
3. Fermán Cienfuegos, *En Borrador: Apuntes sobre el movimiento de liberación nacional y la construcción de la república democrática en El Salvador* (San Salvador: Ediciones Roque Dalton, 1989).
4. Among important analyses of the problems of the urban guerrillas are Eleuterio Fernández Huidobro, *Historia de los Tupamaros* (Montevideo: TAE Editorial, 1986), and Mario Palleras, *El trueno en la ciudad* (México: Juan Pablos Editor, 1987). Palleras's work examines the case of Guatemala at the beginning of 1980.
5. See Carlos Rafael Cabarrús, *Génesis de una revolución. Análisis del surgimiento y desarrollo de la organización campesina en El Salvador* (México: Ediciones de la Casa Chata, 1983).
6. Mario Lungo, *El Salvador: Historia del Movimiento Obrero de 1920 a 1977* (México: Anastacio Aquino, 1984).
7. Mélida Anaya Montes, "La gran huelga de ANDES" (San Salvador, 1972, mimeographed).

8. Mario Lungo, *La lucha de las masas en El Salvador* (San Salvador: UCA Editores, 1987).

9. Particularly the struggle against militarism within the ERP, described in its internal documents of 1986.

10. Various Sandinista leaders have recalled their experiences of the splits and reunifications of the FSLN in valuable firsthand accounts.

11. Mario Lungo, "Movimiento popular y movimiento sindical en El Salvador en los años 80," paper delivered to the seminar "El sindicalismo y la crisis centroamericana en la presente década," CEPAS-CLACSO-CEDAL-OIT (San José) (mar 1989).

12. Lungo, *El Salvador: Historia.*

13. I am aware that in this book (and up to this moment in the text) I have merged the workers movement and the union movement, which does not fit the current reality of El Salvador. It must be remembered, however, that during the 1960s, and even in the 1970s, there were no labor unions for state workers or for farm workers.

14. The struggles launched by the Partido Revolucionario Abril y Mayo (PRAM), allied with the clandestine Partido Comunista Salvadoreño (PCS) and the Asociación General de Estudiantes Universitarios Salvadoreños (AGEUS), at the end of the 1950s and the beginning of the 1960s provide a good example.

15. UNO (Unión Nacional Opositora), an electoral coalition of the PDC, the MNR, and the UDN which participated in the presidential elections of 1972 and 1977.

16. Shafik Handal, "El viraje de las grandes masas," *Fundamentos y Perspectivas* (San Salvador), 2 (1982).

17. Mario Lungo, "El resurgimiento de la lucha política de masas y sus nuevas manifestaciones en El Salvador," *Rojo y Negro* (Caracas), 2 (mar–abr 1985).

18. Mario Lungo, "1985: El continuado resurgimiento de la lucha política de las clases trabajadoras salvadoreñas," *Crítica* (Universidad Autónoma de Puebla, México), 26–27 (ene–jun 1986).

19. Mario Lungo, "1986: La lucha de masas avanza en El Salvador" (unpublished).

20. Oscar Fallas, "Características del movimiento y la lucha de masas en 1987 en El Salvador" (unpublished).

21. A significant critique (though I do not agree with all its reasonings and conclusions) of the struggle modalities in the popular organizations appears as an editorial in *ECA*, 465 (jul 1987), "La cuestión de las masas."

22. Joaquín Villalobos, "Perspectivas de victoria y proyecto revolucionario," *ECA*, 483–84 (ene–feb 1989).

23. Leonardo Hidalgo, "Los movimientos sociales urbanos y las organizaciones de pobladores," *El Salvador: En construcción*, 4 (abr 1989).

24. Comandancia General del FMLN, "El único camino para construir la democracia en El Salvador." (The four quotations that follow are also from this document.)

25. Joaquín Villalobos, "El estado de la guerra y sus perspectivas," *ECA*, 449 (mar 1986).

26. Villalobos, "Perspectivas de victoria."

27. Interview with Joaquín Villalobos by Marta Harnecker, "La propuesta del FMLN: Un desaño a la estrategia contrainsurgente," in *ECA*, 485 (mar 1989).

28. Shafik Handal, "El poder, el carácter y vía de la revolución y la unidad de la izquierda," *Fundamentos y Perspectivas*, 1 (1982).

29. Published as an appendix in an article by Adolfo Gilly, "El Salvador a modo de conclusión," *Nexos* (México), 82 (oct 1984).

30. I have criticized this vision in my book *El Salvador, 1981–1984: La dimensión política de la guerra* (San Salvador: UCA Editores, 1985).

31. Handal, "El poder, el carácter."

32. Interview with Villalobos by Harnecker, "La propuesta del FMLN."

33. Comandancia General del FMLN, "El único camino."

34. Fermán Cienfuegos, *La república democrática* (México-Managua: Ediciones Roque Dalton, 1989).

35. Villalobos, "Perspectivas de victoria."

36. Comandancia General del FMLN, "El único camino."

37. Lungo, *El Salvador, 1981–1984.*

38. Comandancia General del FMLN, press release, San José, October 16, 1989.

39. Handal, "El poder, el carácter."

40. The FMLN statement was published in various newspapers in Central America.

41. "Propuesta del FMLN para convertir las elecciones en una contribución a la paz," *ECA*, 483–84 (ene–feb 1989).

42. Interview with Villalobos by Harnecker, "La propuesta del FMLN."

43. Handal develops this theme of "new popular subjects" in his article "El poder, el carácter."

44. Eduardo Sancho (Fermán Cienfuegos, pseud.), "Propaganda, democracia y revolución," *ECA*, 489 (jul 1989).

45. Joaquín Villalobos, "Acerca de la situación militar en El Salvador," *Cuadernos Políticos* (México), 30 (oct–dic 1981).

46. Comandancia General del FMLN, "Situación revolucionaria y esclada intervencionista en la guerra salvadoreña," *Ediciones Sistema Radio Venceremos* (México), 1984.

47. Villalobos, "El estado de la guerra."

48. Villalobos, "Perspectivas de victoria."

49. There are a number of works on Central American integration, particularly on the experience of the 1960s. I have evaluated the current prospects of the integration process in an unpublished article, "Centroamérica: La unidad regional sólo es posible con la participación popular."

50. Carlos Granados, "Hacia una definición de Centroamérica," *Anuario de Estudios Centroamericanos* (San José), 11 (1985).

51. Roque Dalton, *Miguel Mármol* (San José: EDUCA, 1982). This work has been republished in English as *Miguel Mármol*, trans. Kathleen Ross and Richard Schaaf (Willimantic, Conn.: Curbstone Press, 1987).

52. Comandancia General del FMLN, "Situación revolucionaria y esclada intervencionista."

53. Comandancia General del FMLN, "Balance de julio de 1985."

54. Villalobos, "El estado de la guerra."

55. Villalobos, "Perspectivas de victoria."
56. Ibid.

CHAPTER 6

 1. Samir Amin, "El problema de la democracia en el Tercer Mundo contemporáneo," *Nueva Sociedad,* 112 (mar–abr 1991).
 2. Boaventura de Sousa Santos, "Subjectividade, cidadanía e emancipacao," *Critica de Ciencias Sociais,* 32 (jun 1991).
 3. The facts are taken from *Proceso,* various editions, and *El Salvador on Line,* publication of the Washington Center for Central American Studies, Washington, D.C., various editions.
 4. Mario Lungo, *La lucha de las masas en el Salvador* (San Salvador: UCA Editores, 1987).
 5. "Primer Foro Nacional por la Paz," memoria (San Salvador, February 1988), and "Documento Final: Debate Nacional" (San Salvador, September 1988).
 6. Mario Lungo, "Los modelos alternativos de desarrollo y el papel de las ONG's," paper presented to the Congreso de CIPHES, San Salvador, April 1991.
 7. The facts appear in *Proceso,* various editions, and *El Salvador on Line,* various editions.
 8. *Proceso,* 477 (junio 12, 1991).
 9. Pedro J. Hernández, "La situación actual de cooperativismo en El Salvador," CSUCA/INVE-UES, 1991.
10. Amin, "El problema de la democracia."
11. James Petras, "Los movimientos sociales y la clase política en América Latina," in *El socialismo español, camino de Marbella* (Madrid: Editorial Revolución, 1990).
12. Mario Lungo, "El movimiento popular y la construcción de poderes locales" (manuscript).
13. The basic chronology is taken from the newspaper *Diario Latino* (San Salvador) (enero 16, 1992).
14. Mario Lungo, *El Salvador, 1981–1984: La dimensión política de la guerra* (San Salvador: UCA Editores, 1985).
15. "Los dilemas políticos del sandinismo," *Envío* (Managua), 116 (jun 1991). Actual mechanisms of the *concertación* in Nicaragua are described here and in other articles.
16. *Proceso,* 491 (oct 16, 1991). This expresses the opinion of the Jesuit community of the country.
17. Ibid.
18. "El Salvador: La paz nacerá con democracia," *Panorama Internacional* (Costa Rica) (oct 2, 1991). Interview with Francisco Jovel, member of the Comandancia General del FMLN.
19. André Gunder Frank, "La revolución en la Europa del Este," *Leviatan* (Madrid), 39 (primavera 1990).
20. Norberto Bobbio, "Entrevista," *Leviatan,* 39 (primavera 1990).
21. Some have suggested that movement from representative democracy to participatory democracy accompanies the current "modernizing" neoliberal

processes. One example offered is the emphasis on decentralization and the reinforcing of local governments. It is necessary to examine this point critically with reference to concrete situations. Proyecto "Democracia en países en conflicto," coordinated by ILSA of Santa Fe, Bogotá.

22. Santos, "Subjectividade, cidadanía e emancipacao."
23. Ibid.
24. Xabier Gorostiaga, "América Latina frente a los desafíos globales de los 90: Una coyuntura estratégica," *Este País* (Panamá), 33–34 (jun–ago 1991).
25. Santos, "Subjectividade, cidadanía e emancipacao." As Santos poses it.
26. Ibid. Santos proposes the suggestive concept of socialism as a "democracy without end."
27. David Harvey, *The Condition of Postmodernity* (London: Basil Blackwell, 1989).
28. Mario Lungo, "La constitución de un movimiento de base amplio y su papel en la construcción del proyecto popular" (Washington: EPICA, 1992).
29. Gorostiaga, "América Latina."
30. Victor Bulmer-Thomas, "A Long-Run Model of Development for Central America" (University of London: Institute of Latin American Studies, 1991).
31. Anthony Lake et al., *After the Wars: U.S. Third World Policy Perspectives* (Washington: Overseas Development Council; New Brunswick, N.J. Transaction Publishers, 1990).

CHAPTER 7

1. Rafael Guido Béjar, "El tiempo del adios," *Polemica* (San José), 16 (1992).
2. René E. Ponce, "Nuestra visión de las relaciones cívico-militares en la consolidación de la democracia," *El Diario de Hoy (San Salvador)* (oct 2–5, 1991).
3. Adolfo Blandón, "Un nuevo concepto de seguridad pública," *La Prensa Gráfica* (San Salvador) (mar 22, 1992).
4. FUSADES, "Como está nuestra economía, 1990?" (San Salvador, 1991).
5. FUSADES, "Informe trimestral de coyuntura" (San Salvador, 1991).
6. Daniel H. Wolf, "ARENA in the Arena: Factors in the Accommodation of the Salvadoran Right to Pluralism and the Broadening of the Political System" (San Diego: Department of Political Science, University of California, 1992).
7. President Alfredo Cristiani's speech at Mexico City's Chapultepec Castle, *Diario Latino* (San Salvador) (enero 21, 1992).
8. Communiqué of PRS-ERP, member of the FMLN, *La Prensa Gráfica* (marzo 28, 1992).
9. Ministerio de Planificación y Coordinación del Desarrollo Económico y Social, "Plan de reconstrucción nacional" (San Salvador, marzo 1992).
10. FUSADES, "Informe trimestral de coyuntura."
11. Among them (although the list is incomplete and unfair), I point to the work of James Dunkerley, *Power in the Isthmus: A Political History of Central America* (London and New York: Verso, 1988), and Sara Gordon, *El Salvador, crisis y política* (México: Siglo XXI, 1989).

Index